71

Managing Preservation for Libraries and Archives

DISCLAIMER

No undertakings, express or implied, are given concerning the use of the contents of this book and neither the individual authors and editors nor publishers will accept liability for losses which might arise directly or indirectly from use of information herein.

MANAGING PRESERVATION FOR LIBRARIES AND ARCHIVES

Current Practice and Future Developments

Edited by
John Feather

*Professor of Library and Information Studies,
Loughborough University, UK*

ASHGATE

Published by
Ashgate Publishing Limited
Gower House
Croft Road
Aldershot
Hants GU11 3HR
England

Ashgate Publishing Company
Suite 420
101 Cherry Street
Burlington, VT 05401-4405
USA

Ashgate website: http://www.ashgate.com

British Library Cataloguing in Publication Data
Managing preservation for libraries and archives : current
    practice and future developments
    1. Library materials - Conservation and restoration
    2. Archival materials
    I. Feather, John
    025.8'4

Library of Congress Cataloging-in-Publication Data
Managing preservation for libraries and archives : current practice and future
    developments / edited by John Feather.
        p. cm.
    Includes bibliographical references and index.
    ISBN 0-7546-0705-4
    1. Library materials--Conservation and restoration. 2. Archival materials--
Conservation and restoration. I. Feather, John.

Z701.M26 2003
025.8'4--dc21   2003045156

ISBN 0 7546 0705 4

Typeset in Century Old Style by J.L. & G.A. Wheatley Design, Aldershot.
Printed and bound in Great Britain by MPG Books Ltd, Bodmin, Cornwall.

Contents

List of Contributors

EDITOR

JOHN FEATHER

John Feather is Professor of Library and Information Studies at Loughborough University, UK. His areas of expertise include preservation management; previous publications in this field include *Preservation and the Management of Library Collections* (2nd edn, 1996) and, with Graham Matthews and Paul Eden, *Preservation Management: policies and practices in British libraries* (1996). He has undertaken work in the preservation field for IFLA, the British Library and the National Preservation Office.

CONTRIBUTORS

MAJLIS BREMER-LAAMANEN

Majlis Bremer-Laamanen is Head of the Centre for Microfilming and Conservation at Helsinki University Library. The Centre is also responsible for the Library's digitization activities. Majlis Bremer-Laamanen has participated in various projects relating to microfilming and digitization, among others as a project leader for the Nordic TIDEN – Digitization of Historical Newspapers – project 1998–2001. She is also participating in enhancing digitization policy and programmes in Finland, for example as the coordinator of The Finnish Digitisation Program for University, Scientific and Public Libraries 2002. On the international arena she is involved in the Benchmarking group in the EU MINERVA (Ministerial Network for valorizing activities in digitization) and a member of the IFLA Newspapers and Preservation and Conservation Sections.

GRAHAM MATTHEWS

Dr Graham Matthews is Director of Research, Faculty of Computing, Information and English at the University of Central England in Birmingham. He previously worked as a lecturer in information and library studies at Loughborough University and (then) Liverpool Polytechnic, and before this in academic and public libraries. He has a PhD in preservation management in libraries. He has led or been involved in several major externally funded research projects on different aspects of preservation management, including a review of preservation policy and activity in Great Britain, guidelines for disaster management in libraries, preservation management training, and the development of a preservation needs assessment model which has been developed and implemented by the National Preservation Office based at the British Library. He has written widely on the subject. He is joint editor, with Professor John Feather, of *Disaster Management for Libraries and Archives* (Ashgate, 2003). He is a member of the Chartered Institute of Library and Information Professionals Preservation and Conservation Panel and has served on other national preservation committees.

ADRIENNE MUIR

Adrienne Muir is a lecturer in the Department of Information Science at Loughborough University. She teaches collection and preservation management and research interests include preservation, especially digital preservation, digital libraries and information policy. Previously she managed Digital Library and Preservation research programmes for the British Library Research and Innovation Centre and the Library and Information Commission. She has also worked as a researcher in the areas of digital libraries at Loughborough University and information and cultural policy at the Policy Studies Institute. She started her career at the National Library of Scotland.

DIETRICH SCHÜLLER

Dietrich Schüller began his studies at the Technical University in Vienna with a major concentration in physics, later changing to ethnomusicology and cultural anthropology, and graduating from the University of Vienna with a PhD in 1970. While still in school in 1961, he was a student assistant to the Vienna Phonogrammarchiv of the Austrian Academy of Sciences and, following graduation, became its Director in 1972. He is actively involved in the technical and methodological aspects of sound recording for research purposes, particularly field recordings and the problems of sound preservation and re-recording. He is a lecturer on audiovisual carriers at the Universities in Vienna and Krems, and the Technical College for Information Sciences, Eisenstadt. He is also engaged in national and international training seminars on audiovisual archiving. Dietrich Schüller is author of numerous publications on audiovisual archiving, and has worked as a consultant to a number of audiovisual archives world-wide, partly on behalf of UNESCO. A former member of the Executive Board of the International Association of Sound Archives (IASA), he is member of the IASA Technical Committee, of the European Commission on Preservation and Access (ECPA), Audio Engineering Society AES, and Chair of the Sub-Committee on Technology for the Memory of the World-Programme of UNESCO.

JANI STENVALL

Jani Stenvall is a Systems Librarian at Helsinki University Library's database services. His tasks include work in legal deposit framework, especially deposit processes and development for digital publications. He is also working in different metadata or digital library related projects.

RENÉ TEYGELER

René Teygeler is a consultant on international preservation and has worked extensively in Asia and Europe. At present he is working on the disaster preparedness plan for the Dutch Royal Library. His most recent publications are *Preservation Science Survey* (2001), in collaboration with Henk Porck, and *Preservation of Archives in Tropical Climates: an annotated bibliography* (2002). In the autumn of 2002 a searchable database on preservation was launched on the ECPA Web site (www.knaw.nl/ecpa/), for which he was the content manager.

MARIE-THÉRÈSE VARLAMOFF

Marie-Thérèse Varlamoff, Curator General at the Bibliothèque nationale de France, has been Director of the IFLA Preservation and Conservation Core Activity since 1994, and is also Vice-President of the French Committee of Blue Shield. She has written many articles on preservation issues and has contributed to *IFLA Principles on the Care and Handling of Library Materials* (1998), a CD-ROM on *Safeguarding our Documentary Heritage* (2000) and is collaborating in a worldwide survey on digitization and preservation.

COLIN WEBB

Colin Webb is Director of Preservation Services at the National Library of Australia. He was previously Assistant Director of Preservation at the National Archives of

Australia. His previous joint publications include *Guidelines for Preservation Microfilming in Australia and New Zealand* (1998) and papers for a wide range of preservation conferences and journals.

Preface

The management of preservation in libraries and archives is a wide-ranging and rapidly developing field. Some of its techniques – of book binding and paper repair, for example – are as old as the documents to which they are applied. Others are so new as to be barely defined, as we seek methods to preserve the vast quantities of digital data – including sound and moving images as well as text – which are being used to generate data to add to the undiminished flow of printed paper which pours into libraries and record offices.

In this book, an international group of contributors offer authoritative views on policy matters, and discuss both state-of-the-art and well-proven methods of preservation and conservation. A number of experts from around the world have contributed chapters in their own fields of specialism in which they present some of the latest findings in those fields, and address the problems and issues which arise from contemporary techniques of information storage and retrieval. At the same time, traditional preservation and conservation are not neglected, either at the level of the repair of individual items or in terms of how to develop policies which will ensure both preservation and access for the future. A later chapter takes the form of an analytical survey of the rapidly growing literature in the field, and the final chapter looks to the future.

I am grateful to all the contributors for their chapters, and owe a special debt of gratitude to my long-time friend and colleague Graham Matthews of the University of Central England. He has not merely made an important contribution to this book but also made himself available for discussion of its content. His advice and help have, as always, been invaluable.

John Feather
Loughborough University

Introduction: principles and policies

John Feather

INTRODUCTION

Everything we have inherited from the past has come down to us because it has been preserved. This may have been intentional or accidental. It may have been incidental to the reason why the work or artefact was created, or it may have been integral to its purpose and function. A work created for short-term use, accidentally preserved for longer than was originally intended, and perhaps lost and rediscovered, may become an object whose long-term preservation has become desirable by reason of its form, content or rarity, or simply its age. Regardless of the history of an individual work or object, it now forms part of the larger entity which we call our 'heritage'.

The value of heritage can be defined in many ways. Some heritage has a value that can be expressed in financial terms, in the sense that a market exists in which the object can be bought and sold. Monetary worth alone, however, is not usually taken as the defining value of heritage. Less tangibly, but very powerfully, heritage is seen as defining a person, a group, a region, a nation or even the whole human race. The very concept of nationhood is understood in cultural terms, and in terms of an inheritance which has defined that culture over centuries. Where none exists it may have to be invented; powerful myths linking the past and the present can be potent weapons to be used for good or ill.

Inheritance is the essence of heritage, but its custodians must concern themselves with what the future will inherit from the present as well as with what the present has inherited from the past. This is not a passive process of transmission without change. Each generation makes its own contribution to the interpretation of the past, and leaves its own mark on the future. One of the key contributions of the generation which spanned the end of the twentieth century and the beginning of the twenty-first will surely be the development of new technologies of information and communication, which have created a new medium for information storage and transmission and at the same time have facilitated the development of new

1

techniques of heritage management and conservation. Some would argue that at the turn of the millennium a profound cultural transformation is taking place, often repudiating the past and yet ineradicably growing out of it.

Heritage, then, consists of more than merely the objects which we have inherited from the past. It also includes the ideas and sentiments which have been handed down to us, sometimes imperfectly and sometimes with distortions, but often with the power to continue to influence the way we live as individuals and as societies and nations. Oral transmission, by word of mouth from generation to generation, is an integral part of this process even in the most literate and technological cultures, but material objects and written texts play a critical part. At the same time, the received heritage is changed and augmented as it is handed on to future generations. To understand the issues which surround the preservation of materials in libraries and archives – the central theme of this book – we must begin by placing both the materials and the institutions in this broader context of cultural heritage.

CULTURAL HERITAGE AND THE DOCUMENTARY HERITAGE

MATERIAL HERITAGE

Cultural heritage is understood to mean everything that has been transmitted from the past which informs us about how people lived, worked and thought, and may still influence the way in which we do those things. The *material heritage* covers a huge range of artefacts. At one end of the scale, we have buildings and even whole landscapes which have been made and used over many generations. Some may survive only in part, or have been subjected to many modifications over the centuries by many hands and for many reasons. On the other hand, there are tiny but sometimes hugely informative objects, such as the flint tools which give us insights into the lives of our most remote ancestors, or the domestic objects which can be so evocative of past lifestyles.

DOCUMENTARY HERITAGE

The documentary heritage, which is the focus of this book, has to be seen in this wider context of our material inheritance from the past. It consists essentially of documents which contain texts and images intended to convey information and ideas. The purpose of these images varies considerably, from a purely factual record to a text designed principally as a work of art. The visual presentation of the material may be central to its purpose, or of no relevance whatsoever. The format of the information container may be of intrinsic interest, or may be wholly irrelevant to understanding the content. An insight into the purpose of both the content and the container is therefore essential if the essence of the work is to be preserved.

Books and other documents

The physical form of the information is our starting-point. Throughout this chapter, the word 'document' will be used as a comparatively neutral term for all information carriers, regardless of format or medium. In practice, of course, format and medium are by no means irrelevant to the preservation and transmission of their contents, and we must take them fully into account. The most familiar information-carrying documents are books, which are so integral to our literate culture as to need no definition. It is important, however, to remember that for our purposes the word 'book' is being used to define a particular kind of document. It consists of folded sheets, sewn or glued together and usually (but not necessarily) contained in some kind of outer casing or binding to which they are attached by thread or adhesive. This is the classic form of the book, or *codex*, in widespread use in the western world for most of the last two millennia. The information content on the folded sheets may have been written by hand, produced in a printing press, be the end-product of a photographic process or be the output of an electronic system. In each of these cases, however, although the process of production does have an impact on the preservation of the artefact, the material and mechanical object is the same.

This remains the case even if the book is a later creation than its own contents. Libraries, for example, have traditionally taken a number of parts of a serial publication and bound them together. The end-product is treated very differently in many ways from a monograph published and bought as a single item. In cataloguing, storage and, indeed, in use, serials and monographs are very different from each other. Physically, however, there is no meaningful distinction between a monograph bound by the publisher as part of the production process, and a book created by bringing together the parts of a serial into an annual volume. An understanding of the issues that face libraries in preserving their contents must begin with an understanding of the physicality of the materials involved. This phenomenon is not confined to libraries. Archives also contain what are, in physical terms, books, when documents are mounted in guard books or similar protective devices. Many manuscripts, of course, are in precisely the same codex form as the printed books which largely supplanted them from the middle of the fifteenth century onwards. Materials, contents and methods of production may differ between manuscripts and printed books – sometimes profoundly – but the basic mechanics of all codices are essentially identical.

Codices are not, however, the only written or printed documents in libraries and archives. There are also single sheets which are not folded or bound in the codex format. Groups of these may be held together in some way (using thread, pins, staples and various other devices), or they may be genuinely separate sheets. Although there are printed single sheets – many of great historical importance – probably most of the single-sheet material is in manuscript, and is to be found in record offices and archives rather than libraries.

Artefacts and information carriers

Almost all documents were created because of their contents rather than their form. It is therefore important to distinguish between the document as artefact and the document as information carrier. As an artefact, a document in any format is a physical object, part of whose interest lies in its information content. As an information carrier, a document is a device for storing and transmitting its contents and the format is of interest only to the extent that it contributes to, or inhibits, that objective. This distinction is critical, for it underlies many of the ways in which librarians and archivists approach the task of preservation. If the interest of the document lies primarily in its information content, then the artefact may be considered dispensable provided that the information content is preserved. In practice, this is how much of the literature of the past has been transmitted to us. We have, for example, no manuscript of any complete play by Shakespeare, and only a comparatively small number of copies of the first printed editions survive. With the exception of a handful of scholars, no one has read Shakespeare in those early printed editions for centuries, because the works (usually edited but sometimes photographically reproduced) have been transferred to other artefacts in which they are (in several senses) more easily accessible.

The example of Shakespeare has been chosen deliberately because of the many complex issues which it raises. Generations of scholarly endeavour have been devoted to trying to ensure the accuracy and authenticity of the text, but there is still no final agreement on many issues, including some fundamental principles of editing and presentation. Other literary examples could be adduced which would further complicate the issue, especially of works which survive only in manuscripts written (or rather copied) many years or even centuries after the text was composed. This is precisely the case with many of the Greek and Latin classics, and indeed much of the vernacular literature of medieval Europe, both sacred and secular writings in the Jewish and Islamic traditions, and much of the surviving written material from the traditional cultures of south and east Asia. The value of the surviving artefacts lies in the evidence they offer of the information content created by the author; indeed, textual scholars refer to such documents as 'witnesses'. But many have also acquired an artefactual value simply because they are rare, and indeed have become commercially valuable. Some may even be of aesthetic interest because of their calligraphy, illustrations or historic bindings, or of interest as historical objects because of the history and past ownership of the artefact itself. There are many and complex reasons for wishing to preserve both the artefact and its contents.

We should not, however, fall into the trap of assuming that all artefacts are of equal interest, an assumption which has sometimes significantly influenced the approach of librarians and others to the preservation of documents. The fundamental fallacy in this approach is perhaps best understood by suggesting a similar approach to content, and thus suggesting that the information in all documents is equally valuable. This is clearly untrue, even though at the time of creation it has to be presumed that the content was of interest and concern to the creator. The significance of a document, both an as artefact and as an information carrier, is determined by its form and content, by its age, and by its intrinsic, as opposed to monetary, value. That value judgement is, of course, one of great difficulty and sensitivity. Librarians and archivists rightly err on the side of caution, but that does not exempt them from the duty of gaining an awareness and understanding of the issues involved.

The balance between the significance of the artefact and the significance of its information content effectively determines whether preservation activity is to focus on the former or the latter. If the content is deemed to be the principal point of interest, then it may be appropriate – and perhaps even necessary – to transfer it into some other format or medium to ensure its continued survival and accessibility. In a sense, it was printing that was the first technique for format conversion, as this process is sometimes called. During the first fifty years or so after the new technique was developed, thousands of ancient and medieval texts, previously only in manuscript formats, were put into print. At the same time, and increasingly so over the next five hundred years, new works were written which were intended to be printed, so that the manuscript was seen only as a temporary device which enabled the author to make the work available to the printer. In the last hundred and fifty years, however, a whole range of new media has been developed which has allowed the principle of format conversion to be carried forward in a quite different way. The first, and in some ways still the most important, was photography. In particular, the development of 35mm film and subsequently of other microphotographic formats in the 1920s and 1930s made it possible for librarians and archivists to transfer the information content of large numbers of documents in all other formats into one in which it seemed that the information content was not disturbed, and even the appearance of the original artefact (though not its material form) was preserved. The creation of photographic surrogates – as they are generically called – remains a significant, though increasingly controversial, strategy to preserve the information content of documents in archives and libraries. More recently, and equally controversially, and with great cost and less technical certainty, the conversion of analogue information content into digital formats has offered a superficially attractive alternative route to format conversion for preservation and access.

HERITAGE INSTITUTIONS

Cultural heritage is generally understood to belong to a whole society, even though particular artefacts may belong to individuals, organizations or institutions rather than the state. This is manifestly true of intangible aspects of the heritage; no one 'owns' the plays of Shakespeare even though millions of people and thousands of libraries own books which contain them, editors and publishers own the copyright and performing rights in particular editions and recensions, and so on. This stands in clear contrast to a house and estate owned by an individual or a family, even though both the house and the surrounding landscape may be part of the general heritage. In most countries, the duality of the 'ownership' of the heritage – general and specific, public and private – is recognized in the relationship between the state and the material and documentary heritage.

State institutions almost always bear some part of the burden of responsibility for heritage preservation. This may take the form of an umbrella body which superintends and partly funds the maintenance of heritage objects, buildings and environments, including perhaps parts which are in private ownership. Thus the owner of a historic house, although unquestionably its owner, may not be permitted to make alterations to it without the permission of the body charged with representing the general interest in this specific activity. In addition, however, there are public bodies which actually own heritage objects, which means in practice that they are trustees on behalf of the nation of goods which are owned by the state. This is the position of a national gallery or a national museum, or indeed a national library or a national archive.

The custodial institutions – the museums, galleries, libraries and archives – have a central role in the preservation of the material heritage, and this is particularly true of the role of libraries and archives in the preservation of the documentary heritage. There are, of course, important private collections, and some institutions fall in the ill-defined borderland between the public and private sectors. Whatever their formal legal status, however – and it varies from country to country – such institutions as national, university and public libraries and archives have a clear and often explicit obligation actively to preserve the heritage and indeed to promote public use and understanding of what is essentially public property. The position of libraries is perhaps more ambiguous than that of archives. Some libraries have a well-defined and legitimate mission of which cultural heritage forms no part, although those libraries are clearly part of a national and indeed international system of information provision which cannot operate effectively unless information content, in whatever format or medium, is made available to users. Archives, on the other hand, are fundamentally preservation institutions. Although they exist to make documents available, their primary purpose is to ensure their preservation and transmission. Any understanding of preservation in archives and libraries begins from the proposition that it is a central part of their mission as heritage institutions.

Although much of the material heritage of most countries is either owned or partly protected by the state, a great deal of it is actually created by private organizations and by individuals for their own purposes. Those purposes may be artistic or literary; they may be commercial; or they may be essentially incidental to the purposes for which the object is made or the document is written. It is the third of these categories that presents a particular issue for the custodians of heritage to address. While it is obvious that records created by a government in transacting public business have a potential long-term interest and are in the public sector (if not in the public domain), it is far from clear that the same is true of a set of documents generated by, for example, a business firm. Yet in archives and research libraries the records of insurance companies, banks, manufacturers and other professions, trades and industries are invaluable to historians for the information which they contain about economic, social and political life. Their survival is largely serendipitous until they are taken into the comparatively safe haven of a library or archive. Yet if we lay claim to having a greater awareness of the importance of heritage than past generations had, we must consider how contemporary records created by businesses, charities, voluntary organizations and the like can be preserved for the future in a way which will give a meaningful insight into the work of the bodies by which they were generated. To attempt this task, something beyond the work of individual institutions may be needed.

PRESERVATION: CONCEPT AND PRACTICE

THE PRESERVATION DILEMMA

Preservation, as it is understood by librarians and archivists, has to do with the means by which the documentary heritage is handed on to future generations while being made available to current users. Simple as it may seem, this statement is underpinned by many complexities. First, and perhaps most importantly, there is a dynamic process implicit in this concept. Although the transmission of the heritage is the ultimate objective of preservation, the means by which this is done are not merely passive. It is clearly intended that provision must be made to do all that is necessary in order to ensure that both artefacts and information content, in an appropriate mixture, are available to future generations. At the same time, this concern for the future cannot be allowed to exclude current usage. The present generation is the heir to those who undertook preservation in the past precisely so that the heritage would be made available. Their work is being nullified if access is prevented.

In practice, there is a balance to be struck between preservation for the future and availability for current use. Heritage institutions, libraries and archives among them, have a clear responsibility to develop policies which reflect this, and which reflect the legitimate demands of society on them as societal, and often publicly funded, organizations. For museums and galleries, this dilemma is perhaps not quite so acute, in the sense that there is a lesser conflict. Museum objects, or the pictures in a gallery, are 'used' by being looked at by visitors and interpreted to them. Of course this requires appropriate conditions of display (air conditioning, lighting levels and so on) and often high levels of security; and it almost always precludes handling, other than by trained experts. In archives and libraries, the opposite is the case. Documents exist to be read, and they cannot be read without being handled. Every use of a document involves handling by at least one person, and often by many. Users are typically not trained in how to handle documents without damaging them, except by exhortation to exercise their common sense, sometimes reinforced by rules about the use of book rests, pencils for note-taking, and so on. For public libraries, in particular, the core of their mission is to make information and information carriers available to everyone, and indeed to encourage their use. While this is particularly true of public libraries, a similar consideration does in fact apply to all libraries and archives; they have no purpose if they are merely storehouses of artefacts, because the only purpose of the artefacts is to carry information and ideas with the intention that they will be conveyed to other people. The mission to transmit the heritage of the past to the future, therefore, has to be seen in the context of making the artefacts of that same heritage available at the present time.

THE DYNAMIC OF HERITAGE

Perhaps the most important aspect of the dynamic of heritage which concerns us here is that heritage is never completed but continuously growing and changing. The attempt to freeze it is a mark of societies which have lost their sense of development and advance, where new information is not sought and new ideas are unwelcome. Some libraries certainly have their origin in that ethos, and were founded primarily as institutions in which the learning of the past would be preserved. In the last two hundred years, however, it has come to be recognized – albeit slowly in some cases – that this narrow concept of the purpose of a library is ultimately self-defeating. Each generation adds its own contribution to the documentary heritage, and the contents and the responsibilities of libraries and archives increase in proportion.

For some institutions this presents a very serious problem indeed. Legal deposit libraries, with their obligation to take a copy of every item published in the jurisdiction in which they are located, can look forward to continuous and perhaps exponential growth as the output of books, journals, newspapers and other printed matter (to look no further) continues to grow despite the even more rapid growth in the output of electronic and audio-visual media. Archivists have developed their own solution to their equivalent of this problem. They do not accept every document created by an organization or a government. They select those which are judged to be of historical significance, and preserve them and them alone. There may be a second weeding-out process some years, or even decades, later, but in broad terms the intention to is to select for permanent preservation before documents enter the archive and then to create the circumstances in which such preservation is possible. Librarians approach the same task in a very different way. The legal deposit libraries – national libraries and in some countries selected university and public libraries as well – have an obligation to preserve as well as to accept. Other librarians operate under more flexible regimes. Acquisitions are carefully and professionally selected to serve the clientèle of the library; they are then made available in a way that meets the library's objective in buying the items. This may mean careful storage and supervised consultation on the premises for a handful of rare and valuable books; or it may mean making them available without restrictions for borrowing and use, subject only to basic rules about periods of loan and avoidance of damage.

PRESERVATION OBJECTIVES IN LIBRARIES AND ARCHIVES

Another way of expressing this is to say that while all archives, *ipso facto*, have a heritage function, only some libraries have one. Moreover, the significance of that function can vary between different sections of the same library, different kinds of materials, even materials on different subjects or in different formats. A university library will typically envisage a limited life-span for undergraduate textbooks (often defined in practice by the publication of a revised edition or a replacement text); a permanent, although largely unprotected, existence for scholarly journals and monographs; and a carefully protected and controlled environment (in every sense) for materials of particular interest because of their age, subject-matter, provenance or artefactual significance. In other words, such a library has a least three different high-level preservation objectives for different parts of its collections. They cannot be entirely separated from each other, but they do need to be considered separately.

Institutional missions

Certain issues must be considered in determining the preservation objectives of an archive or library. The first of these is the institutional mission. As we have

9

suggested, these differ greatly even between apparently similar institutions. In the public library domain, for example, although making information available and promoting its effective use is a core service in all public libraries, the understanding of how this is to be achieved, and what else is to be done, can differ significantly. While one system may emphasize the provision of printed books for home use, another will see its role as providing an essential support and supplement to education for people for all ages, while yet another will see itself as the community's centre for IT access, use and training. Such self-perceptions develop out of many different pressures: government policy, community needs expressed through local and regional democratic institutions, the social and economic characteristics of the area being served, and so on. Moreover, the professional judgement of the librarians on these and other matters has a key role to play in the determination, interpretation and implementation of the mission.

Similar but even greater differences in emphasis can be seen in the education sector at all levels. Particularly in the universities, however, with their dual function of research and teaching, library and information services are necessarily tailored to institutional missions. As the distinction between research-led and teaching-led universities becomes ever more apparent throughout the world, this takes on an additional significance. Collections designed to promote and underpin research, and indeed to provide the primary materials for researchers, especially in the arts, humanities and social sciences, will necessarily make a greater call on the resources and skills of preservation experts than the comparatively transitory materials intended to support student learning. This does not mean that one is inherently less important than the other, merely that they are different activities and need different kinds of library service. Libraries cover the whole spectrum, from those whose mission envisages permanent preservation of everything in an essentially archival institution to those that see virtually everything as expendable when it has fulfilled the purpose for which it was acquired.

The development of digital collections has created a new and complex dimension in this sphere. Although the words 'library' and 'archive' are often used to describe such collections ('digital *library*', 'text *archive*', and so on), the terms are little more than metaphors. Certainly, all the conventional implications of an institution as a physical entity at a geographical location have been stripped away. What is left is a form of knowledge and information which is dependent on access to technology, not on the right to use an institution. How we preserve the digital heritage, and indeed how we select what parts of it to preserve, are matters discussed in detail elsewhere in this book. At a more general level, however, the issues raised by the digital heritage include the need to consider how preservation can be assured when no institution 'owns' the physical form of the information which is made available. The owners of the servers and files (who may or might own the rights in the information content) are rarely heritage organizations. The gradual development of formal data archives and digital library 'collections' in the public domain is beginning to address the issue. This has to be done at least at the national level, and given the essentially supranational nature of networked digital technologies, any significant achievements will necessarily be international in the long term. The development of national policies and international conventions for the preservation of digital objects is an urgent matter. It is the context in which institutional policies will be developed and implemented in the future.

Access and use

Libraries and archives exist to be used, but the understanding of appropriate use varies between institutions in line with their missions. The public library is the most open, in the sense that it is there to serve the whole community. It cannot, however, provide all the services that might be needed, and has to take account of a wide range of factors. Among the most important of these are the level of demand for its services, and the political and social priorities assigned to them. Most public library systems recognize that one of their core obligations is to provide information and documents about the region which they serve, and from whose taxpayers they derive the bulk of their funding. One way in which this obligation is met is by the provision of collections of local materials, consisting of items published in the area, or whose subject-matter is particularly relevant to it. Such collections, especially if they have cumulated over time (sometimes for more than a century), come to form valuable historical collections as well as being of current interest.

The historical parts of a local studies collection present a classic example of the potential for conflict between preservation and use. In almost any local studies collection there is rare, and possibly even unique, material. Much of this will be genuinely local, including runs of local and regional newspapers, pamphlets and other ephemeral matter, much of which will not have been deposited in national libraries. A great deal of this material does not appear in national bibliographies. Research suggests that the percentage of material not captured by the legal deposit system is alarmingly high unless special measures are taken to ensure that it is recorded and acquired. If such material is to be preserved for long-term use and consultation, conditions have to be created in which that is possible, so that the local studies collection – including not only material now considered to be historical, but also current materials of potential historical significance – may have to be differently administered, and conditions of access and use may have to be different from those of the bulk of a public library's loan collections. This presents managerial, and perhaps even ethical, problems for public librarians, and highlights the potential for conflict between different demands on the same material and the same institution.

The dilemma is perhaps less acute, but no less real, in other libraries. University libraries, and many college libraries, hold special collections of materials of importance for research – and often assembled for that purpose – which cannot be treated like the bulk of the stock. The obligation is recognized, but it can only be met if resources are available. These resources include not only appropriate storage space, but also special reading areas, higher levels of staffing and probably specialist staff, and mechanisms for allowing users from outside the institution to have access to materials which are not available elsewhere or which represent collections of national or international significance. In practice, meeting obligations outside the owner institution may be assisted by additional resources from public funds, or by funds from foundations which support research or by some combination of the two. Indeed, without support of this kind, many universities could not continue to maintain and develop their special collections of research materials.

It follows, therefore, that the conditions of access to such collections are different from those that apply to general collections. They are more open, in the sense that people from outside the host institution will be granted full access rights; they are less open in the sense that not everyone, even in the host institution, will be allowed to use the materials, the materials will typically not be available for loan or for photocopying, and they may have to be read under strict supervision and perhaps with limitations on the number of items that can be in simultaneous use, and so on. In fact, much of the organization of a special collections section in a library is designed to reconcile the conflicting demands of preservation and use, and appropriate strategies have to be developed to ensure this.

In many ways, the approach of archivists is analogous to that of special collections librarians. There is typically a public right of access to public records (protected by law in many countries), but in practice archivists have to ensure that in meeting this obligation for one user, the rights of other (and future) users are not infringed by irreversible damage to the materials. The provision of indexes, calendars, transcripts, photographic facsimiles and digital surrogates can all contribute to this strategy, and are widely used in archives and record offices.

Selectivity

It is fundamental to understanding preservation to realize that we cannot preserve everything, and that nothing can be preserved for ever. This is true throughout the heritage sector, but has a particular resonance for libraries and archives. The sheer scale of the production of books and documents in literate societies makes it impossible to contemplate indiscriminate preservation, which forces librarians and archivists into making hard decisions.

For archivists, this process of choice begins before documents reach the repository at all. The traditional professional practice has been to select only those records that seem likely to be of permanent historical value. This obviously includes many categories of formal public records relating to such matters as taxation, land ownership and personal histories, records of diplomatic transactions and the formal records of the making and implementation of policies at all levels of government. In terms of central government records, what is typically not selected for preservation includes the informal papers which underlie many more formal policy documents, although drafts and earlier versions may be selected in important cases. In central government in the UK this process is initiated by departmental record officers, as part of the increasingly complex process of records management. In due course, materials selected for their potential historical significance are sent to the Public Record Office. Even then, they are subject to further review and possible discard before they are finally made available to the public, normally after a thirty-year interval. Similar practices prevail with those records of local government which find their way into local record offices, and there are analogous processes in all countries which have national, regional and local archive collections of official papers. For records created by other bodies, archivists exercise their professional judgement about the importance of the organization which created them as well as the significance of the records themselves.

Once records have been taken into an archive, the assumption is that they will be preserved in perpetuity at least in terms of their information content. In libraries the approach is very different. Librarians select material for acquisition, but for most items in most libraries it is assumed that their useful life will be comparatively short. This is true even in those libraries that have special collections, but in which the bulk of the materials is not in those collections; this includes most university libraries and all public libraries. Materials which are selected for special collections, or which are transferred from general to special collections at some subsequent time, are indeed intended for permanent preservation for long-term use, and will be treated differently. In other words, selectivity may be exercised at several stages in the existence of a book, from before it is acquired until the point at which it is discarded or designated for permanent retention.

The legal deposit libraries are very different. In most countries, the right to receive publications is linked to the obligation to preserve them and make them available to users. Although in some countries (including the UK) libraries can exercise some choice and exclude the most ephemeral material, in practice they seek to obtain all but a handful of the published output. The long-term preservation problems which this presents are enormous in terms of storage space alone, quite apart from technical issues about the physical preservation of the materials, and the arrangements for access and use.

Long-established professional procedures have been challenged by the development of digital objects. Many records which were formerly kept on paper are now created in electronic formats. Archiving of digital data presents a quite different range of problems. A digital record may never be finalized in the way that a paper record can be. Indeed, the capacity of digital records to be dynamic – to be regularly amended and updated – is one of their practical advantages for the creating organization. To address this, archivists have developed new concepts of how to identify a record, and how to designate it for preservation. We must add to this the technological problems of the retrievabilty of digital data, and dependence on the continued availability of both the hardware and the software which make that possible. And finally, the scale of the creation of paper records is outweighed substantially by the sheer bulk of digital data which can easily be created and stored, at least in the short term. Selectivity will become even more important than it has always been if we are to preserve a reasonable sample of the official and unofficial records which we are creating. This is essential if the research libraries and record offices of the future are to contain the late twentieth-century and later equivalents of the printed books and manuscripts which now fill their shelves.

OBSTACLES TO PRESERVATION

The desire to preserve selected materials for the foreseeable future drives the need for preservation policies. But many obstacles stand between the intention and its fulfilment. Some of these are inherent in the materials of information storage, from baked clay tablets to optical disks; some are an inevitable consequence of using or even displaying these materials; others are complex issues of resource allocation and the political and social decisions which drive them.

Resources

Preservation costs money. Even as a book stands unused on a library shelf, it absorbs resources: the shelf itself, the building in which the shelf is located, and the maintenance of that building all have to be paid for. When books are used, or have to be repaired, even greater resources are consumed. In archives and record offices, long-term preservation of collections is a core objective of the institution; in most libraries, however, this is, at best, the objective for a small part of the collection. Special collections absorb a disproportionate amount of the resources available for the library as a whole, a factor which cannot be ignored in determining the place of those collections in the institution. In all publicly funded institutions, there is a political dimension to library funding; in public libraries, this is explicit and direct. Public funds are almost inevitably applied first to the areas of greatest need and use, which means provisions for students in universities and colleges, and for the general public in the public libraries. It is inevitable that special collections, with their typical combination of fewer users and seemingly insatiable demand for controlled storage and reading areas, specialist staff and physical preservation, will come comparatively low in the order of financial priorities.

Even in libraries for which special collections are indeed central to their mission, the sheer cost of preservation is a major problem. It does not only require staff with specialist knowledge even before any actual work can be done on the collections or on individual items. Many historic collections are housed in older buildings, some of which are historic in their own right. They can therefore only be adapted in very limited ways, thus creating a further obstacle to ensuring appropriate conditions for storage and use. To remove the collections from their historic context – quite apart from the cost of providing new or adapted buildings – can itself damage their historical significance. This is manifestly true, for example, of the libraries of country houses, cathedrals or colleges where collections have been created and housed in the same space for centuries. However much money can be provided, nothing can make a medieval or Victorian room into a book storage area comparable in environmental conditions to a contemporary building designed and built for the purpose. Sometimes the only way to preserve the collections and to make them available is to break the historic continuity of association with a particular building or room, and transfer collections to more suitable storage, perhaps in another library. These are the parameters within which preservation has to be undertaken.

Materials

The materials of information storage often militate against their own survival. This should not, however, be overemphasized. There are millions of books and manuscripts in our libraries and archives which have survived for many centuries, often in conditions which we would now regard as wholly unacceptable. They may have suffered damage, and there have of course been great losses, but they have nevertheless survived. It remains the case, however, that the materials from which books and documents have been made are vulnerable to damage.

Paper is particularly susceptible. Until the late eighteenth century, paper was normally made of linen rags, and was always made by hand. The resultant material was physically strong and chemically stable. In normal usage and reasonable conditions of storage it would survive over long periods of time with little or no damage. The same is not true of papers made during much of the nineteenth and twentieth centuries. For economic reasons, papermakers sought both to mechanize the process of manufacturing and to find less expensive and more readily obtainable raw materials. Large-scale commercial papermaking was mechanized by about 1820, in mills which consumed vast quantities of water both in the papermaking process itself and in driving the machinery. They were therefore typically located by fast-flowing streams and rivers; consequently, the chemical properties of the water in those rivers – including impurities which were deleterious to the paper – influenced the chemistry of the paper itself. As the chemistry of the process came to be better understood, damaging impurities could be removed, but this increased the cost of the paper at a time when there was intense pressure to reduce it.

At the same time as the manufacturing process was mechanized, new materials were being used for the paper itself. Varieties of grass, reeds and other fibrous materials were used in the middle decades of the nineteenth century, but eventually it was wood in various forms which came to be the basic material of papermaking. In principle, processed wood is a very suitable material for making strong and physically durable paper. Again, however, there is a problem of chemical impurity, and particularly of the very high acid content of much of the wood used for papermaking for a century or so from about 1850 onwards. These impurities can be removed, but the chemistry was not fully understood until the middle of the twentieth century, and chemically stable paper was not regularly produced on a commercial basis until the 1960s.

The physical and chemical history of paper is central to the practice of preservation in libraries and archives, and has sometimes been misunderstood. The instability of some paper does not mean that all European and American books and documents made between 1850 and 1950 are decaying to dust, although some certainly are and many others will. It means that there is a real danger that many of them are too fragile for regular use (even in the terms in which that phrase is understood in an archive or research library), and that without some form of intervention further decay is inevitable, with consequent loss of the information content which is the reason why they are in the collections in the first place. Some of these materials can be repaired; some can be stabilized; some, however, can only be subjected to processes which will preserve their information content before the information carrier itself is damaged beyond the possibility of rescue or use. The scale of the problem, however, has called for large-scale responses. These have included the development of equipment and techniques for removing acid from paper on an industrial scale, called mass deacidification, although neither the machinery nor the techniques themselves have always been wholly successful; and the practice of format conversion, especially to 35mm microfilm, which then creates preservation management problems of a different kind.

Paper is not the only vulnerable material. The very structure of the codex book is easily damaged. A bound book is essentially a mechanical device, and like all mechanical devices it is most vulnerable to damage in its moving parts, in this case the hinges which link the boards with the spine, and the sewing or adhesive which links the binding with the body of the book itself. Books bound in inappropriate materials, or using inappropriate substances (boards which are too light for the weight of the book, or low-quality sewing thread, for example), will deteriorate by merely standing on a shelf. Books which are carelessly handled, or simply handled too often by too many people, will suffer inevitable damage even if reasonable care is exercised. They can, of course, be repaired or the item can be re-bound. But some bookbindings are of historical interest, or indeed are significant works of art in their own right, and cannot simply be replaced. Preservation and in some cases protection of bookbindings is an integral part of the whole process of preserving materials in libraries.

If the traditional materials of information storage are vulnerable to damage and decay, this is even more true of almost all of those media and formats developed since the middle of the nineteenth century. All the photographic media, from the earliest daguerreotypes to the most recent films, are susceptible to damage from light and air because of the very nature of the materials and the chemical processes used in their creation. The preservation of photographic material is a highly specialized activity. For libraries and archives, the principal concern is typically with the various forms of negatives and with photographic prints. Photographs have been created using many different materials in the one hundred and fifty years since the art was invented. For much of the nineteenth century, glass was a common medium and indeed its use persisted (in the form of lantern slides) into the second half of the twentieth century. For the librarian or archivist, glass plates present not only chemical but also physical problems of preservation, storage and safe use. Flexible film, such as is now universally used, evolved from the late nineteenth century onwards. Some early film is notoriously unstable or even, in the case of nitrate-based stock of the early and mid-twentieth century, potentially dangerous. Even if it is not susceptible to spontaneous combustion (as nitrate film is), it is still a potential major fire hazard, and storage conditions need to take this into account.

Photographs on paper, like those on glass or celluloid, also suffer from the double problem of the need for both chemical and physical preservation. Chemically, the issues are similar to those of film, where the major hazard is exposure to bright light which will cause images to fade and dyes to change colour. Physically, photographic paper is exposed to all the same hazards as other paper, with the additional complications which arise from its special chemical characteristics. For archivists and librarians, the most sensible – but not the cheapest – means of dealing with these problems is to ensure that users do not normally have access to the originals at all. Copies – whether photographic or digital – are less vulnerable and in any case can be replaced. The ideal practice is to create a copy negative from which all subsequent copies are made, so that the original is used as little as possible. This strategy can be applied to any photographic medium, and is generally regarded as essential where photographs are unique or are considered to be of exceptional archival importance.

Some photographic materials have, of course, been created specially for library and archival use. The use of so-called microfilm (which is typically standard 35mm roll film) to make copies of rare or vulnerable materials began in the 1930s, and became common after the Second World War. Other formats, some film-based (such as microfiche) and some paper-based (such as microcard) were also developed, each with its own specialized reading equipment. Photographic materials which can only be viewed using special equipment raise further issues for librarians and archivists. The equipment may be a movie projector, a slide viewer or one of the special devices for microphotographic media. In any case, equipment must be properly maintained and properly used; otherwise irreparable damage may result.

The same is true, for different reasons, of all the various media used to store recorded sound. Some, such as shellac discs, are physically easy to damage; others have comparatively unstable magnetic recordings imprinted on them. All require special equipment when they are used, and the very act of use can cause unavoidable damage, as happens in the case of a vinyl disc.

Digital media are even more problematic. Quite apart from the issue of selecting digital materials for preservation, actually keeping them in usable condition is a major task in itself. As with photographs and recorded sound media, we have to consider both the carrier and the content. The carriers may be comparatively permanent, but the digital content is less stable, an issue made more complicated by the fact that the damage is invisible and can only be discovered when the data are actively sought. To prevent this, the regular renewal – or refreshment – of the contents of digital media has been adopted as a technique for long-term preservation, but it is costly. Refreshment, however, is a satisfactory strategy only if the hardware and software needed to read the files remains available. With the rapid evolution of both over the last twenty years of the twentieth century, many digital data have already become inaccessible. Although greater awareness of this problem has probably made it less of an issue for the immediate future, refreshment remains, at best, an uncertain preservation strategy. The alternative seems to be to preserve the digital data in a format which is compatible with current hardware and software by transferring it into an appropriate format. This process – known as migration – is increasingly regarded as the most robust approach to a problem which is already large, will continue to grow and may never be entirely solved.

For many photographic media, and for all sound and digital media, the availability of functioning viewing and playback equipment is essential to facilitate access. In practice, this can threaten to turn libraries and archives into working museums, and indeed some specialist sound archives and film archives have in effect chosen this route. For regular consultation and use, however, transfer to standard modern carriers and the use of standard modern equipment is regarded as the ideal, and as the only practical means of making available materials of historical interest. In its turn, however, this raises significant issues about the quality of a second- or third-generation copy, and indeed about the permanence of the carrier to which the material has been transferred.

Damage by use

Even the most appropriate and careful use of library and archive materials causes damage. A book cannot be removed from the shelf and read without being opened, an act which in itself puts a strain on the binding. Documents are continuously exposed to chemical and physical influences which can be minimized but not eliminated, and which have deleterious long-term effects. But if we were to follow through the logic of this line of argument – for all its unquestionable truth – we would arrive at the illogical position that materials which exist to be read cannot be read at all. In practice, librarians and archivists have to recognize that all use leads to some damage, and must try to minimize the consequences.

The greatest cause of damage is handling, and this can be controlled up to a point. Certainly in research collections of long-term importance, properly trained staff and properly supervised use by readers can address the problem to a significant extent. Reading rooms must be properly equipped (with large tables and book rests or lecterns, for example) to ensure that materials can be used without being unnecessarily exposed to danger. The problem is of course greater in lending libraries or in loan collections in any library, but is made somewhat less by the fact that many of the books in these libraries are not in any case intended for long-term preservation. All that is needed is to ensure that they are usable during their useful life, which can be achieved by a combination of physical intervention (strengthening of bindings, rebinding and so on) and exhortation to users, perhaps with some sanctions against gross misuse.

Even when materials are not handled, or are handled only infrequently and professionally, damage will occur. When documents are exhibited, for example, as they are in many libraries and archives, the conditions within the display case (temperature, humidity, light levels and so on) can have a significant impact on the materials. So also can the precise form in which the display is mounted: a book in which the same opening is displayed for many weeks or months will prove difficult to close when the time comes, so that regular turning of pages is a necessary condition (and cost) of the safe display of important volumes. Apart from obvious prohibitions like not using adhesives in contact with displayed materials, it will often be necessary to make special book rests, page weights and so on to ensure that display is safe and effective.

Accidental and deliberate damage

Damage by use is almost unavoidable. Accidental damage is probably inevitable, although precautions are possible, and individual items of great importance can be protected if appropriate measures are taken regarding storage and use. Some accidents, however – what insurance companies call 'Acts of God' – can be neither predicted nor prevented. Of course, precautions can be taken. Buildings should be properly maintained to protect their contents against the elements, and have efficient and appropriate systems for the detection and retardation of fire. Librarians and archivists need to be aware of the potential for natural disasters affecting the building, such as a nearby river liable to flooding, the prevalence of earthquakes in the region, and so on. A well-managed library or archive has policies which deal with both the prevention of disasters and the management of the consequences should a disaster occur. Indeed, disaster preparedness and management is a subject in is own right, but one that is integral to the management of preservation.

In the final analysis, precautions can be taken against accidental damage, and systems put in place to mitigate its effects. Deliberate damage presents a different range of problems. Perhaps the most common form is the marking of books and documents by users. While this is always wrong, it is sometimes only marginally malicious; perhaps its most typical form is the marking of a textbook by a student user. Removal of a particular article from a volume of a periodical is another common act; it is more reprehensible since it does permanent and irretrievable damage. Acts of vandalism, however, can happen in many different ways. From the mild damage of the pencilled scribble to the destruction of a whole library by arson is a long step, and one that few will take, but precautions are needed against the consequences of both. Even more insidious, and even less preventable, is damage caused by acts of war. Historically, many books and documents have been destroyed in wartime, although in the twentieth century, and especially with the development of aerial bombing, active steps were often taken to protect cultural property. For much of the second half of the twentieth century, this problem seemed to be diminishing, and to be confined to south and east Asia and Africa. The 1990s, however, brought destructive wars back to the mainland of Europe and western and central Asia, with many libraries and archives damaged or destroyed in the Balkans and to a lesser extent in some of the successor states of the Soviet Union. Acts of terrorism can of course be equally destructive.

Not all of the destruction of heritage documents, buildings and objects is what is called, in military jargon, 'collateral damage', that is, the unintended side-effect of battle. Some is deliberate. Precisely because heritage embodies the very identity of a state or a nation, its destruction or desecration is seen to be part of the process of subjugating or even eliminating a people. This was certainly the case in the Balkan wars of the mid-1990s, and perhaps elsewhere in the world as well. It is one of the less desirable measures of the importance attached to our cultural heritage.

PRESERVATION POLICIES

It is against this background of cultural, physical, professional and even political considerations that libraries and archives must develop policies for the preservation of artefacts and their information contents. Such a policy is, *ipso facto*, a product of the institution which develops it; it reflects its history, ownership and function, as well as its financial and human resources, and the nature of the buildings in which it is housed and the place and circumstances in which those buildings are located. Nevertheless, there are some general principles which underlie preservation policies and can offer a broader context for their development and implementation.

Objectives and strategies

A meaningful preservation policy will be based on working towards clearly identified and well-understood objectives which have been agreed both within the institution itself and between the institution and its governing body or owners, such as a university or a local government authority.

The three key objectives which need to be defined are:

- the institutional mission;
- conditions of storage, access and use;
- selection and retention of materials.

The first of these, the institutional mission, is the basis for everything that follows. Its implications have already been discussed; in essence, the mission of the institution determines what it seeks to preserve, in what form and for what purpose. The conditions of storage, access and use are critical. They deal with such matters as whether materials are in storage areas open to users or only to staff, where and under what conditions materials can be inspected, consulted, read, copied or borrowed, and – above all – who has the right of access to the institution and to some or all of its collections. The third objective relates to the materials themselves. The principles upon which materials are selected for the library or archive, and the long-term intention of preserving them (in whatever format may be chosen), will ultimately determine the need for active intervention with individual items, conditions of storage and use, and policies for format conversion and other techniques for the preservation of information content.

To meet these key objectives, a number of strategies has to be developed to cover a wide range of activities, not all of which will be relevant in every institution, or even across the whole of an institution to which they are relevant in part. There are various strategies which, in an appropriate combination, can be a powerful force to enable the preservation of materials in terms of the institution's overall objectives. These include:

- creating and maintaining appropriate storage conditions;
- controlling the extent and nature of the use of materials;
- policies for the identification of materials intended for long-term preservation;
- agreed procedures for repair of damaged materials;

- identification of appropriate techniques to ensure longer life for materials before they suffer damage;
- the development of programmes for creating surrogates for original materials through format conversion;
- developing policies and procedures for providing security for the collections, for disaster prevention, preparedness, reaction and recovery;
- the identification of partnerships with other institutions and of cooperative programmes at regional, sectoral, national and international levels;
- identifying resource needs and possible sources of both money and expertise to implement these strategies.

Which parts of this long and complex list of activities (which could be further extended) is appropriate in any particular library or archive is determined by the purpose of the institution itself. In the loan collections of a public library, for example, policies relating to the strengthening of newly acquired paperbacks or for the rebinding of heavily used reference books will almost certainly be of far greater significance than, for example, trying to create ideal environmental conditions for the books in a branch library. In other words, policies should be developed in a realistic context and with meaningful objectives. There is no 'one size fits all' solution, and indeed the attempt to develop such solutions in the past has been – and perhaps still is – a deterrent which prevents some librarians from recognizing that they can offer even better services to users if some of these factors are taken into account.

For many of the strategies suggested in this list, there are established standards (for example, on environmental conditions for the storage of paper, photographic film, and so on), although there is often a measure of disagreement among experts about the finer points of detail, and international standards tend to be something of a compromise. For others, there is a wide and sometimes confusing range of choice. A librarian or archivist should take professional advice on such matters as appropriate binding techniques and styles, the repair of damaged documents (especially those which are of materially historic significance) or the appropriateness and techniques of format conversion by photography or digitization.

The preservation policy

In some senses, all preservation policies are different, but, in some respects, they are all also the same. Any one preservation policy will cover much of the same ground as any other, but they may have different targets, take divergent paths and be looking for different things. It is, however, important to identify the common ground.

Any meaningful preservation policy document will be based on a clear understanding of the three key objectives suggested in the previous section. The policy statement needs to be explicit about the scope, contents and strategies of the policy. Beyond that, however, the policy will need to address issues of implementation, and at this level there will be very significant variations between institutions even in the same sector. General guidelines for the contents of preservation policies are of real use, but their application in any particular situation will inevitably and rightly be selective. Indeed, the more they attempt to cover every aspect of the field – as the best of them do – the more likely it is that the direct relevance of any particular aspect of the guidelines will vary from one institution to another. Two comparatively recent publications are of particular value in this respect:

- *Building Blocks for a Preservation Policy*, published by the National Preservation Office at the British Library, London, in 2001. It was written in 1999 by Professor Mirjam Foot for a Preservation Management Summer School held at the Public Record Office in London in that year;
- *Principles for the Care and Handling of Library Materials*, published by the IFLA Core Programme on Preservation and Conservation, based at the Bibliothèque nationale de France, in 1998.

There are of course many important standards and recommendations, and indeed analytical discussions of policy issues, many of which are listed and discussed by Graham Matthews in Chapter 7.

CONCLUDING COMMENTS

The field of preservation in libraries and archives continues to evolve. Within living memory, it consisted of little more than traditional activities of binding and paper repair, and was usually seen as a rather esoteric activity even in the rarefied institutions in which it was practised at all. For whatever reasons (and the history is somewhat disputed), this position began to change in the United States in the early 1970s and in Britain and the rest of Europe a little later, as there was a growing recognition of what was often called a 'crisis'. Exactly how critical that crisis was has itself been challenged in recent years, but the perception that there was one certainly directed the attention of librarians and archivists to the need to reconsider the whole field. New techniques have been evolved not merely for the physical preservation of materials (such as mass deacidification) but also for preservation management (such as software to facilitate collection surveys). New international and national cooperative agendas have been developed, and there has been a recognition that heritage is not confined by national or sectoral boundaries. Both within the library and archive professions and – perhaps more importantly – among their public and private funding bodies there has been an increased and genuine recognition of the need to invest more time and money in both research and implementation in the preservation field.

A new consensus has emerged in the professional community about why preservation policies are important, and what they are trying to achieve. This is reflected in much of the literature, not least in the shift away from the traditional focus on techniques at document level to a concern for developing and implementing policies at institutional level and beyond. There is also a recognition of the commonality of problems and hence of interests between sectors which in the past have not always sat easily together. This is not only the case between libraries and archives, but increasingly between the documentary heritage institutions on the one hand and the other institutions of material heritage – notably museums and historic buildings – on the other.

During the three decades in which these developments have taken place there have been revolutionary changes in almost every aspect of the information world. This has created new problems for preservation managers – especially in handling digital documents, objects and archives – but also new opportunities. If digitization is not itself a satisfactory mechanism for the long-term preservation of information, as Colin Webb argues in his contribution to this book, it is certainly an important mechanism for giving access to information – including information originally published in traditional formats – on an unprecedented scale. Both archivists and librarians find themselves not merely having to address old questions about new kinds of material, but also needing to formulate new questions about new kinds of data. In a field which has historically been concerned with the materiality of information storage, this represents a significant shift in intellectual focus and professional practice. Adrienne Muir (Chapter 4) explores these and other concerns in defining the issues which now confont us as we seek to devise long-term management strategies for information that is 'born-digital' as well as for digitized versions of analogue media.

Other scientific developments have had a significant impact on the preservation of historic materials. Our knowledge and understanding of the physical carriers of information – paper, film, magnetic tape and so on – is continually being augmented, and the implications for both document-level and collection-level preservation and conservation continue to be explored. This is exemplified in the chapters by René Teygeler and Dietrich Schüller on paper and sound recordings respectively (Chapters 5 and 6). Dr Schüller's contribution, however, also serves to remind us that another consequence of the information revolution is the dissolution of traditional boundaries between formats and media. Digital sound – and for that matter digital photography and video – is technologically identical to any other form of digital data. It has the same merits and demerits and creates the same sort of problems in long-term management and retrieval. The practical issues of digital data preservation which are explored by Majlis Bremer-Laamanen and

Jani Stenvall (Chapter 3) offer some particular instances of generic issues, and suggest many interesting lines of future development.

That the future is both uncertain and exciting is clear from Marie-Thérèse Varmaloff's essay in futurology (Chapter 8). In the midst of the digital debate, we must not forget the inherited problems that still beset us. Libraries and archives for the foreseeable future will, for the most part, be institutions committed to the storage and use of paper and other traditional materials of information storage. The fact that we understand much more about how we can ensure the survival of these materials does not solve our problems; it merely imposes on us an even greater obligation to do so.

2 The malleability of fire: preserving digital information

Colin Webb

The other was a Scheme for entirely abolishing all Words whatsoever . . . [S]ince words are only Names for *Things*, it would be more convenient for all Men to carry about them such *Things* as were necessary to express the particular Business they are to discourse on . . . [This] would serve as a Universal Language to be understood in all civilised Nations . . .

> Jonathan Swift, *Travels into Several Remote Nations of the World in Four Parts by Lemuel Gulliver*, part iii: *A Voyage to Laputa, Balnibarbi, Luggnagg, Glubbdubdrib, and Japan* (Benj. Motte, London, 1726)

Preservation in libraries and archives is concerned with information and the artefacts of communication. The preservation of digital information takes that process a step further, into a world where there are only symbols of symbols, only understandable 'in any civilized nation', or anywhere else, via the mediation of machines and the programs that run them.

Gulliver's Travels is one of the great books of the English language. Along with the tiny people and giant people so loved by children is a much less known *Voyage to Laputa* and its neighbouring lands, where Gulliver encounters the scientific genius of the Laputans. His visit to the Academy of Lagado is replete with descriptions of crazy endeavours – attempts to extract sunbeams from cucumbers, make clothes from cobwebs, and build houses from the roof down. Many of the projects of the Academy are delightfully, even uncomfortably, resonant for anyone involved in trying to preserve our emerging heritage of digital information, somewhat like a project to prove the malleability of fire.

This chapter seeks to describe digital information in reasonably simple terms, looking at some impacts on libraries and archives, and explaining why digital information presents preservation problems. We will look at the threats to the survival of digital information, and the nature and objectives of digital preservation. This introductory material leads into a more detailed discussion of the main technical, organizational and societal challenges to which digital preservation must respond, as well as some of the responses that have already emerged.

The chapter ends with some conclusions tentatively drawn from this discussion, as well as some pointers to further information for readers with an ongoing interest in this complex and evolving field.

SOME FOCUS QUESTIONS

As we explore this field, it may help to carry some questions with us, such as:

- Is digital information really worth preserving?
- Is there a reasonable prospect that digital information will survive?
- Is digital preservation really the responsibility of everyone or just a well-equipped and well-resourced few?
- Is digital preservation different from 'traditional' preservation?

DEFINITIONS OF DIGITAL INFORMATION

This chapter does not attempt to define information *per se*, but digital information can be defined as information presented in digital form: in other words, information encoded in discrete *bits* (binary digits) recognizable by a computer.

While it is not surprising that numbers can be represented by bits (after all, digital computing originated with the encoding and processing of numbers), nor that someone quickly found a way of representing text by sequences of bits, one of the achievements of the *computer revolution* has been the successful encoding of all kinds of information in digital form, including still and moving pictures, sound, lines, coordinates, colour, and even relationships among data.

The ability to encode information in digital form, either by creating it that way (often referred to as being *born digital*) or by capturing it as a copy in digital form (*born again digital*), has many profound implications for libraries and archives, and for their users. For example, it is relatively easy to send digitized information across communication networks at great speed and with great accuracy, to make changes, to copy digitized information perfectly, to reuse it, to distribute multiple copies, to store it, or to make it available to machines for searching, further processing or manipulation, with relatively little human intervention. Such capabilities make digital information very attractive for institutions and for users.

On the other hand, the nature of digital information also makes it virtually impossible for humans to extract the intended meaning from what is encoded without the mediation of a computer and the various layers of programming that tell the computer how to interpret the code and represent it in a form that can be understood by humans. To achieve this, digital information is usually stored as a sequence of bits, with other bits that tell a reading system what to do with the code, even where the code starts and finishes. If this is not recognized by available computers and layers of software, it cannot be presented as intended, if at all.

HOW DIGITAL INFORMATION AFFECTS LIBRARIES AND ARCHIVES

While it is conceivable that there are some libraries and archives that have not yet been affected by these qualities of digital information resources, they must be very few. Most cultural-memory institutions dealing with documentary resources find that digital technology affects them in a number of ways that are particularly important to their preservation responsibilities.

First, digital information is affecting the kinds of information format found in collections, whether at a physical level, such as the presence of CD-ROMs, online publications, hard disks, tapes; or at a genre level such as datasets, databases, electronic journals, GIS products, electronic manuscripts, multimedia, e-books, electronic records, digitized pictures, sound, email collections, web pages, and many others.

Second, digital information is affecting the processes required to manage collections. While many collection management processes – such as selection against a collection development policy, acquisition, cataloguing, storage, preservation and providing access – remain applicable, the nature of digital information has forced changes in most of these processes. It has also created new opportunities and needs, such as links between items, linking of metadata directly to collection items, automated management of collections, automated access, personalized resource discovery, and the processes required for preservation.

Third, digital information is affecting relationships among custodians and between custodians and other stakeholders. Libraries and archives are used to having to manage relationships with stakeholders such as users, creators/ depositors and other institutions. In managing digital collections, the nature of many of these relationships is changing. For example, users tend to expect more rapid, unmediated access to information but may be more inclined to question the authenticity of what they find. Creators of digital information may have a more active role to play in ensuring that information resources survive until they can be collected. And custodians may find themselves acting as collaborators on some issues and competitors on others as they seek ways of managing a raft of simultaneously changing demands and opportunities.

While digital preservation may appear to be principally about managing technical challenges, success probably depends as much on understanding and managing institutional and societal impacts.

WHY IS PRESERVATION NEEDED?

Information resources can be lost through a very wide range of causes. Some of these are set out in Box 2.1.

Box 2.1   Threats to digital information resources and their usability

The survival of digital information resources may be at risk because:

- Their value is not recognized before they are lost.
- They are changed, intentionally or unintentionally, without previous versions being saved or without the changes being documented.
- They can only be accessed using specific hardware that becomes unavailable.
- They can only be accessed using various layers of interdependent software such as an operating system, application software, other presentation software, and plug-ins, any of which becomes either unavailable or not workable on changing hardware and software platforms.
- They are stored on unstable media.
- No one takes responsibility for them.
- Those taking responsibility do not have the knowledge, systems, or policy frameworks to fulfil their responsibility.
- There are insufficient financial and other resources available to sustain action over the required period.
- So much contextual information is lost that the resources themselves are unintelligible even when they can be accessed.
- The information resources are well protected but cannot be found by users.
- They would be lost in the event of a disaster such as fire, equipment failure, flood, or virus attack that disables stored memory.
- Potential users are not confident that the resources are authentic.
- Critical aspects of their functionality, such as the formatting of a poem, are not recognized and are lost in preservation processes.
- The way they are configured, stored and described makes them so expensive or so time-consuming to find and use that potential users simply give up.
- They are structured in so idiosyncratic a manner that individual handcrafting is needed to provide access to them.
- Access barriers such as password protection, encryption, security devices, or hard-coded access paths cannot be removed or circumvented when they are no longer applicable.
- It is not possible to negotiate legal approval to do what is necessary for preservation.
- The size and complexity of maintaining accessibility are too great for the management skills and the time available.

While the digital preservation 'problem' encompasses all of the challenges listed in Box 2.1, and may appear to be overwhelmingly complex, it is possible to characterize it in much simpler terms:

> The longevity of digital information is constantly threatened by the combined assaults of limited media life and the inexorably rapid evolution (and consequent obsolescence) of the software and supporting hardware systems needed to access and interpret digital data. These factors conspire to limit the effective lifetime of digital records despite the fact that they can be copied perfectly; this has prompted my ironic contention that digital information lasts forever – or five years, whichever comes first.
>
> (Rothenberg, 1996)

As Jeff Rothenberg's comment suggests, digital preservation has two fundamental tasks: keeping information safe, and keeping it accessible. These underlying challenges are not new. Despite a shift in focus from the information carrier to the information itself, and despite an array of different techniques, digital preservation deals with the same fundamental objectives pursued by preservation managers dealing with non-digital collections in libraries and archives. Ultimately, the point of preservation is overwhelmingly about access – by someone, somewhere, sometime.

But, we may ask, access to what?

In dealing with books and paper records, we have been able to assume that this is an easy question to answer: preserving accessibility means maintaining the opportunity to consult the original document or at least a copy of it. On deeper reflection we can see that the answer may not be so straightforward. In 2000, American writer Nicholson Baker critically questioned the use of microfilm as a suitable preservation surrogate for newspapers (Baker, 2000). His questions triggered an unprecedented public and professional debate over the kind of access that preservation programmes should offer. The debate was not about the long-term availability of microfilm, but about its capacity to capture and re-present the full range of newspaper qualities that some users valued. The debate raised a central question: had preservation managers chosen strategies that helped or hindered users in understanding the significant properties of newspapers?

Conservators undertaking treatment to repair books and documents face a similar, if often unacknowledged, question about the characteristics that must be maintained, even at the level of deciding whether annotations or stains should be removed or kept.

Deciding what characteristics give particular digital objects their value and meaning, and therefore must remain accessible, is a particularly serious question for digital preservation programmes. The interaction of hardware and software in accessing any digital object presents the preservation manager with choices that may enhance, misrepresent, or obliterate the intended meaning. Unless we can define the significant characteristics that will re-present the intended meaning, we cannot:

Box 2.2   Significant properties

It is important to see the defining of significant properties in context. From the perspective of the individual object, recognizing which characteristics are significant may depend on factors such as:

- understanding the intentions of the *creator*;
- understanding why the object is being kept – what led to its *selection* as worth keeping;
- understanding for *whom* it is being kept, and how they will want to use it;
- the capabilities of the *keeper*, who might be forced to ignore some properties because they cannot be sustained. (Ideally, the properties that are significant to meaning should at least be documented even if they cannot be sustained or re-presented.)

In reality, most digital information collections are too large to allow this kind of individual definition except in a few cases. Typically, the imperative for mass handling will drive the process of defining significant properties towards simplification: a small number of classes of objects that can be automatically recognized using pre-set criteria.

At one extreme is the proposal that it may be sufficient to categorize digital objects into a small number of very broad classes for re-presentation to users. Such classes might include unformatted data, data with relationships, formatted data where the *look and feel* is significant, or complex and possibly dynamic interactive multimedia.

Taking this approach, one might expect to be able to distinguish between suitable preservation processes for:

- a simple text document which does not need to reflect any formatting;
- a set of data in a database where the data themselves and the relationships between them must be maintained accurately;
- a text document such as a poem where formatting may be critical to its meaning;
- a sound or image file which must maintain its sound or image qualities;
- a complex multimedia web page that includes sound, video, animations, text, hypertext links, a database structure, interactive elements, and so on.

On the other hand, it may be necessary to identify all the technical parameters that make the object do what it does when it is accessed. (Such an approach underlies the *Data Dictionary for Technical Metadata for Digital Still Images* [NISO, 2002], which lists more than one hundred characteristics needing to be documented. Of those, however, it is debatable whether more than a quarter describe significant properties that must be maintained.)

It should be apparent that defining the essential characteristics of digital information objects may not be a simple or trivial task for preservation managers.

- understand what our preservation processes have to achieve;
- design our preservation processes to do the job appropriately or cost-effectively;
- judge whether we have been successful; or
- report on the authenticity of what is preserved.

These are critical requirements for any preservation programme.

Box 2.2 discusses some approaches to defining what must be preserved.

Some people argue that it is not enough to see information as data: the experience of using information is also important and should be preserved or re-created as well as the data (for example, Christensen-Dalsgaad, 2001). Describing and re-creating the experiential aspects of static information resources may be challenging enough; it is not yet apparent how the experience of using highly interactive, constantly updating resources can be described and maintained cost-effectively.

THE NATURE OF DIGITAL PRESERVATION

Clearly, digital preservation is about more than simply maintaining data. The view of digital preservation so far discussed encompasses:

- preservation of data as a stream of bits;
- preservation of information about the data (usually called *metadata*);
- ensuring that data can be found;
- ensuring that there are workable ways of retrieving and accessing the data; and
- providing means to re-create or re-present the experience of using the data.

Demanding that preservation managers define the experience that must be re-presented seems to take us far beyond what is expected of the conservator of books or paper records. On the other hand, the best preservation programmes have probably taken a similarly holistic approach in dealing with non-digital materials.

SOME TECHNICAL CHALLENGES

This section looks at some of the main challenges that emerge from the technical nature of digital information, and at some of the responses to those challenges.

THE CHALLENGE OF UNSTABLE MEDIA

There is no particular reason why digital information must be carried on unstable media, but it usually is. Early computers used punched cards or punched paper tapes. (Some of them still sit quite safely in museums half a century after they were used.) Other systems have used glass or stable plastic disks. However, the imperative of the marketplace demands inexpensive data storage, and magnetic media have served the computer industry extremely well. Vast amounts of data are stored on magnetic tapes and disks with a useful life measured in years or decades, not centuries. Magnetic media are vulnerable to magnetic interference, physical damage by reading devices, and chemical deterioration of the layers of polymers of which they are made.

The introduction of optical media (using light interference rather than alignment of magnetic particles to store data) such as the compact disk in the 1980s was initially expected to solve the longevity problems of magnetic media, but evidence of problems in poorly made optical disks soon led to questions about their longevity as well.

(Critics of digital storage media often ignore the fact that other media considered to be relatively long-lasting, such as clay tablets, papyrus, parchment, paper or microfilm, are also subject to damage from factors which, if not adequately controlled, will lead to loss of information.)

Two common responses to the threat of unstable storage media are *refreshing*, which refers to the continual copying of data from one carrier to another, or *media transfer*, where data are copied from less stable to more stable media.

The search for more stable carriers for digital information has continued. Small, stable metal plates engraved by ion beams to record either digital or analogue information, marketed under the name of HD-Rosetta (Norsam Technologies, 2001), are one emerging option for storage of digital information of very long-term value. (It should be noted that HD-Rosetta uses analogue storage even of digitally generated files, etching a permanent image into the surface of the plate.)

Does the offer of more stable storage solve any digital preservation problems? Certainly there may be information that needs to be stored safely for very long periods. Stable storage media may also help in containing the costs of constant refreshing.

Underlying the concern with media stability is a proper concern with protecting the data stream. Without that, there can be no accessibility. However, storage on stable media is not the only option. The computer industry has developed sophisticated means of managing and maintaining safe data streams by the use of stable *systems* in the place of stable media. In fact, such stable systems have typically used media that are intrinsically unstable. By constantly moving data through refresh cycles with automatic error checking and correction, supported by multiple back-ups and redundant storage, such systems can maintain data integrity for much longer than the life of any particular carrier used in the system.

These quite normal IT practices replace the search for an archival carrier with the development of archival systems and procedures that achieve an equivalent or greater level of data security. Underlying such an approach is a commitment to spreading the risk of damage or loss across multiple carriers.

Another interesting approach to spreading the risk of damage or loss is the LOCKSS project (Lots of Copies Keeps Stuff Safe) led by Stanford University, which seeks to exploit the insight that multiple copies of digital objects stored in different systems stand a much better chance of survival than any single copy (LOCKSS, 2002).

While looking after the data stream is critically important, it is almost always insufficient to ensure accessibility over more than a reasonably short timeframe unless it also addresses the key characteristic threat to digital accessibility: obsolescence.

THE CHALLENGE OF UNSTABLE TECHNOLOGY AND OBSOLESCENCE

This chapter has already referred to the common dependence on machines in order to access digital information. Changes in the machines that store, read, process and present digital information are the main threat to ongoing access. Change is almost the defining characteristic of the very systems relied upon. Typically, the interdependent layers of software and hardware used:

- do not remain usable for more than a few years;
- are replaced by newer versions and products, often accompanied by withdrawal of technical support for the superseded versions and products;
- do not work in the way the superseded version worked;
- do not work well together across succeeding generations of versions or products.

Access to digital information depends on all components of an access system working together. When one component such as an operating system does not work, access is lost even if the other parts of the system survive. Typically, the different components of systems become obsolete at different times. Taken together, large and diverse collections may contain hundreds, thousands or even millions of such interrelated dependences. Trying to manage all of these in the interests of sustained accessibility is surely a task worthy of comparison with the Projects of the Lagado Academicians reported by Lemuel Gulliver.

There have been many responses to this critical problem of technological obsolescence. These are outlined below.

Use of standards

Although it is often said that the IT scene is chaotic and lacks standards, this is probably misleading. While computer and software companies do try to distinguish their products from each other, they are also driven by the demands of the market for reliability and compatibility. To achieve these, standards have proliferated, both at the individual product level and in support of interoperability of products and systems.

Rather than a lack of standards, preservation managers face the problem of choosing appropriate ones that will foster what they are trying to achieve. It is still very much a field encumbered, not facilitated, by standards. However, much of the concern expressed about the paucity of standards is well placed, because it is still not possible to find reliable, universally approved methods to do many of the things that digital preservation must do.

While there is an ongoing international effort to identify where standards are needed and to reduce some of the gaps, another response has been to accept the proliferation of standards and formats, looking for progress in two areas:

- Identifying and promoting the use of particular formats and features likely to make preservation easier rather than harder. A number of file formats that provide good functionality, are very widely used, and have publicly available specifications have been promoted as *de facto* preservation standard formats (such as the TIFF image format). On the other hand, files in formats containing in-built restrictions on copying and access may be impossible to maintain without special circumvention devices, which are illegal in some jurisdictions.

- Encouraging the use of standards in ways that comply with the standard specification, in order to minimize individual variations that may complicate batch preservation processing. The use of HTML (HyperText Markup Language) for web-based documents illustrates this: although the HTML standard is quite specific, the software programs (browsers) widely used to read HTML documents are very tolerant of variations. As a result, web archives often contain very idiosyncratic HTML documents that may have to be identified and individually treated to work with later generations of browsers.

Metadata

Another response to technological change looks to the use of metadata to document what is needed to provide access. The metadata required for preservation management go far beyond the resource discovery metadata that search engines and other browsing systems use to automatically find and recognize specific digital resources. Preservation metadata record all the information about a digital object that will be needed in order to manage it over time, and to re-present it appropriately to a user.

While resource discovery metadata such as the Dublin Core set of descriptive elements were early enablers of networked access, preservation metadata have taken much longer to evolve. By mid-2002, there was still no widely accepted standard despite almost universal agreement that good metadata are critical to virtually all digital preservation efforts. In 2002, an international working group convened by the Online Computer Library Center (OCLC) and the Research Libraries Group (RLG) recommended preservation metadata elements from which preservation management systems should choose (OCLC/RLG Working Group on Preservation Metadata, 2002), although it was still not clear whether the recommendations would be widely adopted.

Encapsulation

An especially promising concept that exploits the use of metadata response is *encapsulation*. This refers to the bundling together of digital information resources, the preservation metadata associated with them, and possibly even the software required for access. (One proposal from the late 1990s even suggested bundling access hardware into the package: such a *tablet* would make the digital object virtually independent of any other machines or systems [Kranch, 1998].)

Some degree of encapsulation is now almost universally accepted as necessary for efficient and safe management of digital resources. (However, the bundling is often virtual, consisting of links between separately stored components.)

Technology preservation

Another response has been an attempt to keep superseded technology available and operational. If all computers, all operating systems, all software and all information carriers could be kept in working condition, the digital preservation problem would hardly matter.

While such comprehensive technology preservation can be dismissed as an unrealistic fantasy, it would be foolish to discard the only means of providing access in the absence of other viable strategies. Keeping critical pieces of hardware as well as archives of software may provide an essential bridge between technologies, so its potential importance should not be dismissed.

However, in the long term there is probably no more than the slimmest chance of being able to keep ageing computers in working condition in sufficient numbers to make a difference, or of being able to persuade manufacturers to maintain a supply of superseded technologies. So technology preservation cannot be expected to serve as a reliable ongoing strategy, even if it may be a vital interim strategy in some circumstances.

Migration

The response of first choice in the computer industry has generally been two-fold: quite severe deselection of non-critical data, combined with migration or copying of what must be kept from one file format to another. Migration usually requires some rewriting of the way data are coded so that they work in a new operating environment. This kind of transformation has been successfully used to maintain access to large datasets for many decades, using well-understood practices. At a conceptual level, these practices are based on understanding the data and how they are organized, understanding what must be achieved in the new environment, understanding the constraints the new environment will impose, and checking that the data still work as intended once they are migrated.

There have been many questions about whether migration can offer a cost-effective pathway for maintaining reliable access to digital information without significant changes in meaning over time. Jeff Rothenberg in particular has highlighted the risks and costs involved, even if an organization can sustain the 'heroic effort' required to support migration strategies over long periods of technological change (Rothenberg, 1998).

For some kinds of digital resources, and in some circumstances, the criticisms are probably justified. Information in complex file formats for which there is no successor format will almost certainly be significantly changed in migration. However, it does seem likely that migration will work well for at least three kinds of resources:

- Relatively straightforward, well-developed and very widely used formats, especially those based on non-proprietary standards. Image formats such as the Tagged Interchange File Format (TIFF) and audio formats such as WAV have achieved such widespread industry use that it is most unlikely that successor formats will sacrifice their significant properties. Many well-managed digital collections containing very large numbers of such files should find it relatively simple to batch-migrate them, taking advantage of economies of scale and opportunities for automated migration and checking.

- Large, heavily used, business-critical databases and datasets, where the investment in developing and managing migration programs will not be challenged.

- Very large numbers of files where minor changes during migration will be seen as an acceptable trade-off for added functionality or for ongoing access to core information content. Most popular proprietary word-processing documents probably fit into this category for most users.

Critics of migration often seem to assume it is a monolithic, blunt instrument, but like most strategies under review, migration is capable of many subtle variations.

For example, some record-keeping systems expect to hold data objects in a relatively stable format while applying migration approaches to the presentation software that users will use to view them.

Emulation

It is unlikely that migration will provide a workable, sustainable access pathway for all kinds of digital information resources. Some things are so complex, or so idiosyncratic, that our best hope for providing access once their machine dependences have been superseded may be to re-create the environment in which they originally worked. Emulation programs attempt to do this.

Like migration, emulation as a preservation strategy is an extension of long-used practice in the IT industry. In this case, the technique has been widely used to provide access on what would otherwise be incompatible operating systems (such as Apple Macintosh files viewed on PC systems and vice versa).

Advocates of emulation point to its superior leverage, referring to the fact that the work invested in developing an emulator for a particular type of computer or operating system should ensure accessibility for all files originally dependent on that system. Migration, on the other hand, requires action on every individual file (although that action will usually be automated and global, not handcrafted).

Emulation approaches are also capable of subtlety. Recent research on emulation includes attempts to design emulator bridges between original operating systems and contemporary ones via a 'Universal Virtual Computer' – a theoretical, lowest-common denominator set of principles that underlies all computers (Lorie, 2001).

Several projects are trying to develop emulation approaches that will work for large digital collections over many changes in technology. If they can be advanced to a production level, such approaches should make it easier to maintain and re-present a more accurate experience of using digital information resources as they were originally used than would be possible with migration.

Format simplification

Migration, emulation, even technology preservation, would all be easier if the number of file formats to be managed could be kept to a minimum, and if the file formats themselves could be simplified. Many digital archiving programs are based on this premise. Many data archives, for example, only accept a very limited number of specified formats; others convert submitted data objects to a file format they know they can maintain, accepting that there may be some loss of significant properties in the process.

A variation on format simplification is to accept a wider range of formats but to structure them into a highly formalized and standardized file structure that is expected to remain recognizable by computer systems for many decades. Such a structure may also serve as an encapsulation, providing a wrapper of metadata that tells a computer system how to interpret the enclosed data objects. Extensible Mark-up Language (XML) shows great promise as a format for achieving this. Such *normalization* of file formats comes at a cost: converting or encapsulating submitted file formats may be an unacceptable overhead for some institutions. It is also possible that some file formats will be so idiosyncratic that they cannot be adequately described and enclosed in such a standardized structure.

Reconstruction of documented and managed archives

The archival and supercomputing communities have developed an approach to dealing with very large collections of data, which involves detailed recording of the context, structuring of data in a durable, versatile format such as XML, and development of software to reconstruct the collection using the data and context information so that the collection can be re-presented to users using available technology. The collection stored as files within the archive requires only regular refreshing to new media, while the supporting hardware and software systems evolve over time (Moore et al., 2000). Proponents of this approach (for example Thibodeau, 2002) believe it offers a comprehensive strategy that looks after the data themselves, and the architecture needed to manage and provide access to them.

Data rescue

Even in well-managed collections it is possible for some digital resources to be neglected and only to be discovered, or collected, when their intended means of access has already been lost. Such situations have led to the development of techniques for recovering data from otherwise inaccessible file formats. Whether we call this approach data archaeology (Ross and Gow, 1999), data palaeontology (Christensen-Dalsgaad, 2001), or data rescue, the techniques require some means of recognizing file formats, and a way of translating the data to a format that can be accessed with currently available software and hardware. Given that such files often turn up on physical format carriers that no longer fit into any available equipment, and often lack any kind of documentation that might tell the rescuer what to look for, it may be difficult even to decide whether the information is worth the effort until after the effort has been made.

Like technology preservation, data recovery programs should not be dismissed, as they may be the only means of regaining access to important information. Nevertheless, like technology preservation, data recovery is a poor substitute for more proactive preservation strategies.

THE CHALLENGE OF UNSTABLE LOCATIONS

Not only are we dependent on machines to read digital information that is before us; we also must rely on machines to recognize where the information is that we want and to bring it to us. Unambiguous naming of files is important in any file structure, but the advent of the Internet means that we expect machines to find the files we want in a haystack of truly staggering proportions. A globally accepted system of unique identifiers is one of the great achievements that has enabled the networked information world in which we live. It is unfortunate that the system of unique resource identifiers (URLs) is based on file location, because changes in location require a changed identifier. Many stakeholders would benefit from a system of identifiers that stayed with the information regardless of its location. Such persistent identification is important for digital preservation, because preserving accessibility requires that resources can be reliably found, over periods of time that will inevitably require location changes.

One response to this challenge has been to look for systems of location-independent persistent identifiers (PIs) and resolver services that reliably direct access requests to the correct current location. Many such systems have been proposed, and some of them, such as the Digital Object Identifier (DOI) adopted by publishers, have been implemented in some sectors. In mid-2002, there was still no globally accepted PI scheme in place. Digital repositories may need to use other means of managing persistence while such a scheme evolves (for example, National Library of Australia, 2001).

SUMMARY – TECHNICAL CHALLENGES

Preserving digital information resources encounters many complex and interrelated technical challenges. Digital preservation must find ways of understanding the threats to accessibility, monitoring their progress, documenting their effects, and overcoming them. To achieve this requires many technical tools and solutions, but as the following sections show, the challenges and the solutions are not purely technical ones.

SOME ORGANIZATIONAL CHALLENGES

The search for technical solutions to the core problems of digital preservation is paralleled by a search for answers to a range of organizational challenges. For many individuals and organizations, these challenges have been just as significant, as they try to envisage, and then manage, effective programmes in what looks like an unknown and high-risk environment. Through much of the 1990s one commonly heard the term 'paradigm shift' as commentators tried to express their sense of a revolution in the way information is created, discovered, shared, used and managed. Paradigm shifts usually imply a whole new way of doing things, so it is not surprising that people have been thinking about the context in which the emerging technical solutions might be effective.

What follows is an attempt to cluster some of the more important issues together and to briefly discuss some of the early responses.

RESPONSIBILITY AND WHO MIGHT TAKE IT

At least one thing has become clear – digital information will not survive through the benign neglect that many non-digital collections have experienced. If digital resources survive it will be because someone accepted responsibility for them and took effective action at the right time.

With the arrival of the much-vaunted 'information superhighway' that accompanied Web-based technology, many voices challenged the custodial and preservation roles of institutions like libraries and archives. Such institutions were said to be information dinosaurs, so firmly locked in 'yesterday's paradigm' that a new kind of institution would be needed. Alternatively, some people predicted that the Web would be preserved through its inherent self-ordered anarchy: collecting institutions would not be needed because everyone would archive and preserve their own resources.

These predictions may still eventuate, but in the early twenty-first century it appears that the existing mandated roles of institutions such as national, research and deposit libraries and large records archives continue to offer a great deal even in the networked, digital information environment. It is much to the credit of such institutions internationally that over the previous decade they had shown that they could not only offer security, but also considerable energy, adaptability and leadership. Somehow, many of these pillars of the old paradigm were drawing together their great expertise in managing information resources and commitment to service to adapt to a quite different environment. They seem likely to remain crystallization points around which responsibility for digital preservation may be constructed.

Early in this chapter it was noted that digital information was changing the relationships among a range of stakeholders. Considerable debate has focused on the roles various stakeholders such as creators, software developers, publishers, indexers, users, legislators and different kinds of institutions might take. Ultimately, it seems probable that digital information resources, like their non-digital counterparts, will tend to be kept by those with the capacity to do so and either a natural interest in or a mandated responsibility for their survival.

Unlike non-digital resources, however, it is quite possible to provide an information service from digital resources held by someone else. This probably has two very important implications in terms of responsibility.

First, it means that digital preservation is not necessarily everyone's core business. Those taking responsibility will need to do so very explicitly and clearly, while others who may have been used to taking an active preservation role may find that they can rely on others to preserve the information resources their clients want to use.

Second, while digital preservation may not be their core business, all stakeholders will have a much greater interest in how well the preservation responsibility is fulfilled by those undertaking it. It is easy to envisage an increased demand for accountability when the services offered by some depend so heavily on the performance of others.

Time will tell whether it is more cost-effective and reliable to centralize or decentralize digital archiving and preservation responsibilities. Whatever eventually appears as a stable responsibility model (if anything), it seems likely that for the foreseeable future there will be many complementary roles to be played by different stakeholders, such as identifying what needs to be kept, choosing appropriate formats, defining significant properties to be maintained, assigning metadata and persistent identifiers, storage and preservation management, and coordination and responsibility for the effectiveness of such a patchwork of roles.

THE NATURE OF THE DIGITAL PRESERVATION RESPONSIBILITY

Concern over a lack of technical standards has an organizational parallel, as organizations look for models that will clarify their responsibilities and offer some consistency of approach between archiving and preservation systems.

By far the most highly developed conceptual model to emerge is the Open Archival Information System Reference Model (generally referred to as OAIS). In early 2002 this model, developed over a period of some years, was issued internationally as a formal standard for describing digital repositories with preservation responsibilities (CCSDS, 2002).

The Reference Model grew out of the needs of the international space data community, but it has been taken up by a wider group of information managers, most particularly the research library and archives communities.

The Reference Model seeks to describe the functions of a digital archive, define the *information packages* that an archive manages, including the metadata needed to make them understandable and manageable. It also seeks to create a terminology that can be used across sectors and programs.

While it would probably be premature to say that OAIS has solved any digital preservation problems (other than the need for a widely accepted, coherent model), it has helped to coalesce the myriad of conversations about how digital archives should be managed into a common dialogue. The coming years will demonstrate just how effective it is as a model on which practical programs can be built.

The functions of digital archiving systems, as set out in OAIS, include:

- submission of data;
- ingest, or the processes of taking data packages into the archive;
- archival storage;
- data management;
- preservation planning;
- administration of the archive;
- provision of access.

The responsibilities of such an archive, according to the Reference Model, include:

- negotiation for and acceptance of appropriate information from producers and rights owners;
- obtaining sufficient control of the information to support long-term preservation;
- determining the community of users who need to be able to understand the archived information when it is made available to them;
- ensuring that the information is understandable to that community;
- following documented policies and procedures to ensure the information is preserved against all reasonable contingencies and to enable the information to be made available as authenticated copies traceable to the original;
- provision of access to the preserved information.

What kind of organization or system can be trusted to fulfil such responsibilities? According to a joint Research Libraries Group/OCLC working group studying the attributes of reliable digital repositories, such a system must:

- accept administrative responsibility for the archived material;
- be viable as an organization;
- be financially sustainable and use programs that it can sustain into the future;
- use technology, techniques and procedures that are suitable;
- have secure systems;
- operate with full accountability.

(RLG, 2002)

Both the OAIS Reference Model and the Attributes Working Group report address high-level principles, leaving others to work out detailed implementation programmes that satisfy their requirements.

Many of these responsibilities and attributes are those also required of anyone expecting to be trusted to look after non-digital collections, the main difference being that there is often much less margin for error in managing digital collections.

COSTS

How much does digital preservation cost? Even after a decade or more of studies, pilot projects, research reports, and even ongoing mainstreamed programmes, costs are not clear. Estimates have been based on theoretical models or extrapolated from necessarily limited experience. It remains impossible to estimate with certainty the costs to store, manage and take preservation action over the whole life of digital collections.

For example, it is commonly assumed that data storage costs will continue to decline to levels where they can be disregarded. At a unit cost level that is a reasonable expectation. However, the amount of data to be stored will increase quite spectacularly on a number of fronts: the size of digital objects is increasing as they incorporate more features, the number of objects will continue to grow, and migration programs will double the data storage requirements each time a migration is completed but the source generation is not discarded (a likely scenario for cautious repositories). It is impossible to estimate the effects of techniques not yet understood on collections of resources that do not yet exist.

Uncertainties about costs may act as a barrier to progress on almost all digital preservation fronts. Organizations and funding bodies are understandably reluctant to commit to programmes that may come with long-term, uncosted responsibilities. To say 'we only know it will cost a lot' is an unsatisfactory answer, even if it the truth. In the light of this dilemma, three ways of going forward suggest themselves:

- accepting that we may have to tailor digital preservation programmes to the available resources;
- squeezing the greatest benefit we can out of our programmes by good management;
- accepting that the only way to get better cost information is by taking action.

At the National Library of Australia it has been possible to make significant progress within very constrained resources by reallocating some priorities and by drawing on skills and commitment already in the organization. This has tended to encourage senior managers to pay close attention to digital preservation programmes, and helped embed such programmes in the core business of the Library.

PRESERVATION MANAGEMENT

Experience suggests that, for all their new technical challenges, digital preservation programmes benefit from a strong preservation perspective and also need good management input.

Good management principles that may be applicable include:

- a focus on objectives, regularly asking 'why are we doing this?';

- development of policy frameworks to guide decision-making;
- a determination to recognize risks, assessing their likely impact and developing plans to manage them;
- making informed decisions when they are needed;
- planning on the basis of good priorities;
- accountability;
- finding appropriate resources – people, skills, energy, systems, equipment, money – and managing and nurturing them;
- recognizing the need for change and fostering a culture of learning from experience and from the experience of others.

In addition, some long-standing preservation perspectives are particularly relevant to digital preservation, such as:

- a long-term view, and an interest in how long information resources need to remain usable;
- a professional commitment to honest and open communication;
- a commitment to documenting any action that affects the material and may interfere with a user's understanding of it;
- looking for minimal and if possible reversible interventions that will achieve what is needed;
- a commitment to keeping technical knowledge up to date;
- a willingness to return to first principles when necessary to solve new problems;
- critical questioning of any proposal involving potential risks to the material;
- insistence on knowing who is responsible.

COLLABORATION

Perhaps because of the highly portable nature of digital information and its access, or the size and complexity of digital preservation issues, but whatever the cause, collaboration has been a strong and strongly influential feature. Collaboration has occurred at all points, from simply sharing information to formal partnership agreements covering actual preservation programmes. So pervasive has this been that it is hard to identify any significant advances that have not involved cooperation of some kind between organizations with an interest in preserving digital information.

For all its apparent benefits, collaboration comes with its own challenges. The most effective cooperative programmes seem to have been based on areas of real common interest, realistic expectations, clear understandings about who is responsible for what, and the allocation of sufficient resources to pay attention to the collaborative relationship itself.

46

In a world of distributed archiving and mutual accountabilities, one can only imagine that collaboration will continue to offer benefits that make the effort worthwhile.

SOME PROJECTS

A small selection of projects has been chosen to illustrate some of the real-world responses to these challenges. They are not meant to be representative of everything that is happening. It is only possible here to make a few relevant comments against each project; readers are strongly recommended to explore these and other projects further.

NEDLIB (Networked European Deposit Library) – a collaboration between a number of European national libraries, archives, large commercial publishers and the IT industry, to explore methods and infrastructure that would enable deposit and preservation of online and offline digital publications. Uses the OAIS Reference Model as a framework. Funded by the European Commission. Has produced a number of important reports. More information available at <http://www.kb.nl/coop/nedlib>.

Digital archiving developments at the Koninklijke Bibliotheek (KB) (the National Library of the Netherlands) and at the British Library (BL). Following the conclusion of the NEDLIB project, the KB established a contract with IBM to develop a digital archiving and preservation programme as part of its DNEP programme. A key feature is the dedication of resources specifically to development of practical technical solutions that address the core digital preservation challenges of technology obsolescence over long periods of time (Long Term Preservation Study). Coincidentally with the KB initiative, the BL also entered a contract with IBM to develop a facility for that library. Information on the KB programme can be found at <http://www.kb.nl/kb/ict/dea/index-en.html>.

Arts and Humanities Data Service (AHDS) – a leadership initiative for the UK higher education (HE) sector set up to collect, describe and preserve the electronic resources which result from research and teaching in the humanities. AHDS has been particularly important in coordinating the work of some long-established data archives and fostering the establishment and management of others, using a standards or best-practice approach. More information can be found at <http://ahds.ac.uk/>.

CEDARS (CURL Exemplars in Digital Archives), and *Project CAMiLEON* (Creative Archiving at Michigan & Leeds: Emulating the Old on the New). CEDARS was another UK HE sector initiative with a brief to test current preservation theory by developing a demonstrator system that would work with a wide range of digital object types. A key feature was its distributed archiving sites spread across a number of universities. Based on the OAIS framework, with a heavy emphasis on preservation metadata development. Its investigations into emulation fed into Project CAMiLEON, a joint UK/US project between the Universities of Michigan and Leeds. More information on CEDARS is available at <http://www.leeds.ac.uk/cedars/>; information about CAMiLEON can be found at <http://www.si.umich.edu/CAMILEON/>.

PANDORA (Preserving and Accessing Networked Documentary Resources in Australia) – a programme initiated by the National Library of Australia to enable the development of a national collection of Australian online publications. Takes a very selective approach based on publicly available selection guidelines, in order to apply a high level of quality control over the functionality of what is archived, and negotiated access rights. Distributes some archiving functions among nine collaborative partners in Australia. Pre-dates publicly available versions of OAIS, but maps well to it. Information on PANDORA can be found at <http://pandora.nla.gov.au/index.html>.

Kulturarw3 – project initiated by the Royal Library of Sweden to comprehensively archive and preserve the entire Swedish Web domain, in contrast to approach followed by PANDORA. Information available at <http://www.kb.se/kw3/ENG/Default.htm>.

Internet Archive – a non-profit US-based commercial venture, which collects and stores publicly available materials from the Internet. Further information available at <http://webdev.archive.org/>.

Development of record keeping standards in the records archives community. For example, the Public Record Office of Victoria (Australia) VERS project in collaboration with IT researchers, business analysts and records specialists. VERS features encapsulation of files in a standardized wrapper with extensive metadata. National Archives of Australia is introducing a digital preservation approach built around *normalization* of all incoming record formats by converting to an XML structure. The InterPARES project (International Research on Permanent Authentic Records in Electronic Systems), headed by the University of British Columbia, is a collaborative attempt to determine the requirements for maintaining the authenticity of records over time, looking at the extent to which appraisal and preservation processes meet these requirements. Information on the VERS project can be found at <http://www.prov.vic.gov.au/vers/>. Information on InterPARES is at <http://www.interpares.org/index.htm>.

SOME SOCIETAL CHALLENGES

Some challenges go beyond the control of individual organizations even acting together. This section looks at some of the wider societal challenges to keeping digital information accessible.

AWARENESS

Awareness remains an important starting-point. Despite many horror stories of lost public data, and despite growing individual experience of lost files, software obsolescence and broken Internet links, digital preservation remains a relatively low-profile issue likely to be dealt with superficially or not at all by the media.

There have been some innovative attempts to change this level of engagement. The General Conference of UNESCO in late 2001 adopted a resolution committing the organization to preparation of a charter on the preservation of the digital heritage (UNESCO, 2001). Likewise, the European Commission's Directorate-General for the Information Society in January 2002 received a report from the DigiCULT study which included a call for 'national governments and regional authorities . . . to take immediate action on long-term preservation and (to) formulate a strategy for digital preservation as part of a national information policy' (European Commission, 2002).

Establishment of the Digital Preservation Coalition in the UK is another very significant step in providing a voice of advocacy that may be heard by governments, funding bodies, the media and the broader community (DPC, 2002).

RIGHTS

Early twenty-first century society continues to struggle with perceived conflicts between rights of reasonable access to information and protection of legally enforceable property rights such as copyright. The resolution of such conflicts will influence what digital information can be collected, what can be done with it, and how it can be used. All of these impact on preservation programmes.

Despite warnings of dire outcomes on both sides of what easily becomes a highly polarized debate, in many areas rights owners and information managers such as libraries have been able to find enough common ground to justify optimism that there will be ways of working together.

The current debate may be a crucial prelude to more widespread extension of legal deposit arrangements to digital publications in a range of jurisdictions.

RESOURCING

While individual organizations have some control over the resources they choose to allocate to digital preservation, there is little evidence that societies are yet prepared to provide adequate resources to manage digital information collections as they grow in size and complexity, and as they reach threshold points where preservation action cannot be delayed any longer without loss.

It will be interesting to see the way different communities respond to this challenge. Presumably some will seek to provide more resources, while others will be unable or unwilling to do so even though it means a substantial loss of access to information. Yet others will probably look for business models that shift the financial burden of maintaining access on to users, depositors, or other stakeholders.

SOME BASIC MESSAGES

Some tentative conclusions could be drawn from this chapter, as follows:

- While there is much room to argue whether all digital information should be preserved, some of it is undoubtedly of enduring value and needs to be kept.
- Keeping digital information requires action, not benign neglect.
- While not everyone needs to feel responsible for taking action, if no one accepts responsibility and acts on it, digital information of enduring value will be lost.
- It makes much sense to work together, and there is a strong developing culture of doing so.
- We already know a great deal about the factors that threaten ongoing accessibility, and we have a good sense of what we need to do, even if we still struggle to recognize techniques that will work well and how to organize ourselves to use them.
- While those with an interest in the long-term accessibility of digital information resources may not have the means to take full action yet, there is much they can do to assess and improve the *preservation readiness* of their resources.

FINDING MORE INFORMATION

This has been of necessity a superficial overview. The literature on digital preservation is extensive and rich in ideas and debate. Useful avenues for further reading include:

- The PADI subject gateway to information on digital preservation, managed by the National Library of Australia. Also includes access points to a number of online discussion lists that act as forums for debate about digital preservation issues. <http://ww.nla.gov.au/padi>.

- The (US) Council on Library and Information Resources range of published reports and newsletters, available at <http://www.clir.org/pubs/>.
- *D-Lib Magazine*, which carries regular articles on digital preservation among a range of other research topics to do with digital libraries. Available at <http://www.dlib.org/>.
- *RLG DigiNews* published by the Research Libraries Group with frequent features on digital preservation. Available at <http://www.rlg.org/preserv/diginews/>.
- ERPANET (Electronic Resources Preservation and Access Network) case studies in digital preservation, available at <http://www.erpanet.org/>.
- The *Preservation Management of Digital Materials Handbook*, online version, maintained by the Digital Preservation Coalition in conjunction with PADI. Available online at <http://www.dpconline.org/graphics/handbook/index.html>.

CONCLUSION

Lemuel Gulliver, visiting the strange lands of Laputa, was impressed with the focused, energetic but intrinsically worthless projects of the 'scientists' at the Academy in Lagado as they struggled with intransigent reality. May the many attempts to find our way towards a secure future for digital information lead us in more promising directions than those who sought to communicate without words and shape fire.

REFERENCES

(All Web sites checked 5 September 2002)

Baker, Nicholson (2000), 'Deadline', *The New Yorker*, 24 July 2000.
Christensen-Dalsgaad, Berte (2001), 'Archive Experience, Not Data', paper presented at the *Preserving the past for the future – strategies for the Internet* conference, Copenhagen, 18–19 June 2001.
Consultative Committee for Space Data Systems (CCSDS) (2002), *Reference Model for an Open Archival Information System, CCSDS 650.0-B-1*, CCSDS Secretariat: Washington, DC. Available online at <http://www.ccsds.org/documents/pdf/CCSDS-650.0-B-1.pdf>.
Digital Preservation Coalition (DPC) (2002), *About the Digital Preservation Coalition*. Available online at <http://www.dpconline.org/graphics/about/index.html>.
European Commission Directorate-General for the Information Society (2002), *The DigiCULT Report: Technological Landscapes for Tomorrow's Cultural Economy – Unlocking the Value of Cultural Heritage*. Available online at <http://www.salzburgresearch.at/fbi/digicult/>.
Kranch, Douglas A. (1998), 'Beyond Migration: Preserving Electronic Documents with Digital Tablets', *Information Technology and Libraries* 17: 138–48.
LOCKSS (2002), *Permanent Publishing: local control of content delivered via the web*. Available online at <http://lockss.stanford.edu/projectdescbrief.htm#Medium>.

Lorie, Raymond A. (2001), 'A Project on Preservation of Digital Data', *RLG DigiNews* 5 (3), 15 June 2001. Available online at <http://www.rlg.org/preserv/diginews/diginews5-3.html#feature2>.

Moore, Reagan, Chaitan Baru, Arcot Rajasekar, Bertram Ludaescher, Richard Marciano, Michael Wan, Wayne Schroeder and Amarnath Gupta (2000), 'Collection-Based Persistent Digital Archives – Part 1', *D-Lib Magazine* 6 (3). Available online at <http://www.dlib.org/dlib/march00/moore/03moore-pt1.html>.

National Library of Australia (2001), *Persistent Identifier Scheme Adopted by the National Library of Australia*. Available online at <http://www.nla.gov.au/initiatives/nlapi.html>.

NISO (National Information Standards Organization) and AIIM International (2002), *Data Dictionary for Technical Metadata for Digital Still Images, NISO Z39.87-2002/AIIM 20-2002* (released as a Draft Standard for Trial Use 1 June 2002–31 December 2003), Bethesda, Maryland. Available online at <http://www.niso.org/standards/resources/Z39_87_trial_use.pdf >.

Norsam Technologies (2001), *HD-Rosetta Archival Preservation Services*. Available online at <http://www.norsam.com/hdrosetta.htm>.

OCLC/RLG Working Group on Preservation Metadata (2002), *Preservation Metadata and the OAIS Reference Model: A Metadata Framework to Support the Preservation of Digital Objects*, OCLC Online Computer Library, Inc.: Dublin, Ohio. Available online at <http://www.oclc.org/research/pmwg/pm_framework.pdf>.

Research Libraries Group (RLG) (2002), *Trusted Digital Repositories: Attributes and Responsibilities – An RLG/OCLC Report*: Mountain View, California. Available online at <http://www.rlg.org/longterm/repositories.pdf>.

Ross, Seamus and Ann Gow (1999), *Digital Archaeology: Rescuing Neglected and Damaged Data Resources*, Library Information Technology Centre, London. Available online at <http://www.ukoln.ac.uk/services/elib/papers/supporting/pdf/p2.pdf>.

Rothenberg, Jeff (1996), *Metadata to support data quality and longevity*. The Institute of Electrical and Electronics Engineers Inc. Available online at <http://www.computer.org/conferences/meta96/rothenberg_paper/ieee.data-quality.html>.

Rothenberg, Jeff (1998), *Avoiding Technological Quicksand: Finding a Viable Technical Foundation for Digital Preservation*, Council on Library and Information Resources: Washington, DC. Available online at <http://www.clir.org/pubs/reports/rothenberg/contents.html>.

Thibodeau, Kenneth (2002), 'Overview of Technological Approaches to Digital Preservation and Challenges in Coming Years', in *The State of Digital Preservation: An International Perspective – conference proceedings DAI Institutes for Information Science, Washington, D.C. April 24–25, 2002*, Council on Library and Information Resources: Washington, DC. Available online at <http://www.clir.org/pubs/reports/pub107/contents.html>.

UNESCO (2001), *Resolution 31 C/DR.79 of the General Conference*. Available online at <http://unesdoc.unesco.org/images/0012/001239/123975e.pdf>.

3 Selection for digital preservation: dilemmas and issues

Majlis Bremer-Laamanen and Jani Stenvall

DILEMMAS AND ISSUES

This chapter focuses on issues of selecting material for collections in the digital environment from a national point of view. Particular attention is given to printed publications which are converted to digital format and to publications originally published in electronic format (born digital). The solutions and dilemmas in Finland are used as an example of the issues influencing decision-making in material selection today.

In libraries all over the world there is a rapid digital development going on, with digitization projects growing ever larger. Libraries are taking important steps in order to meet the expectations of the public, by building core collections that can be accessed via the World Wide Web. In this process the audiences will change and so also will the mission and functions of these institutions.

EASY ACCESS

The expectations of customers are changing with the new media. They are anticipating easy access to core collections in libraries and other heritage institutions such as museums and archives.

Within the library field the need for cooperation is a great challenge, for many reasons. On a governmental level the national, university, research and public libraries are often not administered by the same governmental body. The funding organizations are manifold, such as governmental bodies, universities, companies and local authorities. The funding for digitization is often not organized on a continuous basis. In many cases it is also unclear who should fund digitization, and to what extent, as it is a new task. It is also unclear which collections should be freely available on the Web and which should get their funding from the users.

Restricted financial resources are well known to most heritage institutions and they have their pros and cons. To take the good news first – restriction encourages cost-effective use of the resources which are provided. Technical infrastructure must be developed and automated as far as possible. Heritage institutions must evaluate the most effective way of collecting electronic material. On the other hand, if there is no or little funding, this will stop or delay a good project.

How can a mutual understanding in building a critical mass of collections be reached, when missions and management differ so much in individual libraries? There is also the difficulty of coordinating the selection of collections with other heritage institutions such as archives and museums, representing different kinds of institutional cultures and technical solutions (Smith, 2001).

For smaller countries representing smaller language groups the dilemma is that the general public, academic institutions, researchers and business might turn to using the English collections on the Web as their main source. This could in the long run diminish the knowledge, research and interest in the national culture as part of Europe's cultural richness as a whole. The selection of material for the Finnish collections should support the technical solutions for the multilingual use of European collections. This would enable the development of our manifold collections and deepen understanding and research worldwide.

PRESERVATION ISSUES

The selection of electronic publications for preservation is difficult. The following methods can be considered for preservation of digital collections: keeping available the original hardware and software; migration – converting the collections from one format to another; or emulation – creating programs to keep the original environment updated. There are many problems as yet unsolved. At the time of the selection process it is not known what documents or even what attributes of a document will be important in the future. Rothenberg (1999) states that the 'look and feel' of electronic documents is essential, while Bearman (1999) is satisfied with the intellectual content as evidence. This dilemma, which arises from the different perspectives of computer science and the archiving tradition, will not be dealt with further here.

One of the main problems in the preservation of electronic materials is the obsolescence of hardware and software and the expensive solutions mentioned above. Archiving the bits can be easy but rendering these archived bits into documents in the future is not. The rapid development of electronic publishing is forcing libraries to make decisions without knowing the future preservation options. Digitization is above all a method to improve access to otherwise fragile or rare analogue materials. In contrast, we could transfer digital materials such as simple text and pictures to paper or microfilm formats, which are safer than any file format today (Häkli, 2001).

With all these dilemmas at hand, how do we choose our digital collections, such as those originally on paper and those born digital?

HOW DO WE CHOOSE?

The selection decisions made when starting digitization projects are the most important and critical for success. Content and its accessibility are what interest the end-user most. Selection criteria have been used in the preservation field for many decades. The essential difference between preservation and digitization criteria in the selection process is that preservation deals with the extent of the damage and hazard caused to the collection, while digitization deals with the demand for the collection (Gertz, 1998).

The selection decisions for cultural heritage should primarily be based on demand, which has not always been the case. The need for technical development during the 1990s made selection criteria less important. Small samples were in some cases gathered to show the public the possibilities of digitization. As many of the technical problems are now solved, we can focus on content and its accessibility, and on audiences and their reactions (Lynch, 1996; Demas, 1996).

The problem of preserving electronic publications should influence the selection decisions from the very start. When ordering and receiving the material in electronic format, the need for continuous preservation treatment must be acknowledged (Häkli, 2001). Technical realities, costs, copyright issues and the properties of electronic documents likewise prevent us from proceeding at a faster rate. One can also agree with Calanag et al. (2001) that the act of selecting electronic publications for preservation has become a process of reselecting. We have to intervene continually to keep our electronic resources available for use.

SELECTION CRITERIA FOR ELECTRONIC PUBLICATIONS

Digital publishing on the Web and offline has grown rapidly in recent times and will continue to grow. The enormous increase in the number of digital and electronic documents is putting pressure on libraries and other heritage institutions. Because of the short life-span of born-digital material, especially on the Web, national libraries and libraries with preservation obligations have to collect the digital heritage of the country before it is too late. Several countries are revising (or have already revised) their legal deposit laws to cover electronic documents. This implies that the institutions responsible for legal deposit are willing to try to find ways to preserve this digital heritage.

Russell (1999) writes that in 1999 selection for preservation tended to be based on *ad hoc* criteria, for example file formats. It is quite clear that the file format or carrier should not be regarded as a selection criterion because formats and carriers are changing constantly. However, it is necessary to state which formats or carriers the deposit organization is able to handle and preserve. There is no point in accepting electronic documents or publications that cannot be preserved for technological reasons. Usually this means that standard open file formats should be preferred to proprietary ones. In addition, preservation measures should include access functions. Accordingly, newspaper articles as text in pdf-format, Portable Document Format, is preferred to image-pdf.

Different selection guidelines are defined in various preservation projects. One of them is the National Library of Australia's (NLA) selection guidelines for physical format electronic publications which lists the following criteria for publications to be preserved:

- the publications have long-term research value and have either Australian content or authorship; and
- the authors/publishers of the publications are considered to be authoritative in their field; or
- the information content is substantial and significant to Australian research and is not generally available in any other format.

(Preserving Australian physical format electronic publications – selection guidelines, NLA, http://www.nla.gov.au/policy/selectgl.html)

The so-called Mackenzie report (Mackenzie and van de Walle, 1996) gives general guidelines for any deposit organization to implement. The report is still valid and gives a good picture of different criteria for selection and exclusion. Selection policy is an important tool for an organization to implement fully its preservation actions.

Many deposit organizations (for example deposit libraries) state that their selection policy for electronic publications follows the policies set for traditional materials. The NLA principles are an excellent example of this. Although this approach is justified, it does not cover the whole electronic field because not all of the electronic documents necessarily fall into the traditional categories. Electronic materials are new and still under development; they are not as stable as the traditional publications.

On a national level the legal deposit guidelines can serve as a basis for selecting and preserving the national output. The selection can be limited to national documents, national publishers and mediators, and nationally important materials with a significant intellectual content. Organizations with no legal deposit obligations may find this approach unsatisfying. These organizations are, however, likely to have some other reasons for preserving electronic documents. The selection guidelines can be based on heavy use, specific contents of the documents or other specific attributes such as creators, retention periods, condition of the document, legal evidence, even file formats and so on. As is stated in the report of the Cedars project (Russell, 1999), any preservation actions should be tied to the cultural, research, legal or commercial interests of the organization.

A MATERIALISTIC APPROACH

As early as 1986 Ross Atkinson presented a materialistic preservation approach which is still valid today. In this he divided library holdings into three general classes of material (Atkinson, 1986).

The first category contains objects and collections of high artistic value which are rare and unique materials. The originals will be permanently retained in their original form. Digitization can ensure safety of these collections as well as make them readily accessible internationally.

The importance of the collections in the second category is their intellectual content and high demand. Digitization of these heavily used collections is a priority for libraries. Legal issues have to be dealt with where more recent material is concerned. The selection criteria within this category can be based on one or a combination of the following criteria listed by Demas (1996):

- the genre of the material, for example newspapers, serials or photos;
- core collections chosen by scientists, librarians and so on;
- the discipline, for example mathematics or physics;
- the 'vacuum cleaner approach', that is, digitizing the prominent collections in a specific field from one or two libraries;
- collections from a geographical area;
- collections from a time period.

The third category consists of little-used and usually brittle items, with very low or short-term demand. Usually there is no need for digitization in these cases.

In contrast to the paper and microfilm collections in libraries, the added value that comes with digitization might change the use of collections and also user groups. This added value is dependent on the material digitized. For genres such as newspapers and journals free text search provides a wholly new perspective for research, as places, historical persons and eras can be combined in various ways and applied to a large number of titles. The problems with digitizing, cataloguing and the complementary functions have to be recognized from the beginning. For example, medieval collections and collections in older foreign languages need to involve both specialists in these fields and conservation experts. In the digitization process we must also take into account multilingual features, and the special needs of the disabled.

In the course of time the materials selected for retention need to be re-examined. As mentioned earlier, selection tends to become a process of reselection. The selection and reselection procedure being carried out in the Finnish broadcasting company, Yleisradio, is a good example. The company is archiving and preserving radio programmes (analogue or digital) for its own use and also for national cultural purposes. The producer of the radio programme is the one who makes the selection and preservation decisions. He or she evaluates the cultural importance or unimportance (for example, introductions to musical pieces) and the need for archiving. If the producer is hesitant, he or she can assign a specific number, from 1 to 9, to the programme. This means that the programme is archived, but that the final decision will be made by the same producer, if still working for the company, one to nine years after the first broadcasting of the programme.

Other important questions are the copyrights of digital versions and their funding, the safety of the material when reformatting it, the infrastructure of the digitization, the total cost factor and the availability of the material. Finally there is the preservation of the digital files.

Efficient, selective, qualitative and systematic decision-making is needed more than ever.

SELECTION CRITERIA AND THEIR IMPLEMENTATION ON A NATIONAL LEVEL

When setting up a digitization policy we should always look at the local communities, their institutions and needs. The situation in Finland will stand as an example for ongoing selection criteria discussions and implementation challenges.

In Finland, Helsinki University Library – the National Library – is heavily involved in developments in the electronic field and this has had a substantial impact on library cooperation. The long history of the library – it was established in 1640 and has had legal deposit rights since 1707 – has not been an impediment to its innovativeness; indeed, the contrary has been the case.

DEVELOPMENT AREAS

There are four main development areas in the electronic field in Finland. First, there is a research library network, which includes not only all university libraries but libraries in other sectors as well. These libraries are using a joint server; the university libraries share the same university network, FUNET.

Second, the National Electronic Library, FinELib, has become one of the functions of the national library since the year 2000. Country licences have been purchased for almost 8000 journals and bibliographic databases in 2002.

Third, the Legal Deposit Act is under revision in Finland, supervised by the Ministry of Education. Electronic publications in all formats will be included. Legislation will serve as an ultimate selection guideline for the national heritage.

The law will probably state that electronic publications should be deposited like the traditional publications in all legal deposit libraries. Helsinki University Library will be the organization responsible, along with five other deposit libraries, for the legal deposit of electronic publications, most probably from the beginning of 2003.

Fourth, a centre of excellence for the digitization of the national heritage was established in 1999 within the National Library at the Centre for Microfilming and Conservation, situated in Mikkeli, 200 kilometres from Helsinki.

NATIONAL AND INTERNATIONAL COORDINATION

The Ministry of Education has set up a working group for the Digitization of the Cultural Heritage, within the Information Society Programme, for the production of digital resources. In this working group the National Library, National Archives and the museum sector are coordinating digitization practices and issues on a large scale. On a national level the working group has recommended voluntary cooperation between the participating heritage institutions in building large core collections. This seems to have generated an encouraging response.

The working group for the digitization of the cultural heritage is following closely the corresponding international work on the European Union level, the *eEurope – An Information Society for All* – programme, in which Finnish members from the heritage institutions are participating in the working groups for digitization policy, programmes and technical matters.

The international and national working groups have had a positive impact on digitization issues in Finland, although the restricted resources currently available for digitization are limiting substantially the implementation of the forthcoming digitization programmes.

DIGITAL COLLECTIONS DEVELOPMENT IN THE UNIVERSITY LIBRARIES

To determine the digitization needs in Finnish university libraries, Helsinki University Library sent a questionnaire to them in 1999. This questionnaire was complemented in Autumn 2001 by answers from the public library sector as well.

According to the responses, digitization needs are manifold, involving both small and large problems. It was possible to distinguish marked trends of development as well as well-defined selections of collection groups for national, academic and local needs.

On a national level the choices could be divided into four groups. All groups were based on demand among the library users. The first three groups were based on genre; the first two also raised the question of the time factor in asking for current materials. This of course has implications for the legal rights in the material.

The most persistent request for a genre of collections to be digitized was newspapers up to the present time. Advanced search options and indexes were desired. The second important genre was scientific journals and their indexes. Third came the most-used reference works in libraries. The fourth group included many core collections in the cultural field. Examples of these were collections in literature and science and collections of national and international importance.

On a local and university level the needs were naturally based on the desires of the institutions and the surrounding local community. University libraries consider it their task to digitize the dissertations and scholarly theses produced at their institutions.

On a local level there are many similarities between the wishes of the various libraries in the country. For instance, there is a need to digitize the biographies of famous and influential persons, famous writers and their works and geographical descriptions from earlier times. There is also cultural interest in past centuries, in everyday life, in the industry and commerce of those times, and work in factories, in the fields, in offices. These could be combined with larger projects of historical, social and cultural importance.

MEETING THE DEMAND – A HISTORICAL DIGITAL NEWSPAPER LIBRARY

To build comprehensive digital collections requires a long planning, development and implementation period to get a sustainable result. Fortunately this was possible in the Nordic TIDEN project, which resulted in a historical digital newspaper library. The project launched its database in October 2001. In Finland, newspapers are one of the most-used categories of material in the national collection, and were hence a likely option for digitization. On the initiative of the Finnish National Library in 1998, the national libraries in Sweden and Norway, and the State Library of Åarhus in Denmark, started to test digitizing historical newspapers from microfilm and to apply full text search to the material. All these libraries have substantial newspaper holdings on microfilm. The Nordic Council of Scientific Information (NORDINFO) has financed the Nordic project together with the participating libraries, and the Finnish part of the project received additional funds from the Ministry of Education.

The Newspaper project covers a period from 1645 to 1860, with between one and three titles from each country. Because of copyright restrictions it is not possible to extend the time period into the twentieth century. In Finland the project includes all the 44 titles published during the period and covers newspapers in Finnish, Swedish and German.

Finland and Sweden were to our knowledge the first in the world to be able to use optical character recognition (Finereader software) for old Gothic text, and for free text searching of digitized newspaper collections. Fuzzy search (Excalibur Retrieval Ware) has been applied to enable full text searching to defective text and old-fashioned typography and language. An article search index is also included in the Finnish digital newspaper library.

In Norway and Finland the technical solutions have been developed for larger digital databases and workflow, and in Finland the Web solution has also taken account of the needs of disabled persons.

The project has extended geographically, as Iceland, Greenland and the Faroe Islands have started a digital newspaper project of their own. This means that a comprehensive Nordic digital newspaper library is developing. Newspaper publishers have taken an interest in the ongoing project, especially in Finland, Norway and Iceland.

SERIALS AND A COPYRIGHT SOLUTION

The other project directly responding to the findings in the questionnaire is the PERI+ project, which aims at the conversion of whole series of scientific journals into digital format. For this collection it is possible to manage the copyright issues because of the scientific nature and the smaller scope of the material in comparison with newspapers.

The aim is to build a critical mass of digital scientific journals for researchers and scholars in Finland. At first the aim will be three to five digitized journals, to be augmented later. For PERI+, a full text search option will be added to the options of serials and article titles and authors. An important goal for the project is finding a suitable model for managing copyrights in cooperation with the Finnish copyright organization KOPIOSTO, which is a standing member of the project.

ELECTRONIC PUBLICATIONS

The Legal Deposit Act will function as a selection policy for the national output of Finland. The current draft of the Act defines two types of electronic publications: offline technical resources and online Web resources.

The offline technical resources will cover publications such as games, educational materials and databases distributed on physical carriers such as CD-ROMs, DVDs, disks and tapes. The DVDs consisting mainly of video material will be donated to the National Film Archive, which is responsible for preserving the moving image. The current draft states that electronic materials that have low intellectual content can be ruled out and not preserved. Software will probably fall into this category, although there might be some exceptions. Only one copy is needed of the technical resources in a format suitable for preservation at the National Library. The right to copy the product for preservation purposes has to be included in the law. Thus the product must be supplied with proper documentation and without any copy protection. The same applies to Web resources with use restrictions like e-books, course materials and so on, which have to be supplied to the deposit library ('Vapaakappalelaki 2000').

The selection of freely available Web documents is quite a different matter. The main method for collecting these in Finland at the time of writing is harvesting. Harvesting is popular because it comprehensively collects online Web resources at moderate expense. The testing and production phase of automated harvesters is under way in several countries. Both national libraries and special projects are involved in harvesting, all trying to collect their own Web space into an archive. Harvesting is ideal for static documents and the Web, but not suitable for dynamic pages or the 'deep Web' with documents in databases (Hakala, 2001). The harvesting of national Web space is easy when there is a clearly defined domain space, for example *.fi* or *.se*. But when you are dealing with .com, .org, .net or similar domains there are problems in resolving which domains and sites belong to which national Web space. An alternative approach is selective harvesting. Several projects have examined this (PANDORA, MINERVA). In these cases certain Web pages or sites have been selected for preservation and the contents of those sites have been copied into special archives. In Finland, freely available Web pages will be harvested, archived and indexed in bulk. Some pages or sites can be harvested on a more frequent basis and dynamic pages will be archived as 'snap-shots'.

TECHNICAL INFRASTRUCTURE AND FINANCIAL SUPPORT FOR DIGITAL COLLECTION DEVELOPMENT

TECHNICAL INFRASTRUCTURE

The development of digital collections in Finnish libraries will benefit from sustainable technical solutions. Funding can be directed to the digitization and access of collections on a larger scale than before.

There are a number of significant differences between the management of a specific project and the management of a long-term programme. A separate project has to build the whole structure from choosing the collection, digitization, indexing, metadata, software, search tools and Web sites. Later on this includes the maintenance of the digital files.

The advantage of programme management is the established collections and technical management structure. From the technical point of view there is also the benefit of continuity. A technical infrastructure should be developed with future flexibility in mind and for many kinds of collections. A reliable technical infrastructure and established automated work processes are platforms for all digital projects. The less there is of technical software that has to be updated and converted, the less expense is involved in future projects. Stable technical and managerial structures will ease the arduous work the institutions have in enabling easy access to national and international core collections.

In the field of electronic publications different technical infrastructures should preferably be built. For example in Finland the current draft for the new Legal Deposit Act states that access to electronic technical resources is restricted to deposit libraries and their customers. The draft also stipulates, as mentioned above, that only one copy of an electronic publication has to be donated to the National Library. So in order to study a deposited CD-ROM one has to make a physical visit to one of the deposit libraries. This means that an infrastructure is needed that allows delivery of products in six different locations using only one copy. This will be handled with specific software and a virtual private network.

FUNDING

Funding is essential for the implementation of sustainable long-term digitization programmes. It should be based on continuity. Digitization policies and programmes should be built on a national level but in the context of the national heritage institutions to provide a mutual understanding for future needs and actions to be taken. In the end it is the responsibility of the nation to fund digital access to and preservation of the national heritage, which will benefit the population at large, research, academic institutions, business and others.

At the time of writing the funding of digitization and its continuity is very much dependent on national governmental actions; in Finland, this means the Ministry of Education. Three digital centres received funding in 2001 in the museum, archive and library sector to enable them to develop their competence. The continuation of funding is essential, but at present it is granted for only one year at a time.

The Finnish enquiry into university, research and public libraries discussed in this chapter will, if successful, lead to a digitization programme for the cultural library heritage. This might be a platform for future applications to funding bodies and could enhance the digital environment, development and cooperation between libraries, memory institutions and nations. However, outside funding is always dependent on the programmes of the funding authorities and should preferably function as an aid to the normal digital functions of the institutions and not as a mere funding possibility.

A VISION

Many institutions are digitizing their collections to a greater or lesser extent. Some of these institutions are digitizing collections containing holdings of other institutions and nations. The goal is now to combine these efforts into systematic programmes, for better quality standards, for funding and for more comprehensive access. There is not one simple method for achieving these goals. Cooperation and agreements on the national and international level will be useful in promoting a more systematic approach.

Diversity can be seen as a positive feature, especially when quality, access and preservation actions have been observed. In the Finnish National Library there is a vision for the selection for digitization, which will perhaps assist it to establish a systematic programme for the selection of material into collections. An example would be digitization of the nineteenth century, which consists of many genres of material such as newspapers, journals, manuscripts, maps, photographs, art and so on. These are the items and genres forming the core collections, in such disciplines as science, history, mathematics, geography, ways of life, education, culture and so on. Each institution is contributing to this pattern, which in the end forms a patchwork of the cultural heritage and extends to other centuries and to international cooperation. The cultural heritage in electronic format is thus extending from the digitized past to the future of born-digital material. The task of the libraries is to select, collect, organize and preserve these collections in cooperation for their end-users.

REFERENCES

Atkinson, R.W. (1986), 'Selection for Preservation: A Materialistic Approach', *Library Resources & Technical Services*, October/December.

Bearman, D. (1999), 'Reality and Chimeras in the Preservation of Electronic Records', *D-Lib Magazine* (5) 4 April. Available at: http://www.dlib.org/dlib/april99/bearman/04bearman.html (5.11.2001)

Calanag M.L., Sugimoto, S. and Tabata, K. (2001), *A Metadata Approach to Digital Preservation*, Proceedings of the International Conference on Dublin Core and Metadata Applications.

Demas, Samuel (1996), 'What Will Collection Development Do?', *Selecting Library and Archive Collections for Digital Reformatting*, RLG.

Gertz, J. (1998), 'Selection Guidelines for Preservation', *Joint RLG and NPO Preservation Conference. Guidelines for Digital Imaging 28–30 September 1998*. http://www.rlg.org/preserv/joint/confpapers.html

Hakala, J. (2001), 'Collecting and Preserving the Web: Developing and testing the NEDLIB Harvester', *RLG DigiNews*, 5 (2). Available at: http://www.rlg.org/preserv/diginews/diginews5-2.html (5.11.2001)

Häkli, E. (2001), 'The Evolving Roles of Libraries and Archives in the Face of Technological Change', *Rational Decision-making in the Preservation of Cultural Property*. N.S. Baer and F. Snickars, cop 2001

Mackenzie Owen, J.S. and van de Walle, J. (1996), 'Deposit collections of electronic publications', *Libraries in the Information Society*, European Commission, DG-XIII-E/4.

NLA (2001), 'Preserving Australian physical format electronic publications – selection guidelines', National Library of Australia (NLA). Available at: http://www.nla.gov.au/policy/selectgl.html (5.11.2001)

Rothenberg, J. (1999), 'Avoiding Technological Quicksand – finding a viable technical foundation for digital preservation', Council on Library and Information Resources, CLIR Reports. Available at: http://www.clir.org/pubs/abstract/pub77.html (5.11.2001)

Russell, K. (1999), 'Why can't we preserve everything? Selection Issues for the Preservation of Digital Materials', CEDARS project report. Available at: http://www.leeds.ac.uk/cedars/documents/ ABS01.htm (5.11.2001)

Smith, Abby (2001), 'Building and Sustaining Digital Collections', Models for Libraries and Museums. Council on Library and Information Resources, Washington, DC.

'*Vapaakappalelaki 2000 – työryhmän muistio*' (2000) [A Memo of a Legal Deposit Working Group]. 13:2000 Opetusministeriö [Ministry of Education]. To get a general idea of the revision of the Finnish legal deposit act see articles in the *Tietolinja News* 1/1999. Available at: http://www.lib.helsinki.fi/ tietolinja/0199/index.html (6.11.2001)

4

Issues in the long-term management of digital material

Adrienne Muir

INTRODUCTION

The preservation of digital objects is a new and complex area. By their nature such objects are unlikely to remain accessible or usable over time without ongoing intervention. Digital information faces various threats from unstable media and technological obsolescence. There are also a number of non-technical issues to contend with. In the library domain, the way in which digital information is created, published and distributed makes it more difficult for libraries to preserve material. For example, for traditional media, libraries acquire and physically own a discrete information object. This is not the case for much digital information, where the model is paying for access to information held remotely. If libraries do not physically own digital material, they cannot preserve it.

While this may not be such a problem for the archives domain, there is still the problem of a blurring of boundaries between 'published' material and records to be archived. An example here is the use of Web sites by organizations to make material available. The selection of material has been covered elsewhere in this book, but a related issue that will be covered in this chapter is how preserving organizations, especially libraries, can discover and acquire physical copies of material so that they can be preserved. This includes legal deposit and arrangements with publishers.

The acquisition, storage, preservation and provision of access to digital objects over time involves repeated acts of copying. The precise nature of these acts depends a great deal on the preservation strategies adopted. The copyright issues that arise depend on the scope of copyright legislation and the nature of the material. There may be conflicts between what copyright allows preserving institutions to do and what library and archive laws require them to do. This chapter looks at some of the approaches to tackling this issue.

Archivists especially, but also librarians, are concerned with the authenticity and integrity of the digital material they care for. Transfer of digital objects from producers to preservation institutions and preservation strategies, including refreshment and migration, involve the risk of corruption or loss of data. Preserving institutions need to know that what they receive from producers is what they should be receiving and users need to know that the information they access is what it purports to be. There are computing techniques that can help in this area, but there is also a need for a supporting authentication infrastructure.

Preservation management for traditional media is fairly well developed, with management tools and techniques, standards, guidelines and benchmarks to help in policy development and implementation of preservation programmes. Decisions on what and why to preserve and various proposed digital preservation strategies have been covered elsewhere in this book. It is clear that there are quite fundamental differences between the preservation of more traditional types of information carrier and digital information which requires intermediary technology for access. Some traditional preservation strategies such as ensuring appropriate environmental conditions and security are still relevant. However, there is a question of how far existing tools and techniques such as condition surveys are applicable in the digital environment or how far the preservation of digital material can be integrated into preservation activities. The Preservation Planning process in the Open Archival Information System conceptual model is a step towards understanding how digital preservation can be managed (Consultative Committee for Space Data Systems, 2002). Other promising work is being carried out in areas such as tools for working out cost implications of different configurations of digital preservation operations and managing redundancy in the digital environment.

It seems that metadata are the key to the long-term management of digital objects, both to allow preservation to be carried out and also to document what has happened to digital objects over time to help establish their integrity and authenticity. Colin Webb (Chapter 2) mentions the work the OCLC and the Research Libraries Group have done in preservation metadata. This chapter expands on this and also looks at how the creation and management of metadata over time could be accomplished.

NEW TYPES OF PUBLISHING AND ACCESS VERSUS OWNERSHIP

Publishers can make the same underlying content available in a variety of digital versions and formats using various dissemination channels. So several versions of a 'work' may exist at the same time.

The ephemeral nature of online information has implications for digital preservation. Online resources are updated, added to, deleted and moved, often without warning. The extent of a hyperlinked digital publication can be a factor when deciding what to preserve; maintaining the links is an ongoing management issue.

In the case of digital publication, access may be directly from the publisher or through some sort of intermediary. Libraries may or may not have access to material that is not current. With print material, cancelling subscriptions would only result in loss of access to future material; previously purchased material would still be available on library shelves. This may not be the case with digital material. The question of responsibility for the preservation of information arises here, as libraries cannot preserve what they do not own.

New forms of disseminating information, such as Open Archives, may also present preservation problems. The main aim of the Open Archives Initiative is to facilitate discovery and access to digital information, not its long-term preservation. Publishers and owners of open archives may or may not have a commitment to preserving their own information; this will depend to an extent on the type of publisher and its mission.

DISCOVERY AND ACQUISITION OF DIGITAL MATERIAL

Extending legal deposit to cover digital publications may solve the problem of access to rather than ownership of digital publication, but only to a limited extent. Legal deposit only covers the national published output. Larivière gives the following definition of legal deposit:

> … a statutory obligation which requires that any organization, commercial or public, and any individual producing any type of documentation in multiple copies, be obliged to deposit one or more copies with a recognized institution.
>
> (Larivière, 2000, p. 3)

Increasingly countries are extending their legal deposit arrangements to cover digital material. However, in many cases legal deposit will only include digital information on physical carriers, such as CD-ROMs or DVDs. Legislation in some countries (for example Norway and South Africa) theoretically extends to all digital publications, but currently only certain types are collected or collecting is on a limited basis. Other countries are currently taking a hybrid approach: legislation covers some types of material, with voluntary arrangements for other types. Australia, and now the UK, is currently taking this approach. The Conference of European National Libraries (CENL) and the Federation of European Publishers (FEP) made a declaration in 2001 in which they advocated the immediate implementation of voluntary schemes (Conference of European National Libraries & Federation of European Publishers, 2001). This declaration includes a model voluntary code for local adaptation. The model code is based on the UK scheme and should include offline and online publications. The declaration recommends that there should be a trans-national steering group for these initiatives in Europe.

IFLA has recently issued guidelines on legal deposit legislation (Larivière, 2000). The elements of a legal deposit scheme are set out, as are the different types of material to be included. There is a separate chapter for electronic publications, although they are also included in the general chapter on types of material. This all comes together in a legal framework for legal deposit. The document discusses the various issues and difficulties of implementing legal deposit for digital material.

Legal deposit libraries face some special problems in preserving digital information. In order to acquire all the information they are entitled to, depositories have to discover its existence. They cannot just rely on publishers sending them their material. Publishers may not want to comply for some reason. Alternatively, they may not know that they have to: organizations publishing material may not consider themselves to be publishers, while new players may not even be aware of legal deposit obligations.

Bibliographic control is well developed in the print environment, less well developed for non-print formats and, it seems, virtually non-existent for digital publications. One particular area of concern is that of unique identification of digital publications. While identification of offline digital material such as CD-ROMs may be reasonably straightforward using identifiers such as ISBN or ISSN, Unique Product Code (UPC) or European Article Number (EAN) barcodes, online material presents several problems. One is that there may be different manifestations of the same content. The question is whether each manifestation should have a different identifier, or whether there should be one identifier for the underlying work. This raises the further question of how to identify each manifestation and relate this to the underlying work.

Another problem in the online environment is the lack of persistence of identifiers. World Wide Web documents are identified by their Universal Resource Locator (URL). Unlike traditional identifiers that identify items, the URL indicates the location of the item. URLs change as Web content is rearranged, hence their lack of persistence. This causes problems when documents are linked because the links will break down over time. It also causes problems with finding documents in the longer term.

Several initiatives explore the development of persistent identifiers. The new types being developed include the Digital Object Identifier (DOI). The DOI system is an implementation of the Uniform Resource Name (URN) approach developed by the Internet Engineering Task Force. The DOI can be assigned to any item of intellectual property, but this must be clearly specified. This is done through the use of structured metadata, and a metadata dictionary is part of the system. Once assigned, the DOI is not altered even through successive ownership changes. In order to ensure persistence, the DOI system uses a resolution system – the Handle System (Corporation for National Research Initiatives, 2002). Rather than relying on the original URL, which is not persistent, the DOI resolves to current information such as the current URL. Resolution can be to more than one piece of data (International DOI Foundation, 2002).

Persistent Uniform Resource Locators (PURLs) are also compatible with the URN idea. PURLs are URLs, but they do not point directly to the item. Instead, they point to a resolution service and the resolution service then points the PURL to a URL. OCLC developed the PURL system and assigns PURLs to resources catalogued in its Internet Cataloguing Project (OCLC, 2002). While the URL may change, PURLs cannot be changed, so are persistent. OCLC considers PURLs to be an intermediate step in the move towards URNs, or a way to ensure continued identification until persistent identifiers, such as DOIs, are assigned to all items.

Although work is being carried out to address the problem of unique identification and persistence of identifiers, until coherent systems are implemented there is still the problem of knowing what exists. One suggestion here is that legal deposit could require all publishers to register their publications (Webb, 1997). The existence of publications would then be known, even if they were not all collected. This idea is a good one in theory, but in practice it may be impossible to enforce precisely because of the large numbers involved and the ignorance of many new players about legal deposit systems.

With traditional publications, deposit usually means that some responsible entity sends physical objects to depositories. At present there are three main options for acquiring online information. Publishers can transfer the information on to a physical medium and send that to the depositories. They can arrange to transfer, or 'push', information to depositories via networks. Alternatively, libraries can 'pull' from publishers' sites themselves. A variant of this is 'harvesting'. This is usually done for Internet information, where the depositories use software to identify and pull in information from sites. The push option may not work well on the Internet because it is populated with a huge number of publishers, some of whom are small organizations or even individuals. It would be impossible to set up relationships with all of them.

INTELLECTUAL PROPERTY RIGHTS ISSUES

Digital preservation strategies involve copying. Table 4.1 sets out the potential copying actions that are likely to be required for the various proposed preservation strategies.

Table 4.1   Possible copying actions

Media refreshment and change	1.	Copying from an old medium to a new one of the same type
	2.	Copying from a digital medium to paper or microform or Copying from one type of digital medium to another
Migration	1.	Media refreshment and migration as above
	2.	Producing a new version of the original information or a migration tool in a new format
		• discarding the original
		• keeping the original
Emulation and the Universal Virtual Computer approach	1.	Media refreshment and migration of content, application software, operating software, hardware specifications, software specifications
	2.	Reverse engineering of software for developing emulators

There are a number of potential barriers to carrying out these activities. One of these is copyright law. While the law in many countries includes exceptions for certain types of copying, including copying by public institutions such as libraries and archives, these exceptions may have been drafted with print material in mind. For example, in the UK Copyright Designs and Patents Act 1988 the exceptions related to 'library privileges' include the making of a copy by a librarian or archivist of a *prescribed library or archive* from any item in the permanent collection to preserve or replace that item or to replace an item in the permanent collection of another prescribed library or archive. Copying is only permitted in certain circumstances. For example, materials can only be from the *permanent* collection in the libraries of both the donor and the receiver, and must be for reference use only. The status of electronic subscription materials such as online journals is not clear. The only type of copying that seems to be clearly allowed under the preservation exception is the first act of media refreshment or migration.

The situation in individual countries is likely to differ. In the United States, the much-criticized Digital Millennium Copyright Act (DMCA) expressly allows authorized institutions to make up to three digital preservation copies of an eligible copyrighted work. It allows the institution to loan those copies to other institutions and permits preservation, including by digital means, when the existing format in which the work has been stored becomes obsolete (United States 1998, Title IV). In Canada the Copyright Act allows electronic publications to be converted into a contemporary format if necessary for preservation purposes. However, the work must be in the library's permanent collection and the copy must be made in order to maintain the collection (Institute for Information Law, 1998).

From a purely technical point of view, even if a preserving institution has a copy of the digital information, and it is allowed to undertake copying under copyright exceptions, it may be prevented from doing this by copy-protected physical carriers and other protection mechanisms. When the latest European Commission Directive on copyright is enacted, libraries in Member States may be able to circumnavigate copyright protection to exercise their privileges (European Commission, 2001).

If preserving institutions do not have the legal right to copy for preservation purposes, then they could ask rights-holders for permission to do so. This was a recommendation from the CEDARS Project (2002, p. 16). According to the CEDARS recommendations, if an institution physically owns a digital object, a clause should be included in the licence agreement to allow making preservation copies. If the digital object is accessed remotely, there should be a clause which allows the institution to access the content for preservation purposes. Alternatively, there should be an agreement clearly stating who has archival responsibility. The JISC Model Licence for Journals (Joint Information System Committee, 2002) seems to cover these points. Under the terms of the licence, the licensee may make back up copies of the licensed material in order to make them accessible locally. The publisher undertakes to provide access to the archive of subscribed material once a subscription ends. Access can be via the publisher's or a third party's server. Alternatively, the publisher may provide the former licensee with an archival copy of the material which was subscribed to, in a mutually agreed format.

A licence negotiated on the basis of perpetual access – in the case of electronic journals this would provide for continuing access to back issues even when a subscription has lapsed – is not the same as a licence for preservation purposes. It relies on other players, such as information providers, publishers, hosts or other intermediaries taking responsibility for and ensuring preservation. Even if guarantees are given, organizations go out of business or just may not have the resources to do the job.

Clearing rights for the preservation of digital materials is likely to be resource-intensive. Text, sound, still and moving images can be combined in so-called multimedia products. Complex digital material may also be dependent on software for search and retrieval and other functionality. The rights in the different elements of multimedia objects or products may belong to a number of different individuals or organizations, rather than the publisher. Even if the publisher has the rights to all of the content, it may only have licences with third parties for the use of software. Preservation institutions may have to spend a great deal of time identifying and locating rights-owners and requesting permissions. The institutions would then have to keep records of all the various agreements, which would also be a drain on resources.

An alternative to individual libraries seeking permissions is some form of central rights clearance operation. There are reproduction rights organizations in various countries that are already involved in licensing for digitization. They may be able to take on licensing for digital preservation purposes.

Organizations wishing to harvest material from the Internet without setting up agreements with rights-owners are taking different approaches to dealing with the rights issues. The Internet Archive tries to take comprehensive snap-shots of the Internet. Material is made accessible unless a rights-owner objects. The Swedish government has issued a decree authorizing the Royal Library not only to collect Swedish Web sites on the Internet but also to allow public access within the library premises (*New decree for Kulturarw3*, 2002). The French government has adopted a law requiring every French Web site to be archived (*Entire French web to be archived*, 2001). While many organizations are expected to do this, the Bibliothèque nationale de France (BNF) and Ina, the national audio-visual depository, are to harvest material at regular intervals.

Another approach to the issue of rights could be the inclusion of rights information in metadata associated with digital material. This information would have to come from rights-holders, but is not included in emerging standards from this sector. The status of material with regard to rights may change over time. The use of persistent identifiers, such at Digital Object Identifiers and Open URLs that could point to related metadata both on the rights-holder and on the preserving institution, may be useful here.

MAINTAINING AUTHENTICITY AND INTEGRITY OVER TIME

The strategies used or proposed for digital preservation may cause problems for maintaining the integrity and authenticity of digital material. Integrity refers to the completeness of material and whether it has been altered. While authenticity can have different meanings in the archive and library communities, it refers here to whether something is what it purports to be. It involves belief or trust on the part of the user. In the opinion of most commentators, it is easier to copy and change digital information than materials in which there is obvious degradation in copies and changes can be detected easily. Preservation actions may cause changes in the materials being migrated or even loss of information. Migrated material may not look, or function, in the same way. While the aim of emulation is to retain look, feel and functionality of the material, this depends on the skill of software engineers. If preservation strategies are repeated over time, more changes can be introduced.

When preserving institutions are deciding what to preserve and how, they have to consider what they require in terms of authenticity or what authenticity means to them. Thibodeau (2002, p. 13) states that the 'outputs of a preservation process ought to be identical, in all essential respects, to what went into that process'. Defining these 'essential respects' is likely to be part of the consideration of significant properties discussed elsewhere in this book (Chapter 2). Intended use is important here. For archives there is usually a legal imperative to preserve records. For libraries it is more difficult to predict why and how future users will want to use digital material.

There is a range of strategies for asserting the authenticity of digital resources. The strategy used depends on the purpose for which authenticity is needed. The International Research on Permanent Authentic Records in Electronic Systems (INTERPARES http://www.interpares.org/) project has focused on this issue in depth. At the least the actions taken and the resulting changes should be documented. Reversible migration processes and keeping the unmigrated and/or all migrated versions are also possibilities. Unique document identifiers and associated metadata can be used to keep track of material and versions. Hashing is a computing technique used to establish the uniqueness of material. A 'digest' of the material can be computed and made public. Anyone who wishes to check the material can recompute the digest and compare it with the published one. Watermarking can be used to guard against unauthorized copying or amendments of material. A digital watermark is inserted into material and can only be detected by appropriate software. The software can be used to check on unauthorized use. Hashing can be incorporated into time stamping and digital signatures. Time stamping records the unique relation between material and a combination of time, date and site data. This allows distinctions to be made between different versions over time. The Dutch Royal Library (KB) intends to 'stamp' migrated material to indicate to users that the information has been altered and to reassure publishers. Digital signatures can support authentication in that some sort of 'official' declaration of authenticity at a particular time is made. The ongoing work of the Research Libraries Group on trustworthy digital repositories (http://www.rlg.org/ longterm/certification.html) may contribute to the development of an infrastructure to support the authentication of digital material.

PRESERVATION MANAGEMENT IN THE DIGITAL ENVIRONMENT

In the archives domain decisions about the future of records are taken at an early stage in their life cycle. This is traditionally less likely to be the case in the library sector. Decisions about how long material is to be kept and how it is to be preserved may be taken some time after the material is acquired. This is not the case with digital material; decisions have to be taken at the time of selection of material for acquisition. The way in which digital material is created and distributed will affect how it is preserved. While archivists may have a degree of control over the material that they accept, librarians are dealing with published material and have little control over how it is created. Selection criteria and preservation strategies are covered elsewhere in this book. What we are concerned with here is how the preservation of digital material can be managed. The problems arising from licensing access to rather than purchasing a physical copy of digital information are dealt with earlier in this chapter. This section assumes that an institution does physically own digital information.

The OAIS reference model (Consultative Committee for Space Data Systems, 2002) includes a high-level preservation planning component, aiming to:

- monitor designated community;
- develop preservation strategies and standards;
- develop packaging designs and migration plans;
- monitor technology.

The designated community monitoring activities are aimed at identifying the changing service requirements of the users or consumers and trends in the product technologies of producers. These activities help the Develop Preservation Strategies and Standards and the Develop Packaging Designs and Migration Plans functions stay abreast of trends in the Designated Community and changing preservation requirements. The Monitor Technology function includes tracking and assessing emerging standards and technologies, in response to requests from Develop Preservation Strategies and Standards and Develop Packaging Designs and Migration Plans. The relationship between these two functions may be similar to that of conservation and technical staff and preservation managers. However, it seems that neither is involved in the implementation of policies and plans or of routine maintenance of collections (for example refreshing storage media). They both feed their recommendations to the OAIS Administration function and implementation is carried out by other functions, such as Archival Storage.

In traditional preservation management an initial step in developing preservation policies is to assess the condition of collections and the risks to which they may be exposed. There is still a need for these activities in the digital environment, and this can be seen in the OAIS functional model. The assessment of risk is traditionally mostly concerned with internal factors such as building security and maintenance or environmental conditions. There are already standards for the storage of digital media. For example, in the UK there are British Standards 4783 for storage and 7799 for security management.

The need for this assessment remains in the digital world, but risk also comes from the outside world, and the community and technology monitoring activities have to be incorporated into the assessment process. The methods of assessing the condition of collections have traditionally involved manual inspection of physical objects for signs of damage. While preserving institutions may retain digital information on discrete physical carriers for some time, physical inspection of these carriers will not yield the kind of information needed for digital preservation. The OAIS model indicates the use of surveys to monitor the external environment. Presumably these will be administered and analysed by staff. Monitoring the condition of physical storage media and application of preservation strategies is likely to be at least partially automated. The degree of automation that is possible will probably depend on the complexity of the material being preserved.

While the OAIS functional model gives some clues as to what is likely to be involved in the management of digital preservation, it says nothing about how the model could be implemented. However, some institutions have been working on procuring storage systems based on the OAIS model. The Royal Library in the Netherlands seems to be furthest down the road, having taken delivery of a system developed by IBM. The British Library has also been working with IBM and the Dutch Royal Library on developing its Digital Library System. While the Dutch have a system in place, it does not yet include a preservation function. Research work is ongoing with IBM to develop this.

The LOCKSS project was mentioned in Chapter 2. It is one way of addressing risks in that it is an approach to organizing redundancy in the digital environment. Researchers at Stanford University are also carrying out interesting work on underlying technical infrastructure for preservation activities through the Stanford Archival Repository project (Cooper et al., 2002). The repository design developed by the project has been implemented through the Stanford Archival Vault and implementation issues are being investigated. The project also includes the development of a simulation tool for modelling configuration options and a model for cooperation between different repositories. This model provides a framework for the negotiation and implementation of storage space trading agreements for redundancy purposes.

METADATA

The role of metadata in preservation is not new to conservators and archivists. Jones and Beagrie (2001) set out a number of reasons why metadata are crucial in digital preservation. These include the dependence of digital information on hardware and software and the need for documentation of technical requirements for decision-making. Preservation may not be affordable or even possible without these data. The likelihood of changes in digital material caused by preservation actions and the potential role of metadata in managing rights have already been discussed. Digital preservation will require active intervention on an ongoing basis and this intervention should be documented to provide continuity for all those who will be involved with decision-making and management of digital material and for the purpose of accountability. Another role for metadata is in any reuse of the material.

Much work is ongoing in this area in both the library and archives domains. A prominent initiative is the OCLC/RLG Working Group on Preservation Metadata, which was tasked with developing 'a comprehensive preservation metadata framework applicable to a broad range of digital preservation activity' (OCLC/RLG Working Group on Preservation Metadata, 2001, p. 1). The aim was that the metadata framework should not be specific to any particular type of data object. There has been some comment on how applicable this high-level framework is in the archives domain (Hofman, 2002); many members of the Working Group are based in libraries and the framework builds on previous library-based work. A report published in June 2002 (OCLC/RLG Working Group on Preservation Metadata, 2002) sets out the framework, which uses elements from existing schemes and also adds new elements. It is based around the OAIS information model.

So there is a library-oriented high-level metadata schema, but it is not clear how such a schema could be implemented. Some of the data elements match the sort of bibliographic information currently needed to describe material; there is then the question of if and how preservation metadata could be integrated with bibliographic data systems.

The recording of metadata for digital objects is a problem for digital libraries as well as digital archives. The Digital Library Federation has developed the Metadata Encoding & Transmission Standard (METS), 'an XML document format for encoding metadata necessary for both management of digital library objects within a repository and exchange of such objects between repositories (or between repositories and their users)' (Library of Congress, 2001). This document includes different types of metadata:

- Descriptive metadata – these may be embedded in the METS document and/or there may be a pointer to descriptive metadata external to the METS document (for example a MARC record).
- Administrative metadata – information on the creation and storage of files, intellectual property rights, provenance of the files (that is, master/derivative file relationships, and migration/transformation information). This can also be embedded or external.
- File groups – a list of all files comprising all electronic versions of the digital object.
- Structural map – outlines a hierarchical structure for the object, linking the elements of that structure to content files and metadata for each element.
- Behaviour – used to associate executable behaviours with content in the METS object.

METS may be used to encode preservation metadata, but the metadata schema must be populated. While libraries would have to supply some of the metadata, the nature of some elements of the OCLC/RLG schema suggest that cooperation with publishers will be necessary to do this. There is no indication in the literature of how this could be achieved. The publishing industry is involved in the development of metadata schemes, but the focus is on the exploitation of intellectual property rather than its long-term management. The ONline Information eXchange (ONIX) is a standard format for the exchange of product information between different players in the information industry. ONIX defines:

> both a list of data fields about a book and how to send that data in an 'ONIX message.' ONIX specifies over 200 data elements, each of which has a standard definition, so that everyone can be sure they're referring to the same thing. Some of these data elements, such as ISBN, author name, and title, are required; others, such as book reviews and cover image, remain optional. While most data elements consist of text (e.g., contributor biography), many are multimedia files, such as images and audio files.
>
> (Editeur, 2002b)

As it stands, ONIX provides some, but by no means all, the metadata that libraries would require for preservation purposes. However, there have been various studies looking at how ONIX metadata could be used by libraries. Examples include mappings of ONIX to various MARC bibliographic data schemes (Editeur, 2002a). If publishers adopt ONIX and libraries are looking at the use of ONIX as a way of acquiring metadata generally, then there is the possibility of exploring the extension of ONIX to provide preservation-related information. ONIX is expressed in XML, so presumably could be incorporated into a METS document. The British Library has been involved in development of a tool to help publishers produce ONIX metadata. There are moves towards collaboration between publishers and preserving institutions to investigate options. Even if the trade standard is extended, the bigger challenge is getting publishers to populate the preservation elements.

CONCLUSION

While existing preservation management principles and practice still apply in the digital environment, there are new challenges in the preservation of digital material. There are differences in the challenges faced by archives and libraries, but also some common ground. The focus of the chapter has mainly been on libraries because of the background of the author. It is clear that the preservation community is becoming increasingly aware of the problems to be overcome and there has been much useful work on exploring issues and developing the building blocks of solutions. However, certainly in the libraries domain, much work is at a conceptual level and the various building blocks that are under development are not yet being turned into integrated systems. There is still much technical work to do, policies and good practice to be developed and supporting infrastructure to build.

ACKNOWLEDGEMENTS

I would like to acknowledge the input of Margaret-Mary O'Mahony, Claire Everitt and Gavin Brindley into this chapter.

REFERENCES

CEDARS Project (2002), *CEDARS guide to intellectual property rights*. <http://www.leeds.ac.uk/cedars/guideto/ipr/guidetoipr.pdf> [accessed 6.12.02].

Conference of European National Libraries & Federation of European Publishers (2001), *International declaration on the deposit of electronic publications*. <http://www.ddb.de/news/epubstat.htm> [accessed 6.12.02].

Consultative Committee for Space Data Systems (2002), *Reference model for an Open Archival Information System (OAIS)*. CCSDS 650.0-B-1 Blue Book, January. Washington, DC: CCSDS. <http://wwwclassic.ccsds.org/documents/pdf/CCSDS-650.0-B-1.pdf> [accessed 6.12.02].

Cooper, B., A. Crespo and H. Garcia-Molina (2002), 'The Stanford Archival Repository project: preserving our digital past', *Library and Information Research News* 84 (Winter), pp. 17–25.

Corporation for National Research Initiatives (2002), *Handle System: introduction*. <http://www.handle.net/introduction.html> [accessed 6.12.02].

Editeur (2002a), *ONIX mappings to MARC*. <http://www.editeur.org/onixmarc.html> [accessed 6.12.02].

Editeur (2002b), *What is ONIX International?* <http://www.editeur.org/ONIX%20International%20FAQ.html> [accessed].

Entire French web to be archived (2001), <http://www.europemedia.net/shownews.asp?ArticleID=4075> [accessed 6.12.02].

European Commission (2001), *Directive 2001/29/EC of the European Parliament and of the Council of 22 May 2001 on the harmonisation of certain aspects of copyright and related rights in the information society*. <http://www.eurorights.org/eudmca/CopyrightDirective.html> [accessed 6.12.02].

Hofman, H. (2002), 'Metadata and the OAIS model', *DigiCult Info: a newsletter on digital culture* 2 (October), pp. 15–20. <http://www.digicult.info/pages/index.php> [accessed 6.12.02].

Institute for Information Law (1998), *Copyright aspects of the preservation of electronic publications*. IViR Reports 7, University of Amsterdam. <www.ivir.nl/Publicaties/koelman/KBeng2.doc> [accessed 6.12.02].

International DOI Foundation (2002), DOI overview. <http://www.doi.org/overview/sys_overview_021601.html> [accessed 6.12.02].

Joint Information Systems Committee (2002), *The JISC model licence for journals*. <http://www.nesli.ac.uk/modellicence.html> [accessed 06.12.02].

Jones, M. and N. Beagrie (2001), *Preservation management of digital materials: a handbook*, London: British Library.

Larivière, J. (2000), *Guidelines for legal deposit legislation*, rev., enl. and updated edn, Paris: UNESCO.

Library of Congress (2001), *Mets: an overview and tutorial*. <http://www.loc.gov/standards/mets/METSOverview.html> [accessed 6.12.02].

New decree for Kulturarw3 (2002), 287. <http://www.kb.se/Info/Pressmed/Arkiv/2002/020605_eng.htm> [accessed 12.11.02].

OCLC (2002), *PURL*. <http://www.purl.org/> [accessed 6.12.02].

OCLC/RLG Working Group on Preservation Metadata (2001), *Preservation metadata for digital objects: a review of the state of the art: a White Paper*. OCLC. <http://www.oclc.org/research/pmwg/presmeta_wp.pdf > [accessed 6.12.02].

OCLC/RLG Working Group on Preservation Metadata (2002), *Preservation metadata and the OAIS information model: a metadata framework to support the preservation of digital objects*. <http://www.oclc.org/research/pmwg/pm_framework.pdf> [accessed 6.12.02].

Thibodeau, K. (2002), 'Overview of technological approaches to digital preservation and challenges in coming years', in *The State of Digital Preservation: an International Perspective*, Washington, DC: Council on Library and Information Resources, pp. 4–31.

United States (1998), *Digital millennium copyright Act (DMCA)* <www.loc.gov/copyright/legislation/dmca.pdf> [accessed 6.12.02].

Webb, C. (1997), *Long-term management and preservation of publications on CD-ROMs and floppy disks: technical issues.* <http://www.nla.gov.au/niac/meetings/tech.html> {accessed 2.6.03}.

5 Preserving paper: recent advances

René Teygeler

INTRODUCTION

The art of preserving is as old as human civilization itself. In a way it may be said to derive from the instinct of self-preservation common to all animate beings. In spite of everything it seems we want to keep the past alive. For nearly two millennia the preservation of works of art on paper has been practised in the Far East. Originating first in China at the beginning of the Christian era, conservation techniques and materials quickly spread to Japan and subsequently to other areas. A fifth-century Chinese writer, Chia Ssu-hsieh, raised points in conservation that are familiar to paper conservators today: care in handling objects, choice of correct materials for conservation, correct storage and vigilance against infestation, exposure at correct levels of humidity, and exclusion of sunlight (Wills, 1987).

As a full-grown profession, however, preservation does not have a very long history. It was only some thirty years ago that paper and book preservation established itself as a true profession in the public domains of education, law, administration and cultural heritage. In the process of professionalization the conservator increasingly made use of science. These days, preservation science is a speciality in its own right in which scientists develop an understanding of why and how archive materials deteriorate and then, in cooperation with conservators, research into methods and materials for arresting that deterioration. In resolving questions, preservation scientists may apply the pure sciences such as chemistry and biology, applied sciences and environmental science as well as several technological areas such as radiography (AIC-RATS, 2001; Tagle, 1999).

The multitude of preservation research activities, carried out worldwide, indicates an international awareness of the need for scientific tools to tackle the problem of degradation of the world's cultural heritage. Many researchers and research institutes are making efforts to supply conservators and restorers with properly tested means to treat individual artefacts as well as with techniques for mass conservation. Ongoing research is providing new insights into the theoretical background and mechanism of the process of deterioration, allowing a goal-directed approach towards the development of active and passive (preventive) conservation procedures. Some of the recent advances in preservation science, especially those relevant to paper conservation, will be discussed below.

Science or not, we have to keep in mind that the cycle of nature dictates that all things made of organic matter must decay. We can only expect to slow down the rate of the deterioration of our paper-based material heritage, the core of our archives.

PAPER PRESERVATION

At the end of the twentieth century a number of trends in preservation were noticeable. Around 1990 governments and institutions alike realized that the paper treasures in archives and libraries were threatened by insidious decay. If nothing were done, before very long large numbers of books, magazines, journals and archival papers would be irreparably damaged, or would even disappear altogether. As a result of this awareness substantial financial resources were allocated to preservation and preventive conservation. In order to make responsible choices, risk assessments and damage surveys were developed. One of the results was that paper-based materials after 1850, in particular, were found to age extremely fast due to the high degree of acidity, an effect of essential changes in the paper production process. The scale of the problems was immense. Thus preservation officers had to develop mass conservation treatment programmes. From that moment on the attention shifted from analytical investigation of individual artefacts and individual conservation problems to large-scale national and even international preservation activities (Porck et al., 2000).

At the same time preventive conservation had made its entry into the field, partly for economic reasons. A more critical, hands-off approach evolved, based on a better understanding of conservation problems and of decay mechanisms of objects, as well as on the acknowledgement of the failure of some modern materials that had previously been introduced into the field. The primary question at the time of writing is how to prevent damage – thereby limiting direct intervention on objects to the absolutely necessary (Tagle, 1999).

Thus most advances in preservation knowledge and practice concentrate on the following three categories:

- decay: cause and mechanism of degradation;
- treatment: active conservation;
- storage: passive conservation and damage prevention.

To lessen the possibility of linguistic confusion it is necessary to define the terms preservation and conservation. In this chapter we follow very broad definitions, which more or less cover the whole field of conservation, in which *preservation* refers to everything that contributes to the physical well-being of the collections, and *conservation* refers to direct physical intervention with the material that is only one part of preservation (MacKenzie, 1996).

DECAY

Many causes and mechanisms of natural degradation of paper are known to us today. Researchers from the nineteenth century already wondered why certain papers degraded more than others. Still, there is no generally valid description of the normal, natural ageing process of paper. There are so many paper-dependent internal factors, partly as yet unknown, as well as external factors varying with time and place that influence the stability of paper. Nevertheless, the study of paper decay does help to determine the permanence of paper. As damage surveys and risk assessments are performed more often today, more and more factors of paper degradation become known to us. General tools to ascertain the life expectancy of paper are also of crucial importance, especially during damage surveys. Once we know the life expectancy of a collection, or part of a collection, we can decide what needs our attention first. The need to test paper-based materials, however, can easily conflict with the first rule of preservation, that is, to prevent damage to the objects. That is why, in most cases, only non-destructive testing methods can be employed. Unfortunately, not many non-destructive testing methods are available for paper.

Non-destructive paper testing

Monitoring the degradation of paper is essential for improving our understanding of how paper ages. Until now a suitable instrument for diagnosing the state of paper deterioration has not been found. Existing standardized testing methods often cannot be applied because of the large number of test specimens required.

A research project initiated at the Netherlands Institute for Cultural Heritage (NICH) aims to develop a non-destructive testing method to identify specific chemical compounds in book papers that are precursory to changes in optical and mechanical properties. Recently they experimented with the Solid Phase Micro Extraction (SPME) book-mark method, a well-known sampling technique, for the determination of furfural and acetic acid concentrations in books, a promising class of chemical markers of volatile paper degradation products. With the SPME method volatile compounds can be identified and their concentration levels within the paper quantified in a non-destructive way and as such they become useful as chemical markers to indicate the rate of deterioration. The SPME book-marker looks like a heavy fountain pen and is very easy to handle.

So far the results show a good repeatability. For short exposures the uptake of the SPME fibre increases linearly with time, but for exposure times longer than a week the uptake levels off. In order to relate SPME uptakes to concentrations in the paper, the transport mechanism still has to be elucidated (Ligterink et al., 2001).

In PAPYLUM, a research project supported by the European Commission under the Fifth Framework Programme, research institutes from five countries are working together on 'Chemiluminescence'. The construction of an adequate prototype is the primary goal of the project. Due to its extreme sensitivity, chemiluminescence (that is, weak light emitted during a chemical reaction) may well become a non-destructive tool for monitoring the degradation processes at conditions close to those of natural ageing. Since chemiluminescence measurements can easily be performed at temperatures lower than the typical accelerated ageing temperatures, the technique is well worth in-depth study. The preliminary results show that the technique may be able to provide the data on stability, usually obtained by long-term accelerated ageing methods, in a much shorter time (Pedersoli et al., 1998; Strlic et al., 2000a, 2000b and 2001).

Artificial ageing of paper

Artificial or accelerated ageing tests are used to determine the permanence (that is, the rate of the degradation) of paper and to predict the long-term effects of a particular conservation treatment. The natural ageing process of paper is speeded up by subjecting it to extreme conditions in a climate chamber. Since the 1950s a great variety of artificial ageing methods have been developed for paper. The field of application of these methods in the practice of conservation of archival materials has broadened enormously. Nevertheless, research into the reliability of this method is only performed on a limited scale. Today, there are many questions about the actual predictive value of these tests. Differences in opinion still prevail, and there are obvious disagreements as to the conditions under which artificial ageing should be performed. Recently, the Koninklijke Bibliotheek (KB), the National Library of the Netherlands, reviewed the various methodologies for accelerated ageing and the current discussions (Porck, 2000a).

There is a fundamental problem in the use of accelerated ageing. The argument for the use of elevated temperatures in artificial ageing relies on the fact that in general a reaction proceeds faster at higher temperatures than at room temperature. This makes it possible to observe its effects more quickly, which in this case is the loss of paper strength. Such artificial ageing experiments are sometimes called Arrhenius tests. The difficulty is that while the Arrhenius principles apply to the kinetics of chemical transformations, the complex properties of paper that are often registered in accelerated ageing (for example folding endurance, tear resistance and paper discolouration) cannot simply and unambiguously be related to its chemical composition. None the less, studies have indicated that, under certain conditions, the rate of the changes of such paper characteristics does relate to the chemical processes that take place during accelerated ageing (Baranski et al., 2000; Zou et al., 1996).

At the time of writing the issue of temperature and relative humidity in artificial ageing is still topical. Up to now the ageing tests have been done at a variety of temperatures and relative humidities. Because chemical paper degradation reactions vary according to these conditions, extrapolating results of accelerated ageing to natural ageing has severe limitations. In this respect the ongoing research at the Smithsonian Center for Materials Research and Education (SCMRE) shows great promise. Their studies are based on the premise that the results of accelerated ageing can only serve as a basis for reliable predictions if the accelerated ageing method speeds the deterioration of paper without fundamentally changing the process. This means that every individual reaction involved in the decay ought to be accelerated by the same factor and that the relationship between the reaction velocities must be kept constant. It is expected that the results of these studies will form a basis for the formulation of more uniform and relevant accelerated ageing protocols (Erhardt et al., 1999).

At the Institute for Standards Research (ISR) an extensive research programme has been set up that focuses on the development of accelerated ageing tests. The programme is committed to the development of accelerated tests in three areas: the ageing of paper, the effect of light on paper, and the effect of environmental pollutants on paper. Its purpose is to develop testing techniques that will make it possible to develop standards for permanent paper that are based on performance rather than on composition (Arnold, 1996). As part of the ISR research programme, the Library of Congress (LC) has developed an alternative accelerated ageing test for paper. Instead of relying on expensive ageing chambers that often lack the desired precision in maintaining preset relative humidity (RH) levels at high temperatures, the investigators retain control of moisture at elevated temperatures by sealing paper samples inside airtight glass tubes. These glass tubes have the added advantage of retaining degradation products, just like books do under ambient storage conditions, according to the LC staff. The first data demonstrate that ageing within airtight glass tubes simulates natural ageing better than ageing of paper in loose sheets or in stacks, although there is a general similarity between the products of degradation found in naturally aged papers and those aged artificially in the presence of moisture. At present, this test method is being evaluated at the Canadian Conservation Institute (CCI). In the same ISR programme the CCI is engaged in a collaborative study to examine the thermal-accelerated ageing of paper in sheets and in stacks for some of the ISR papers (Kaminska et al., 1999; Shahani et al., 2000).

A complicating factor is the way in which the paper is exposed to the ageing conditions. Confirming earlier studies, recent investigations have shown that paper in stacks (that is, books) ages differently from single, loose sheets. Some of these studies have shown that under both accelerated and natural ageing conditions, the centre of a stack of paper undergoes greater deterioration than do the regions located near the outside. This 'stack-versus-single-sheet' phenomenon in the ageing of paper is considered of major importance (Brandis et al., 1997; Hanus et al., 1996; Pauk et al., 1996).

Natural ageing of paper

To compare identical copies of books that, as part of separate collections, have been stored under different conditions and perhaps show different stages of deterioration would be a logical enquiry in the field of paper ageing. The Koninklijke Bibliotheek in collaboration with the TNO (Netherlands Organization for Applied Scientific Research) Institute of Industrial Research got the opportunity to study pairs of books from the collections of the New York Public Library (NYPL) and the Koninklijke Bibliotheek (KB). The conclusion was that the books from the NYPL showed a higher degree of deterioration than the ones held at the KB. This was caused by a higher concentration of the air pollutant sulphur dioxide, in combination with low or fluctuating high and low relative humidity in the NYPL storage rooms (Havermans, 1997; Pauk et al., 1996).

In our search for causes of natural paper ageing a historical approach also appears to create possibilities. Recent studies have drawn on historical sources from the mid-nineteenth century that document the inferior quality of Dutch paper at that time. These records can be compared with the findings of present-day examinations of the same material, traced in archival collections. Such comparisons should yield useful indications on the rate of paper decay (Grijn et al., 1996 and 1998; Porck et al., 1996). To 'make history' the ASTM has set up a natural ageing project. For the next one hundred years, ten North American institutions in different climates will store volumes of fifty test-paper types and submit monthly and yearly storage condition reports. Throughout this time, specimen pages will be extracted from each site and tested for optical and physical durability (McCrady, 1999).

Hydrolytic and oxidative paper degradation

In spite of the campaign for alkaline paper, more recent research shows that the acid papermaking process is not the only factor that significantly contributes to the degradation of paper. It is noted that the spontaneous formation of acids in cellulose during ageing cannot be overlooked as a cause. Researchers at the Library of Congress investigated the role of acid formation in the process of paper ageing. Their findings suggest that weak acids accumulate at a sufficiently high rate to contribute significantly to the increasing acidity in paper as it ages. Also, alkaline papers showed appreciably higher rates of accumulation than did other papers, since the acids formed are immediately neutralized and cannot enter into other reactions or dissipate. It was also shown that these weak acids attach themselves strongly enough to paper and that they are not easily dislodged from the paper matrix, even upon airing. Because of this tenacity and because they catalyse their own formation, these acids present a constantly escalating source of damage that can be dealt with only through deacidification. Thus neutral papers cannot remain acid-free for long (Shahani et al., 2000).

Oxidative paper-degradation processes have become the subject of increased attention in preservation science research. This new focus on oxidation is not only confined to specific problems, such as ink corrosion and photodeterioration, but also concerns the study of paper decay in general. Recently, Slovenian researchers turned their attention to the study of oxidative processes in paper. The main factors leading to the deterioration of deacidified paper made from bleached pulp were identified. It is pointed out that autoxidative reactions are accelerated in alkaline media. In addition, certain transition metal ions as well as groups, which are capable of autoxidation, also promote the free radical reactions. Since the oxidative degradation process of cellulose is enhanced in the presence of ferric compounds, the efficiency of several possible preventive antioxidants was also tested. The studies clearly demonstrate the protective effect of antioxidants (Destiné et al., 1996; Kolar, 1997; Kolar et al., 1998 and 2000a; Strlic et al., 1999 and 2001; Wang et al., 1996).

Permanent paper

Permanent paper is the term archivists use to denote the physical substratum for information that will last for a long time to come (Dahlø, 1998). Impermanence in paper became a problem, with industrial papers replacing traditional papers with good properties for long-term storage. An internal threat to the preservation of information was added to all the external threats to our records. That is why the search for and research into the permanence of paper, often based on natural and accelerated ageing, is so vital for the preservation community.

It is well known that papers become more acid with age, through hydrolysis and formation of acids. It is often presumed that only the acids introduced in the manufacture of paper and those absorbed from the environment are responsible for the deterioration of paper. In this context, the term 'acid-free', which in effect equates neutral and alkaline papers, is often used to imply permanence. None the less, alkaline and permanent papers are not the same. Alkaline paper, according to the National Archives and Records Administration (NARA), is defined as paper that will last for at least one hundred years under normal use and storage conditions, and groundwood-free with a minimum pH of 7 and an alkaline reserve of 2 per cent or more. Permanent paper, on the other hand, is paper that will last for several hundred years without significant deterioration under normal use and storage conditions. This paper is also groundwood-free with a pH of 7.5 or above, an alkaline reserve of 2 per cent or more, and other strength or performance properties that guarantee the use and retention of records generated on this paper for a maximum period of time (Carlin, 1995). In the 1980s it was thought that with the universal use of alkaline paper for new publications, the acidity problem for the future was solved (Stevens, 1988). In 1996 the Alkaline Paper Advocate concluded that its mission had been largely accomplished. Printing and writing papers that are produced for books and documents were then over 80 per cent alkaline in contrast to the early 1980s when they were only 25 per cent (McCrady, 1996).

At the time of writing, the ISO catalogue of International Standards lists 202 standards relating to paper. Three of them are also indexed on 'permanence'. In 1994 the library committee of ISO published ISO 9706 on permanent paper and in 1998 ISO 11108 on archival paper. Whereas ISO 9706 concentrates on permanence alone, ISO 11108 unites the concepts of permanence and durability. The concepts are defined as follows (Hoel, 1998):

- permanence: the ability to remain chemically and physically stable over long periods of time;
- durability: the ability to resist the effects of wear and tear when in use;
- permanent paper: paper which during long-term storage in libraries, archives and other protected environments will undergo little or no change in properties that affect use;
- archival paper: paper of high permanence and high durability.

The discussions on permanence in the different ISO committees should be of interest to all conservators as they codify the findings of preservation research.

The International Standard, ISO 9706, which was approved with the cooperation of the paper industry, does not state any limit for lignin content. Instead, the standard has a limit defined as a Kappa number, a figure that expresses the material's sensitivity to oxidation. The logic was that if the paper is sensitive to oxidation, it is likely to become oxidized with time and thus be unstable over long periods. But the dispute remains whether lignin is harmful or not. At present the stand taken that as long as it is not proven that lignin is harmless, the risk of continuing to jeopardize our cultural heritage cannot be taken. What is known today is that lignin is easily oxidized and causes severe colour change, and that lignin-containing papers discolour other papers in contact with them (Svensson, 1998).

The proposed Canadian Standard for Permanent Paper (CAN/CGSB-9.70-2000) was adopted in 1999 after several years of scientific research, study and discussion. The communal enterprise of the Canadian Conservation Institute and the Pulp and Paper Research Institute of Canada offers new insight into several factors responsible for the degradation of paper. An important conclusion is that the fibre composition of paper is of minimal importance to its permanence, as long as the paper is buffered with at least 2 per cent calcium carbonate. This result is scientifically very significant in that it allows paper containing lignin, in contrast to ISO 9706, to be included among those classed as 'permanent'. Yet it remains to be seen whether or not the new standard will be adopted. If accepted, it is likely to have a profound impact on the permanency of archival collections (Bégin et al., 1998, 1999; Zou et al., 1996).

Ink corrosion

The degradation of paper objects by iron-gall inks, called 'ink corrosion', is a well-known problem among paper conservators. Iron-gall ink is arguably the most important ink in Western history. It came into use in the late Middle Ages and was widespread until the early twentieth century. Iron-gall ink is not easily erased and this property made it an obvious choice for record keeping of any sort. International research has revealed a substantial part of the problem. Two ingredients in iron-gall inks are known to cause degradation of paper artefacts: sulphuric acid and iron(II) ions. Sulphuric acid, which is produced as a by-product during the manufacturing process of the ink, catalyses the hydrolysis of cellulose and iron(II) ions, which derive from a basic component of the iron-gall ink, catalyses the oxidation and forms radicals.

Dutch scientists from the NICH and the Shell Research and Technology Centre applied scanning electron microscopy (SEM) and X-ray fluorescence analysis techniques to study the presence of iron and sulphuric acid outside the inked areas. They discovered that in certain samples the sulphur had moved off the inked areas, and the iron had not (Neevel et al., 1999).

Researchers from the TNO Institute of Industrial Research and the Shell Research and Technology Centre studied the effects of iron-gall inks on the emission of volatile organic compounds (VOCs) from paper artefacts. The findings indicate that the presence of iron in the ink appears to stimulate certain paper degradation processes, namely acid-catalysed hydrolysis and dehydration. The harmful effects of some of the released VOCs have been discussed in relation to the conservation of ink-corroded paper (Feber et al., 2000; Havermans et al., 1999 and 2000; Penders et al., 2000).

Paper discolourations

Local yellow or brown discolourations of paper, often referred to as 'foxing stains', have been the subject of several investigations. However, preservation science research has not yet reached a consensus on the cause of this phenomenon. Several factors presumably are involved in their harmful effect on paper-based materials.

At the Russian State Library researchers found a positive correlation between foxing formation and

- paper production
- duration of light exposure
- dusting and storage condition
- presence of iron (III) in the centre of the stain after dyeing.

Further investigations with ultraviolet rays (UV) revealed that foxing stains show heavy fluorescence at an early stage and that luminescence decreases as the colour intensity increases. No fungal or other microbe cells were observed during microscopic analysis. Thus foxing is a chemical process which still has to be researched further, and not a result of microbiological activities (Rebrikova et al., 2000).

In a joint project Parisian scientists applied two non-invasive techniques, fluorescence and Fourier Transform Infrared Spectrometry (FTIR), to identify the chemicals in foxed papers from the seventeenth to the twentieth centuries. Although fluorescence appeared to produce little chemical information, the researchers maintained that the quantitative measurement of fluorescence would be of significant interest if fluorogenic compounds were the precursors of the brown stains. FTIR provided more insight into the chemical characteristics of the foxing stains than did fluorescence (Choicy et al., 1997).

The phenomenon of discolouration, which takes place at the border between wet and dry parts in paper materials, has been known since the mid-1930s. This wet/dry interface process, as it is called, is the subject of recent and current investigations into underlying degradation mechanisms. At the NICH, a variety of solvents was used to study the formation of brown lines on filter paper at the wet/dry interface. The effects on ageing and the conservation treatments of washing and bleaching with sodium borohydride were also studied. In additional studies on the nature of the brown-coloured oxidation compounds formed at the wet/dry interface, the use of analytical tools has been evaluated (Dupont, 1996a, 1996b).

Air pollutants

While temperature, relative humidity and light have long been major concerns in preventive conservation, indoor air pollution has now become another recognized factor. It is clear that the outside air quality has become a growing problem, especially in heavily urbanized areas. Many institutes are currently concerned with paper deterioration induced by carbonyl pollution, that is, acetic acid, formic acid and formaldehyde, and perform air sampling and/or materials testing experiments. In 1998 the Indoor Air Pollution Working Group (IAP), coordinated by the NICH, was formed. Next to ongoing inter-laboratory comparisons and the development of standard operating protocols for acid and aldehyde vapour testing, a database is constructed to collate information on materials that have been deemed 'safe' for short-term and long-term use in proximity to susceptible artefacts (see IAP Web site).

Researchers from the CCI reviewed and updated the knowledge on coatings that are often used as a means of passive conservation. It is generally known that direct contact with unsuitable coatings or the emission of harmful volatile compounds from coatings can damage artefacts. A summary of control procedures to prevent damage caused by contaminants as well as the use of different spot tests has been published (Tétreault, 1999a, 1999b). Others at CCI assessed the potential impact of acid-emissive materials on cellulose-containing materials. Little research has been done on the effect of acetic acid environments on paper-based materials. Acetic acid probably causes hydrolysis of cellulose polymers, but the action of weak acids on cellulose has not been investigated to the same extent as that of strong acids (Dupont et al., 2000).

Rapid ageing of poor-quality paper materials, such as acidic mat boards, lignin-containing papers and file covers are known to affect the ageing of higher-quality unbuffered paper that is in contact with or in close proximity to them. Scientists from the Carnegie Mellon Research Institute are studying the migration of degradation products from poor-quality materials into higher-quality papers by determining chemical properties.

Although the problem of air pollutants is commonly acknowledged, the mechanism of deposition and threshold concentrations – in particular, the impact of air pollutants on deacidified paper – is not well understood. Useful information can be expected to emerge from a current research project of the Dutch General State Archives in cooperation with the TNO Institute of Industrial Research. In this study identical archive materials are being stored at two locations, one of which is provided with an installation to filter air pollutants. Continuous monitoring of environmental conditions such as temperature, humidity, and concentrations of air pollutants, as well as frequent analysis of the quality of the stored material in both storage rooms, will yield useful data over time. The first results prove the effectiveness of air filtering (Feber et al., 1998).

A Ph.D. student at the Göteborg University devoted her doctoral thesis to the synergistic effects of air pollutants and climate on the stability of paper. The effect of trace amounts of these pollutants on the degradation of paper was studied, as well as the ability of the different mass deacidification processes to provide protection against further acidification of papers. The investigator concluded that RH plays an important role in the uptake of the air pollutants. Clear synergistic effects were demonstrated in the deposition rate. Deacidification treatments did not protect paper against the attack of acid air pollutants, although there were some quantitative differences, neither did it provide an adequate protection from oxidative degradation of the paper (Johansson, 2000).

TREATMENT

The field of conservation has undergone dramatic changes in the last several decades. At the beginning of the twentieth century, when many cultural institutions began to establish restoration studios, treatment was generally focused on aesthetic concerns. The aim of restoration was to return the work to its 'original' appearance, often without regard for the long-term preservation of materials, the integrity of authentic components, or the malignant effects of ageing and wear. At the time of writing, conservators of paper materials are expected to have a strong background in chemistry as well as art history in order to interpret, predict and arrest the destruction of paper and applied media. Next to preventive methods, treatment is a way to improve the aesthetic appearance and the chemical and physical condition of archival materials. However, restoration of individual works is never the ultimate solution to the degradation problem; it must at all times be combined with care procedures such as maintaining proper storage and display environments.

Aqueous treatments

Aqueous treatments have always been important in paper conservation, and there is an extensive literature on their benefits, especially with regard to the improved appearance of the treated papers. Although it is acknowledged that treatment of paper with water also brings about profound, and often permanent, structural and mechanical changes, less attention has been paid to the characterization and quantification of these influences, particularly with a view to optimizing conservation procedures.

In 1997, the Camberwell College of Arts reported on a long-term preservation science project entitled 'Paper Substrates and Graphic Media'. The purpose of the project was to investigate the effects of aqueous conservation treatments on the mechanical properties of paper. A preliminary study on the effects of 'paper washing' showed several main changes, including a reduction in the elastic modulus and an increase in the extensibility, compared with untreated paper. No significant differences were observed between tensile strength before and after washing. These findings provide a better understanding of the 'improvement' that is generally observed by conservators as a consequence of the washing of paper; that is, the changes detected have less to do with an increase in the strength of a sheet than with an increase in its flexibility (Smith, 1997).

Pest control

The number of nuisance organisms in the world is enormous. A small percentage of them are harmful to human beings and their stored goods. Archival collections can be threatened by a variety of pests. They comprise several thousands of invertebrate pests like insects and mites, and several dozens of vertebrates like rodents, bats and birds, and numerous fungi. Archives have traditionally relied on pesticides for routine pest prevention and response to observed infestation. Pesticides often do not prevent infestation, however. Twenty years ago preservation professionals introduced Integrated Pest Management (IPM), originally developed by the agricultural and urban pest management communities. The IPM method of pest control is the least damaging to collections and staff, and involves preventive measures and regular monitoring. Chemical treatments are avoided except as a last resort (see Teygeler, 2001).

To protect documents from the harmful effects of microbiological damage, the vacuum fumigation system using the gaseous sterilizing agent ethylene oxide (EtO) is considered most effective. Although EtO is a significant health hazard and is actually forbidden in several countries, many institutions still use this system for the sterilization of archival materials. At such sites, strict requirements governing the permissible level of exposure are established. To make a comprehensive comparison of the techniques of EtO sterilization and methods of determination of residual EtO in the material treated, an international project has been set up. The results of the different sterilization equipment and procedures applied were compared using different sorts of test samples. Calculations of the content of residual EtO indicated that the samples determined by one method (CNRS, Paris) contained two to nine times higher levels of EtO than did those determined by another method (Chemical Technological University, Prague). Such discrepancies could be explained by differences in technical procedures and time shifts between the various determinations. None the less, the differences underscore the need for a detailed comparison of different techniques and methods, and indicate that a standardized method for quantitative determination of residual EtO in sterilized materials would be very useful (Hanus et al., 1999).

The treatment of microbiological damage is seriously hampered by the fact that the use of ethylene oxide gas is restricted. Consequently, research to develop suitable and safe alternative fungicides is ongoing. Researchers at the Centre de Recherches sur la Conservation des Documents Graphiques (CRCDG) investigated the disinfecting capacity of beta radiation and microwaves. In addition to the fungicidal effect, the influence of radiation on the physicochemical characteristics of the paper samples was determined. Although beta radiation, in a sufficiently high dose, was found to be effective in attacking the fungi, a strong dose-dependent depolymerization of the cellulose molecules was observed in all cases. Consequently, beta radiation, like gamma radiation, which previous studies had found to produce similar adverse effects, cannot be recommended. A fungicidal effect of the microwaves was also demonstrated; the treatment did not show significant negative side effects on the paper itself. Although the practical limitations of the microwave equipment used do not yet permit large-scale treatment, the study has clearly indicated the applicability of microwave techniques (Rakotonirainy et al., 1999).

The antimicrobial properties of essential oils have been known since antiquity. Several researchers from the CRCDG are studying the antifungal activity of these oils. They are seeking to develop ways in which to apply them to prevent fungal growth on cultural properties and in storage areas, as well as ways to use them to treat objects that are already infected. The fungistatic and fungicidal activity of six essential oils (bay, wormseed, citronella, eucalyptus, super lavender and sage) was examined on several fungal strains commonly found in archives. The effectiveness of the oils was studied in relation to their composition. All six oils revealed antifungal properties, although the results varied. It is unclear, from the preliminary findings, how practical the use of essential oils will be because of the large concentrations required for disinfection (Rakotonirainy et al., 1998).

To fight insect infestation attention has recently focused on the applicability of natural insecticides. An extract from the seeds of the neem tree (*Azadirachta indica*), a tropical evergreen, is one of them. The pesticide Margosan-O, a neem extract in ethanol, was developed. The unique qualities of the neem product have been investigated intensively and have yielded encouraging results. In particular, insecticides containing significant amounts of neem oil do not appear to be harmful to human health. In Australia, the oil of the tea tree (*Melaleuca alternifolia*) has been a time-honoured folk remedy for man and beast. At Macquarie University the antimicrobial activity of a large number of commercial tea tree oils was examined. Results demonstrate the importance of terpinen-4-ol for activity against microbes. The powerful antimicrobial activity of p-cymene, a minor component of tea tree oil, was confirmed. Some microorganisms are highly susceptible to a combination of terpinen-4-ol and p-cymene (Ad Hoc Panel etc., n.d.; Gateby et al., in press).

One field that researchers have looked into since the development of IPM in conservation is the use of extreme temperatures in pest control. Controlled freezing has been applied in various institutions over the past fifteen years. Paper that has been heavily damaged by water (for example by a flood) can be treated by freeze-drying. It is a popular method to prevent mould explosion. Possible negative effects of this drying procedure have not yet received full attention. Scientists from the Danish Royal Library investigated the effects of freeze-drying on the mechanical strength and ageing stability of paper. They found that freeze-drying primarily influences characteristics such as moisture content, folding endurance and tear strength. It particularly affected the mechanical strength of paper with low initial strength; its effect on paper with high mechanical strength was relatively small. In general, freeze-drying influenced paper more than did air-drying. High-temperature treatment has been proved to be effective in exterminating insects in collection materials. The CCI designed a bag that will allow solar heating of the contents (slightly in excess of 40° C) in such a way that thermal disinfestation of the bag contents will be achieved. The idea was tested by the Australian War Memorial and proved to be effective (Antonsson et al., 1996; Björdal, 1998; Carlsen, 1999; Pearce, in press; Strang, in press).

It is possible to control insect infestation by reducing oxygen concentration, a form of modified atmosphere. Oxygen reduction is increasingly regarded as a recommendable alternative to insecticides and pesticides. In 1998, the EU financed an international project called 'SAVE ART'. Its purpose is to control pests by reducing the oxygen concentration of the environment through the use of an electromechanical nitrogen generator (VELOXY [VEry Low OXYgen] system). The idea is simple but effective: the oxygen in the air surrounding the object is replaced by nitrogen until a residual concentration of 0.1 to 0.2 per cent is reached, at which level all insects will be killed. The real-scale tests showed promising results. Since the project's inception, twelve VELOXY systems have been assembled and are now operative at several museums, libraries and archives (Åkerlund, 1998; Åkerlund et al., 1998; Conyers, in press; Gialdi, 1998).

Fumigation chambers have always been used in conservation practice to treat objects infested with pests; however, these chambers are expensive to construct, and not all institutions can afford them. A British company, Rentokil, has developed a reusable and flexible fumigation enclosure, the 'Rentokil Bubble'. This portable enclosure is designed for use with methyl bromide, phosphine, or carbon dioxide. For the use of nitrogen, the company designed a different line of fumigation enclosures that have a heat-sealable, aluminized barrier film. These bags are not intended for reuse. Two researchers at the Getty Conservation Institute (GCI) tested the enclosures for nitrogen fumigation. The two sizes were tested for both the oxygen-transmission characteristics of the materials and for the gas-tightness of the enclosure. The tests showed varied results but clearly confirmed the suitability of the bubbles for anoxia treatment. None the less, some practical limitations, especially concerning the size of the units, were detected (Elert et al., 1997).

Ink corrosion treatment

The treatment of ink-corroded paper artefacts remains a concern in the field of paper conservation. The effectiveness of treatments and their possible negative long-term side effects are often a reason for particular anxiety.

Scientists from several European countries have worked together in a framework project to study the effects of various aqueous and non-aqueous ink corrosion treatments. The two well-known mechanisms leading to depolymerization of iron-gall-ink-containing papers are acid hydrolysis and autoxidation. Therefore, a successful stabilization treatment of ink corrosion should involve deacidification and addition of appropriate antioxidants. The Slovenian partners in the project studied preventive antioxidants like the chelating agents phytate and gallate, and

97

the peroxide decomposers iodide and rhodanide. The iron-chelating agent phytate appears to be a potent stabilizer of iron-catalysed degradation. However, some other catalytic metal ions (for example, copper), which are also present in historic iron-gall inks, remain largely unaffected. With this in mind, aqueous and non-aqueous treatments for paper containing a variety of catalytic metal ions were evaluated and the development of new treatments was started. It has been demonstrated that addition of preventive antioxidants (for example potassium iodide – KI) to the phytate treatment of iron-containing paper samples offered advanced protection of the support material. In the case of copper- and manganese-containing iron-gall ink, calcium phytate treatment also offers superior protection over deacidification alone. Iron-gall ink corrosion has also become an important research priority at the NICH, the Dutch partner in the framework project. In one research exercise the effectiveness of nine commonly used aqueous treatments was measured. Standard reference papers and original seventeenth- and nineteenth-century iron-gall ink papers were immersed in different treatment solutions. Results of this study indicate that a combined calcium phytate/calcium bicarbonate treatment, as well as a single treatment with calcium bicarbonate, could effectively delay ink corrosion and minor side effects (Kolar et al., 1999, 2001 and in press; Neevel, 2000a and 2000b; Strlic et al., 1999 and in press; Reissland et al., 1999).

Russian scientists have developed a procedure based on a gelatine preparation to slow down the aggressive influence of iron-gall ink. It works on the principle of albumen paper prints in which gelatine forms durable complexes with heavy metals. The study showed that gelatine paper sizing deactivates the ions of heavy metals. When tests were carried out on historical gelatine-sized rag papers, written with iron-gall ink, both deacidification agents magnesium bicarbonate and calcium bicarbonate effectively stabilized the process of ink corrosion. Phytate and the antioxidant KI offered additional protection and effects were cumulative, confirming the findings of their Slovenian colleagues (Kolbe, in press).

Laser cleaning

The idea of using lasers to clean artefacts has fascinated conservators for two decades. Although the potential has been quite clear, past efforts to apply the technology have been hampered by technical limitations, serviceability and the cost of laser systems. Although the cleaning of paper is a much-discussed subject due to the damage which may arise from conventional wet or dry cleaning techniques, research on the use of lasers for cleaning of cellulose-based materials remained scarce until recently.

In 1997 the EU announced the LACLEPA project (LAser CLEaning of PAper and PArchment). The participating countries will develop a prototype laser cleaning system particularly suitable for use on flexible paper and parchment. The method is based on the use of UV pulse lasers, which will ensure preservation of the delicate artefacts by minimizing the absorption volume, the heat-affected zone and the mechanical shock. The first experiments with an ultraviolet excimer-pulsed laser at 308 nm looked promising. Objects were chosen of which the conventional cleaning was either difficult or impossible. It was demonstrated that surface contamination could be removed by near ultraviolet-pulsed excimer laser irradiation without destruction of cellulose fibre substrate structures including iron-gall ink scripts, but a decrease in ISO brightness was noticed. On the other hand later experiments showed different results. The results for excimer laser treatment at 308 nm show that not only the laser fluence but also the age of the artefact strongly affects the chemical conversion threshold. Most substrates older than several decades exhibited much higher chemical stability than new systems. This is a strong indication that the ageing status of the paper plays a major role in assessing the laser cleaning limits. That means that the laser processing behaviour of model systems can be compared with that of original fibrous artworks to only a very limited extent, and that original artefacts have to be treated rather as individual specimens (Fabre, 2000; Kautek et al., 1997 and 1998; Müller-Hess et al., 1999 and 2001; Vergès-Belmin, 2001).

In cooperation with the manufacturer of laser systems, Slovenian scientists attempted to define optimum parameters for cleaning cellulose-based substrates using Nd-YAG laser. The immediate as well as the long-term effects of pulsed lasers operating at three different wavelengths on paper have been studied. A strong immediate cellulose degradation effect after excimer laser treatment at 308 nm was observed, accompanied by a decrease in ISO brightness. Laser irradiation at 1064 nm resulted in an increase of the degree of polymerization due to the formation of inter- and intra-molecular ether bonds. Nd-YAG processing at 532 nm resulted in no detectable chemical changes after the treatment, although long-term resistance appears to be impaired (Kolar et al., 2000b, 2000c and 2000d). Within the European COST programme (Cooperation in the Field of Scientific and Technical Research) 37 research institutes from 18 countries signed a Memorandum of Understanding to cooperate in the field of laser research under the project name 'Artwork Conservation by Laser'. The project wants to address challenges in three main directions, one of which is laser cleaning. Among other matters, requirements for mobile laser cleaning systems with respect to safety, parameter regimes and performance are investigated as well as laser beam transmission through optical fibres. One study showed that foxing stains from a sixteenth-century paper could be removed successfully with a molecular fluorine laser at 157 nm. This laser was far more effective in comparison to other wavelengths and did not leave any yellowish after-effect on the paper. Another study clearly indicated that certain pigments could undergo chemical and crystallographic changes and concomitant colour shifts. Also a database is being created of all conservation laser cleaning systems in Europe. Very recently a new EU network started: EULASNET E!2566. This is an umbrella organization for Laser Technologies, one of the themes being applications in conservation. It aims to create a platform to stimulate research, development and technology transfer dealing with laser technologies and applications. Both the EU programmes will end in 2005 (see Eulasnet Web site; Salimbeni, 2001).

Mass deacidification

It is well documented that acid hydrolysis of cellulose is one of the key factors responsible for the degradation of paper during ageing. There are a number of strategies one could employ to prevent, or at least forestall, damage to acidic materials. Most deacidification methods work to retard significantly the natural deterioration of paper by neutralizing present acids and by depositing an alkaline buffer to neutralize future acids. Although deacidification stabilizes paper, it cannot strengthen or reverse any damage that has already occurred. At the time of writing there is no one system of choice. There is a strong interest in the commercial world and consequently a certain level of competition. It is clear from existing information that each of the major institutions safeguarding the paper-based heritage has undertaken detailed and exhaustive analyses of the different processes available, demonstrating that their eventual choice was not made lightly (Rhys-Lewis, 2001; Smith, 1999).

Implemented by the Conservation Division of the National Archives, the Wei To mass deacidification system has been in operation in Canada for many years. One of the major challenges has been the replacement of the original chlorofluorocarbon (CFC) solvents, consequent to a ban on CFCs since 1996. One year later a new chemical formula using hydrofluorocarbons (HFCs) was tested. The results of these tests have been fruitful. Inks that had been affected by the previous solvents remained stable in the new solution (Couture, 1999).

The Bibliothèque nationale de France has used a mass deacidification system adapted from the Canadian Wei To process. Research into the effectiveness of this system has produced satisfactory results; however, questions remain about both the amount and the distribution of the alkaline reserve in the paper after treatment. With the assistance of the Research Centre for the Conservation of Graphic Material (CRCDG), the Bibliothèque nationale de France has developed a process to neutralize acids contained in certain types of paper, using a deacidification system, which conforms to conservation standards for national heritage collections. Batches of 100 to 200 volumes are vacuum-treated in an autoclave after freeze-drying followed by immersion in a gaseous solution (Daniel et al., 1999a).

The German Federal Archives have decided to employ Neschen's 'Bückeburg procedure', the main reason being that it is a water-based method designed specifically for archival records. Single sheets are treated separately, guaranteeing individual and uniform results. At the same time harmful substances are washed out and the fibres regain suppleness. The subsequent addition of glue contributes to the stabilization of the paper (Hofmann, 2000).

In 2000 the Swiss Federal Archives and the Swiss National Library together set up a plant for paper deacidification. After extensive evaluation it was found that the Papersave process offered by Battelle Engineering was the most suitable. The Swiss plant benefits from improved controls and greater variability of the treatment parameters. This opens up new possibilities for the treatment of vulnerable material from archives. The Swiss plant belongs to the Swiss Confederation and is run privately. First experiences show that the Swiss model is a feasible business undertaking (Nebiker Toebak et al., 2000).

In the Netherlands both the Koninklijke Bibliotheek (KB) and the Dutch State Archives decided on the Bookkeeper system. Since 1998 mass deacidification of books has been an integral part of the conservation policy of the KB. The KB conservation laboratory has studied the effectiveness and side effects of different mass deacidification processes before the final decision to apply the Bookkeeper system. The results obtained with the Bookkeeper system so far are satisfactory. However, as the treatment procedure causes considerable physical stress on the pages and the book as a whole, books with a deteriorated construction and/or severely weakened paper cannot be treated without the risk of serious damage. After an evaluation of alternatives to the AKZO DEZ method of mass deacidification, the Dutch State Archives preferred the Bookkeeper method to the Battelle method. Although they realized that both techniques had their advantages and disadvantages, they found that the Battelle process left a residue of silicon oil after treatment, that the papers experienced an initial loss of strength directly after treatment (up to 40 per cent), that the printing inks were effected, and that there was no trace of paper strengthening as promised by the Battelle process (Porck, 2000b; Steemers, 2000).

Several initiatives to evaluate the effectiveness of mass deacidification have been taken since the first and biggest evaluation by the Library of Congress in 1991. Most of them were performed with different and often arbitrarily preset conditions, which resulted in many differing conclusions. Although it is very hard to draw a final conclusion, it is not impossible. The following seem to be true for mass deacidification in general:

- Mass deacidification does not fulfil the hope that archive managers had pinned on it, that is, to deacidify the whole collection in a single mighty effort and then to forget about the problem of paper decay.
- Mass deacidification can actually result in the reduced mechanical strength of treated paper.

101

- Frequently mass deacidification provokes slight yellowing of the treated paper.
- With any of the existing mass deacidification plants negative side effects can occur, resulting from the fact that books and files are not only made of paper, but also of leather, plastics, inks, dyestuffs, board of very dirty pulp, and so on, and from poor handling of the books both in the plant and during transportation to and from the plant.
- After accelerated ageing the quality of an acidic paper that has been subjected to a mass deacidification process is better than that of the same paper that has not been treated. This is true even of yellowing.

Generally, it can be acknowledged that deacidification is an appropriate means of fighting the problem of acid catalysed paper decay. Above all, with respect to the tremendous number of books at risk of decay resulting from acidic paper production, it is the only realistic means (Bansa, 2000).

In Germany a new technology has been developed to combine deacidification and strengthening of paper within one process. Deacidification by impregnation with deacidifiers has already reached a satisfying level, but the combination of both steps at the same time still leads to open questions. A dissoluble-gel-based reinforcing system has been developed to carry out the reinforcement not only on single sheets but also on complete books. An anti-adhesive is added to treat the complete book in a dipping process. The experiments show that substantial increases in strength could be obtained. For the deacidification, oxidic nanoparticles such as magnesium oxide added to the impregnation system are being investigated (Schmidt et al., 2000).

In all cases preservation officers stress the need for careful selection of the materials to be deacidified as well as a strict protocol before, during and after treatment. For example, a Swiss study made clear that the colouring agents used in several early non-photographic copies are sensitive to pH and will behave badly during mass deacidification (Dobrusskin, 1999).

While most treated papers degrade less rapidly, some results from the accelerated ageing experiments show an increased degradation of papers whose pH has been changed from acidic to alkaline using deacidification treatments. This behaviour suggests the importance of degradative mechanisms other than acid hydrolysis like atmospheric oxidation. It has also been observed that some acid papers may be destabilized as a result of deacidification treatment. It seems that a pronounced stabilization of deacidified paper can be achieved by either a sodium borohydride reduction treatment or by the addition of potassium iodide to the deacidified paper. In addition conservators do not know the possible impact of previous deacidification on the conservation treatment and care of paper artefacts (Anonymous, 2000; Kolar et al., 1999).

Paper splitting

For the strengthening of deteriorated paper, different techniques are available. One of them is the reinforcement of a plastic foil, another is the infiltration of polymers which re-establish links between the cellulose fibres by polymerization, and yet another is the paper-splitting process. In this practice a paper with a thickness of only a fraction of a millimetre is separated into a front and back side, in order to glue an exactly fitting, very firm and thin reinforcing paper in between. So far reinforcement of deteriorated papers on a large scale has proved to be problematic.

At the Zentrum für Bucherhaltung in Leipzig both mechanical wet treatment and hand splitting paper activities have been practised for years. The paper-splitting process is a very popular conservation technique to restore papers heavily affected by ink corrosion. Some years ago this German centre developed a paper-splitting machine. Today this machine is a part of a mass conservation system for loose sheets of paper. The system uses several consecutive processes, including aqueous washing and deacidification, leaf casting and mechanized paper splitting. Results of independent research into the effectiveness and possible negative side effects of this technique are not yet available; none the less, there is a growing worldwide interest in the paper-splitting system. The Bibliothèque nationale de France supported a study on mechanical reinforcement methods for paper that compared thermal gluing with splitting. The investigation, carried out on different types of printed paper, demonstrated that splitting resulted in a larger improvement of the mechanical properties of papers, combined with an unaltered readability of the text, than did gluing. Moreover, the reversibility of the splitting process was also considered satisfactory (Kolbe et al., 2000; Liers et al., 1998; Vilmont et al, 1996; Wächter et al., 1996).

STORAGE

Until recently little consideration was given to the importance of storage methods and materials, often with the result that further damage was done to the objects. It is now recognized that proper attention to storage plays a major part in a successful (preventive) conservation programme. While proper storage can extend life, slovenly, haphazard and overcrowded conditions soon result in damaged collections. These effects are usually insidious and gradual. In the design and planning of the archive building many measures can be taken to influence the storage areas of archives. The next step is to look at how a building functions on the inside. In recent times, the impact of environmental conditions on records has been studied by a number of archivists and conservators. There are many criteria that can be grouped under the banner of conditions; the most important are temperature, relative humidity, air quality and light. If the building is our first line of defence

103

against the external climate conditions, our second line of defence is the control of the internal climate of the building (Ling, 1998).

Climate conditions

The control of temperature and relative humidity is generally accepted as a means to prevent degradation of collections. Several guidelines are being developed, but the rationale behind these standards is not always clear. The Canadian Conservation Institute (CCI) looked closely at the basis of these standards and at the costs of achieving them. In cooperation with the Canadian Council of Archives it created new recommendations for both temperature and relative humidity. To address the issue of permissible fluctuations for mixed collections, a range of acceptable levels was adopted to replace the old magic numbers (Michalski, 1999 and 2000).

The control of relative humidity (RH) continues to be an expensive and difficult challenge. In many situations, an attractive option is to control the RH within display cases instead of controlling the entire space. Researchers from the CCI are working on a centralized module supplying filtered and humidity-controlled air to each case through small tubes (typically 6 mm diameter) without return air, relying on compensating leakage from the case. The possibility of using an Internet application to provide remote control of the module and remote monitoring of the units is being investigated.

The Smithsonian Center for Materials Research and Education studied the stiffness, strength and elasticity of cellulose-containing materials. The measurements contradict the general assumption that these materials are necessarily brittle or stiff at all low RH values. In fact, if very low RH (less than 30 per cent) is avoided, important physical properties, as well as chemical reactivity (rate of hydrolysis and cross-linking reactions), are relatively insensitive to RH over a wide range (10 to 15 per cent). This represents a much wider range than is generally supposed. Similar results have been found with aged paper, indicating that while paper may become weaker as it ages, its stiffness and response to RH do not change significantly (Erhardt et al., 1995, 1996, 1997 and 1999).

The maintenance of storage conditions to established parameters is the most frequently discussed aspect of storage conditions; proper storage temperature and relative humidity are the subject of continued debate. Most researchers tend to agree that the present norms for all archival materials are too rigid and that stability of both temperature and relative humidity are at least of the same importance. Moreover, norms for both temperature and relative humidity largely depend on local climate conditions. It is of the utmost importance for keepers of archives to be aware of the diverse standards and differing prerequisites. What is a minimum in one country can be a maximum in others, and may be regarded as an optimum in another. One should not lose sight of the fact that any standard is nothing more than a set of compromises among the participants (Banks, 1999; Buchmann, 1998; Fröjd et al., 1997; Shahani et al., 1995).

Lighting technique and guidelines

In the last decade, conservation scientists have given increased attention to lighting issues, particularly the damaging effects of light on paper artefacts. Two processes are responsible for this damage: photochemical action (which causes fading, chalking and loss of strength) and radiant heat (which causes surface cracking and embrittlement).

Standard light levels have been introduced over the past thirty years. Although the intent of such standards is clear, their application to broad ranges of object types has been somewhat arbitrary. Resolving the issue of visibility versus vulnerability of the object has been difficult for the preservation community. The Canadian Conservation Institute has been working with a technical committee of the International Commission on Lighting to develop an improved lighting guide. This guide recommends steps to ensure safe lighting of displays, including the classification of all exhibits according to a four-category scale, determination of the acceptable level of UV radiation, calculation of the annual exposures, and planning for the maximum duration of the display, both for the exhibition and for individual objects (Michalski, 1997).

The Rensselaer Polytechnic Institute examined an innovative lighting technique that promises to reduce rates of light-induced damage without affecting viewing satisfaction. Subjective evaluations of works of art displayed under different lighting conditions were recorded. The study suggests that light concentrated in three spectral bands could provide levels of illumination equal to standard broad-spectrum lighting with substantially reduced levels of damaging incident radiant energy. A tri-band source produced by combining and balancing the outputs of halogen lamps filled with narrow-band-pass filters could allow the display of artefacts for longer periods than is possible with traditional illumination sources (Cuttle, 1998).

Storage materials

Lately preservation researchers became increasingly aware of the importance of archival storage materials. The NARA Research and Testing Laboratory maintains a testing programme to ensure that proposed exhibit and storage materials do not cause damage to permanent records. All the tested products are listed on the NARA Web site.

One of the new products is MicroChamber. First marketed in 1992, MicroChamber is a lignin-free, sulphur-free, alkaline-pulped, alkaline-reserve paperboard with an additional element – molecular traps or sieves. Especially the last component, the zeolite molecular traps, makes it possible to deal with airborne pollutant gases.

The Centre de Recherches sur la Conservation des Documents Graphiques (CRCDG) compared the protective quality of MicroChamber with that of other archival papers. The researchers concentrated on two of the most widely used MicroChamber products. The papers contained 10 to 15 per cent mineral absorbents (zeolites, calcium carbonate). The results showed that the MicroChamber papers absorbed much more sulphur dioxide than did the permanent papers. Interestingly, the verso and the recto sides of each of the paperboards showed different results. This difference appeared to be connected with the weight and sizing of the papers, rather than with the presence of absorbents (Daniel et al., 1999b).

Researchers at the CRCDG have also studied the effects of polyester film encapsulation. In this storage technique an object is encapsulated under low pressure. It is used to protect paper from harmful environmental factors such as air pollutants, dust and microorganisms. The benefit of this preventive measure has often been discussed but contradictory experimental results have been reported. After analysing the effects of several accelerated ageing tests on the degree of polymerization (DP) of different kinds of paper, the authors concluded that in the case of acid papers, encapsulation enhances the deterioration process. The rate of degradation of non-acid paper appeared to increase significantly only when such paper aged together with acid paper, especially when the mixed stack had been encapsulated. Additional experiments have shown that interleavage with alkaline or MicroChamber paper could partly circumvent this influence. Depending on the situation, this kind of interleavage should be weighed against a deacidification treatment before encapsulation (Daniel et al., 1998 and 1999c).

CLOSING REMARKS

Rightly, research is considered an integral part of preservation policy and management. In the future there will even be a greater need for standards, control tools for storage conditions, selection procedures for reformatting, and conservation treatment priorities. The evaluation of the reformatting or treatment procedures themselves, combined with the development of these standards and tools, represents a full agenda for preservation science. It also requires scientists from different disciplines to work together. An essential element is the respect and cooperation between preservation scientists and conservators. The key factors in preservation policy today and tomorrow are interdisciplinary approach, multilateral cooperation and legislation, funding and education. It is only when we work together effectively that we can expect progress in conservation.

REFERENCES

Ad Hoc Panel of the Board on Science and Technology for International Development. National Research Council (n.d.), 'Neem. A tree for solving global problems', online publication: http://books.nap.edu/books/0309046866/html/R1.html#pagetop.

AIC-RATS (2001), *What is Conservation Science?*, The American Institute for Conservation of Historic and Artistic Works, Research and Technical Studies Subgroup. Online publication: http://aic.stanford.edu/conspec/rats/whatis.html.

Åkerlund, M. (1998), 'A New Swedish book on Integrated Pest Management and Health Hazards in Museums', in M. Åkerlund et al. (eds), *Proceedings of the 3rd Nordic Symposium on Insect Pest Control in Museums. Stockholm, September 24–25 1998*, pp. 175–8.

Åkerlund, M., Bergh, J.-E., Stenmark, A. and Wallenborg, I. (eds) (1998), *Proceedings of the 3rd Nordic Symposium on Insect Pest Control in Museums. Stockholm, September 24–25 1998*, PRE-MAL and ICOM Swedish National Committee.

Anonymous, (2000), 'Deacidification Reconsidered', 15th Annual Preservation Conference of the National Archives and Records Administration, Washington, DC, 28 March 2000. Online publication: http://www.nara.gov/arch/techinfo/preserva/conferen/2000.html.

Antonsson, M. and Samuelsson, M.-L. (1996), *Effects of Repeated Freezing on Paper Strength*, SP Report 1996:19, Swedish National Testing and Research Institute, Materials Technology.

Arnold, R.B. (1996), 'Update: ASTM/ISR paper aging research program', *Abbey Newsletter* 20 (3), pp. 29–30.

Banks, P. (1999), 'Overview of alternative space options for libraries and archives', in *14th Annual Preservation Conference, held on March 25, 1999. Washington: NARA*, online publication http://www.nara.gov/arch/techinfo/preserva/conferen/banks.html.

Bansa, H. (2000), 'Mass Deacidification – Effects and Negative Side Effects', paper read at Mass deacidification in practice. Conference in Bückeburg, Germany, 18–19 October 2000.

Baranski, A. et al. (2000), 'Methodology of kinetic investigation of cellulose degradation', in *Preprint of the III Congress of Chemical Technology, Gliwice, Poland, September 4–8, 2000* (distributed by permission of M. Taniewski, Head of Scientific Committee of the Congress).

Bégin, P. et al. (1998), 'The impact of lignin on paper permanence. A comprehensive study of the aging behavior of handsheets and commercial paper samples', *Restaurator* 19, pp. 135–54.

Bégin, P. et al. (1999), 'The effect of air pollutants on paper stability', *Restaurator* 20, pp. 1–21.

Björdal, L. (1998), 'Effects of Repeated Freezing on Paper Strength', in M. Åkerlund et al. (eds), *Proceedings of the 3rd Nordic Symposium on Insect Pest Control in Museums. Stockholm, September 24–25, 1998*, pp. 54–6.

Brandis, L. and Lyall, J. (1997), 'Properties of paper in naturally aged books', *Restaurator* 18, pp. 115–30.

Buchmann, W. (1998), 'Preservation: Buildings and equipment', *Janus* 1, pp. 49–63.

Carlin, J.W. (1995), 'NARA Advises Federal Agencies on Selecting Long-Lived Paper', *Abbey Newsletter* 19 (6–7), pp. 102–3.

Carlsen, S. (1999), 'Effects of freeze drying on paper', in M.S. Koch (ed.), *Preprints vom 9. Internationalen Kongress der IADA, Kopenhagen, 15–21 August 1999*, Royal Academy of Fine Arts, Copenhagen, pp. 115–20.

Choicy, P. et al. (1997), 'Non invasive techniques for the investigation of foxing stains on graphic art material', *Restaurator* 18, pp. 131–52.

Conyers, S. (in press), 'System VELOXY® and its applications', in *Proceedings of the meeting NOOX Anoxic Environment, oxygen scavengers and barrier films, their use in museums, libraries and galleries, Cardiff, November 29–30, 1999*.

Couture, R. (1999), 'Challenges in mass deacidification', in *National Library News* 31 (7–8), pp. 8–10.

Cuttle, C. (1998), *Museum Lighting Protocol Project*, PTT Publications No. 1998-31, National Center for Preservation Technology and Training, Natchitoches.

Dahlø, R. (1998), 'The rationale of permanent paper', paper read at the 64th IFLA General Conference August 16–21, 1998, Amsterdam, Netherlands.

Daniel, F., Flieder, F. and Demarque, A. (1998), 'La conservation des documents encapsulés sous vide', *Nouvelles de l'Arsag* 14, pp. 16–18.

Daniel, F., Copy, S. and Flieder, F. (1999a), 'La désacidification de masse à la Bibliothèque nationale de France: un peu plus de magnésium, s'il vous plait', in *Les Documents Graphiques et Photographiques: Analyse et Conservation. Travaux du CRGDG 1994–1998*, Direction des Archives de France, Paris, pp. 9–24.

Daniel, F., Hatzigeorgiou, V., Copy, S. and Flieder, F. (1999b), 'Étude de l'efficacité d'un nouveau produit d'archivage: le MicroChamber', in *Les Documents Graphiques et Photographiques: Analyse et Conservation. Traveaux du CRCDG, 1994-1998*, Direction des Archives de France, Paris, pp. 25–50.

Daniel, F., Demarque, A. and Flieder, F. (1999c), 'Effet de l'encapsulation sous vide du papier par la méthode "Archipress"', in J. Bridgland (ed.), *12th Triennial Meeting, Lyon, August 29–September 3, 1999, ICOM-CC (Vol. 2)*, James & James, London, pp. 495–500.

Destiné, J.N. et al. (1996), 'The photodegradation of milled-wood lignin. Part I. The role of oxygen', *Journal of Pulp Paper Science* 22 (1), pp. J24–J30.

Dobrusskin, S. (1999), 'Frühe, nichtphotographische Kopier- und Vervielfältigungstechniken', in M.S. Koch (ed.), *Preprints vom 9. Internationalen Kongress der IADA, Kopenhagen, 15–21 August 1999*, Royal Academy of Fine Arts, Copenhagen, pp. 195–205.

Dupont, A.-L. (1996a), 'Degradation of cellulose at the wet/dry interface. I. The effect of some conservation treatments on brown lines', *Restaurator* 17, pp. 1–21.

Dupont, A.-L. (1996b), 'Degradation of cellulose at the wet/dry interface. II. An approach to the identification of the oxidation compounds', *Restaurator* 17, pp. 145–64.

Dupont, A.-L. and Tétreault, J. (2000), 'Study of Cellulose Degradation in Acetic Acid Environments', *Studies in Conservation* 45, pp. 201–10.

Elert, K. and Maekawa, M. (1997), 'Rentokil Bubble in nitrogen anoxia treatment of museum pests', *Studies in Conservation* 42 (4), pp. 247–52.

Erhardt, D. and Mecklenburg, M. (1995), 'Accelerated vs. natural aging. Effect of aging conditions on the aging process of paper', *Materials Issues in Art and Archeology IV, Materials Research Society* 352, pp. 247–70.

Erhardt, D. et al. (1996), 'New versus old wood. Differences and similarities in physical, mechanical, and chemical properties', in J. Bridgland (ed.), *11th Triennial Meeting, Edinburgh, September 1–6, 1996, ICOM-CC (Vol. 2)*, James & James, London, pp. 903 –10.

Erhardt, D. et al. (1997), 'The determination of appropriate museum environments', in S. Bradley (ed.), *The Interface Between Science and Conservation*, Occasional Paper No. 116, British Museum, London, pp. 153–63.

Erhardt, D., Tumosa, C.S. and Mecklenburg, F. (1999), 'Material consequences of the aging of paper', in J. Bridgland (ed.), *12th Triennial Meeting, Lyon, August 29–September 3, 1999, ICOM-CC (Vol. 2)*, James & James, London, pp. 501–6.

Fabre, F. (ed.) (2000), *Lasers in the Conservation of Artworks III, LACONA III. Conference April 19–22, 1999, Florence.* Elsevier, Paris.

Feber, M. de., Havermans, J. and Cornelissen, E. (1998), 'The positive effects of air purification in the Dutch State Archives. Part I: Experimental set up and air quality', *Restaurator* 19, pp. 212–23.

Feber, M.A.P.C. de, Havermans, J.B.G.A. and Defize, P. (2000), 'Iron-gall ink corrosion: a compound-effect study', *Restaurator* 21 (4), pp. 204–12.

Fröjd, I., McIntyre, J., Banks, B., Dureau, J.-M., Ogawa, Y. and Pandzic, M. (1997), *Guidelines on disaster prevention and control in archives*, ICA, Paris.

Gateby, S. and Townley, P. (in press), 'Potential use of the essential oil of Melaleuca alternifolia', in *Biodeterioration of cultural property. Proceedings of the 5th International Conference, 12–14 November 2001, Sydney, Australia.*

Gialdi, E. (1998), 'Project SAVE ART', in M. Åkerlund et al. (eds), *Proceedings of the 3rd Nordic Symposium on Insect Pest Control in Museums. Stockholm, September 24–25 1998*, pp. 78–9.

Grijn, E.v.d., Kardinaal, A. and Porck, H. (1996), 'The 1845 paper crisis in the Netherlands. An historical–technical study into the Dutch paper market and into the nature and extent of the inferior quality of mid-19th century paper', in R. Teygeler (ed.), *IPH Congress Book (Vol. 11)*, International Association of Paper Historians (IPH), Marburg, pp. 153–63.

Grijn, E.v.d., Kardinaal, A. and Porck, H. (2001), 'Research into paper degradation from an historical starting-point. A case-study on discoloration of nineteenth-century paper', in P. Tschudin (ed), *IPH Congress Book (Vol. 12)*, International Association of Paper Historians (IPH), Marburg, pp. 272–7.

Hanus, J., Komorníková, M. and Mináriková, J. (1996), 'Changes in some mechanical properties of paper during ageing in an archival box', in J. Bridgland (ed.), *11th Triennial Meeting, Edinburgh, September 1–6, 1996, ICOM-CC (Vol. 2.)*, James & James, London, pp. 510–16.

Hanus, J., Richardin, P., Bonnassies-Termes, S., Durovic, M., Kubelka, V. (1999), 'Comparison of two different methods of head space gas chromatography for determination of residual ethylene oxide in sterilised papers', in *Preprints of the 12th Triennial Meeting Lyon 29 August–3 September 1999, ICOM-CC (Vol. 2.)*, James & James, London, pp. 507–12.

Havermans, J.B.G.A. (1997), *A Study of the Cause of Damage on Pairs of Books*. TNO-Report BU2.97/009063-1/JH, TNO Institute of Industrial Research, Paper Production Technology, Delft.

Havermans, J.B.G.A. and Dufour, J. (1997), 'Photo oxidation of paper documents. A literature review', *Restaurator* 18, pp. 103–14.

Havermans, J.B.G.A. et al. (1999), 'Emission of volatile organic compounds from paper objects affected with iron-gall ink corrosion', in J. Bridgland (ed.), *12th Triennial Meeting, Lyon, August 29–September 3, 1999, ICOM-CC (Vol. 2)*, James & James, London, pp. 513–16.

Havermans, J.B.G.A. and Penders, N.J.M.C. (2000), 'The role of different accelerated ageing techniques in the evaluation of conservation treatments of objects affected with iron gall ink', paper read at Iron Gall Ink Meeting, Newcastle, UK, 4–5 September 2000.

Hoel, I.A.L. (1998), 'Standards for Permanent Paper', paper read at the 64th IFLA General Conference, 16–21 August 1998, Amsterdam, Netherlands.

Hofmann, R. (2000), 'Stock conservation in the federal archives: the role of mass deacidification', paper read at Mass deacidification in practice. Conference in Bückeburg, Germany, 18–19 October 2000.

Johansson, A. (2000), *Air Pollution and Paper Deterioration. Causes and Remedies*, Ph.D. Thesis, Göteborg University, Department of Chemistry, Göteborg.

Kaminska, E. et al. (1999), *ASTM/ISR Research Program on the Effects of Aging on Printing and Writing Papers. Accelerated Aging Test Method Development* (Draft Final Report to the ASTM Advisory Committee on Paper Aging Research).

Kautek, W., König, E., Bonsanti, G., Fotakis, C., Vergès-Belmin, V. and Watkins, K. (eds) (1997), *Lasers in the Conservation of Artworks I, Restauratorenblätter, Sonderband 1*, Mayer and Comp., Wien.

Kautek, W., König, E., Fotakis, C., Vergès-Belmin, V., Larson, J. and Watkins, K. (eds) (1998), *Lasers in the Conservation of Artworks II, Restauratorenblätter, Sonderband 2*, Mayer and Comp., Wien.

Kolar, J. (1997), 'Mechanism of autoxidative degradation of cellulose', *Restaurator* 18, pp. 163–76.

Kolar, J. et al. (1998), 'Aging and stabilization of alkaline paper', *Journal of Pulp Paper Science* 24 (3), pp. 89–94.

Kolar, J. and Strlic, M. (1999), 'Stabilisation of iron-gall ink corrosion', paper read at the European Workshop on Iron-Gall Ink Corrosion, 16–17 December 1999, General State Archives, The Hague.

Kolar, J. and Strlic, M. (2000a), 'Cellulose Oxidative Degradation Studied by a New Colorimetric Method Based on Hydroxylation of an Aromatic Model Compound', 1st International Conference on Polymer Modification, Degradation and Stabilization, MoDeSt 2000, Palermo, Italy, 3–7 September 2000.

Kolar, J. and Strlic, M. (2000b), 'Laser cleaning of paper. Immediate and long-term effects', paper read at Laser Cleaning of Paper and Parchment. LACLEPA Workshop 2000, 10–11 January 2000 (EUROCARE project EU 1681), Vienna.

Kolar, J. and Strlic, M. (2001), 'The effect of pytate treatment on stability of paper containing copper and iron ions', paper read at the The Iron Gall Ink Meeting, Newcastle, UK, 4–5 September 2000.

Kolar, J. and Strlic, M. (in press), 'Non-aqueous stabilisation of metal tannate inks', *Restaurator*.

Kolar, J., Strlic, M. and Marincek, M. (2000c), 'The effect of Nd:YAG laser radiation at 1064 nm on paper', *Restaurator* 21, pp. 9–18.

Kolar, J. et al. (2000d), 'Near-UV, visible and IR pulsed laser light interaction with cellulose', *Applied Physics A*. 71 (1), pp. 87–90.

Kolbe, G. (in press), 'Gelatin as inhibiting agent for iron-gall ink corrosion in paper', *Restaurator*.

Kolbe, G. and Banik, G. (2000), 'Das Tintenfraßprojekt an der SABK Stuttgart in Zusammenarbeit mit der Staatsbibliothek zu Berlin – Preußischer Kulturbesitz: Die Papierspaltung als geeignete Behandlungsmethode gegen Tintenfraß?', paper read at Tintenfraß und Möglichkeiten seiner Behandlung. Staatliche Akademie der Bildenden Künste Stuttgart, 3–5 Juni 2000.

Liers, J., Wächter, W. and Becker, E. (1998), 'Saving the culture heritage in libraries and archives – illusion or possibility', in *25 Years School of Conservation. Preprints of the Jubilee Symposium 18–20 May 1998*, Det Kongelige Danske Kunstakademi, Copenhagen, pp. 87–9.

Ligterink, F.J. and Pedersoli Jr, J.L. (2001), 'Development of the SPME book-mark method for the determination of furfural and acetic acid concentrations in books', paper read at the 7–10 March 2001 ICOM-CC Interim Meeting of the Working Groups on Graphic Documents and Photographic Documents, in Helsinki, Finland.

Ling, T. (1998), *Solid, safe, secure: building archives repositories in Australia*, National Archives of Australia, Canberra.

McCrady, E. (1996), 'Alkaline Paper Advocate has One More Year to Go', *Alkaline Paper Advocate* 20 (7), p. 1.

McCrady, E. (1999), 'ASTM/ISR Paper Permanence Research', *Abbey Newsletter* 23 (1), pp. 1, 4–6.

MacKenzie, G.P. (1996), 'Establishing a preservation programme', *Janus* 1, pp. 86–99.

Michalski, S. (1997), 'The lighting decision', in *Fabric of an Exhibition: an interdisciplinary approach: Preprints of Textile Symposium 1997*, Canadian Conservation Institute, Ottawa, pp. 97–104.

Michalski, S. (1999), 'Museums, libraries, and archives – new guidelines on humidity, temperature, and HVAC systems', in *ASHRAE handbook: heating, ventilating, and air-conditioning applications*, American Society of Heating, Refrigerating and Air-Conditioning Engineers, Atlanta.

Michalski, S. (2000), *Guidelines for humidity and temperature in Canadian archives*, Technical Bulletin No. 23, Canadian Conservation Institute, Ottawa.

Müller-Hess, D. and Troschke, K.K. (1999), 'Laclepa – Laser Reinigung von Papier und Pergament. Eurocare Projekt EU 1681', in M.S. Koch (ed.), *Preprints vom 9. Internationalen Kongress der IADA, Kopenhagen, 15–21 August 1999*.

Müller-Hess, D., Troschke, K.K., Kolar, J., Strlic, M., Kautek, W. and Pentzien, S. (2001), 'Laserreinigung von Papier. Zwischenbericht des Eurocare-Projektes 1681 LACLEPA', in *Restauro (8)*, pp. 604–20.

Nebiker Toebak, R. and Blüher, A. (2000), 'Papersave swiss – the Swiss variation for paper de-acidification', paper read at Mass deacidification in practice. Conference in Bückeburg, Germany, 18–19 October 2000.

Neevel, J.G. (2000a), 'Irongall-ink corrosion: Development and analysis of the conservation treatment with phytate', in J. Mosk and J.H. Tennent (eds), *Contributions of the Netherlands Institute for Cultural Heritage to the field of conservation and research*, ICN, Amsterdam.

Neevel, J.G. (2000b), 'Phytate based treatment of ink corrosion– an updated review', paper read at Iron Gall Ink Meeting, Newcastle, UK, 4–5 September 2000.

Neevel, J.G. and Mensch, C.T.J. (1999), 'The behaviour of iron and sulphuric acid during iron-gall ink corrosion', in J. Bridgland (ed.), *12th Triennial Meeting, Lyon, August 29–September 3, 1999, ICOM-CC (Vol. 2)*, James & James, London, pp. 528–33.

Pauk, S. and Porck, H. (1996), *Land om land. Verslag van de bestudering van identieke boekenparen, die onder verschillende omstandigheden zijn bewaard*, Koninklijke Bibliotheek, The Hague.

Pearce, A. (in press), 'Heat eradication of insect infestations: the development of a controlable, low cost, solar-heated treatment unit', in *Biodeterioration of cultural property. Proceedings of the 5th International Conference, 12–14 November 2001, Sydney, Australia*.

Pedersoli Jr, J.L., and Hofenk de Graaff, J. (1998), 'Paper Degradation and Light Emission. Possibilities for the Application of Chemiluminescence to the Investigation of Paper Oxidation', paper read at the 20–22 April 1998 ICOM-CC Interim Meeting of the Working Groups on Graphic Documents and Photographic Documents, in Ludwigsburg, Germany.

Penders, N.J.M.C. and Havermans, J.B.G.A. (2000), 'Emission of Volatile Organic Compounds form Objects affected by both – Iron Gall Ink and Ink Ingredients', paper read at Iron Gall Ink Meeting, Newcastle, UK, 4–5 September 2000.

Porck, H.J. (2000a), *Rate of Paper Deterioration. The Predictive Value of Artificial Aging Tests*, European Commission on Preservation and Access, Amsterdam.

Porck, H.J. (2000b), 'Deacidification of books from the collection of the Koninklijke Bibliotheek: selection and quality control', paper read at Mass deacidification in practice. Conference in Bückeburg, Germany, 18–19 October 2000.

Porck, H. and Teygeler, R. (2000), *Preservation science survey. An overview of recent developments in research on the conservation of selected analog library and archival material*, Council on Library and Information Resources, Washington DC.

Porck, H., Grijn, E.v.d. and Kardinaal, A. (1996), 'Analysis of paper destabilizing factors in mid-19th century paper production. A contribution to the development of a conservation policy', in R. Teygeler (ed.), *IPH Congress Book (Vol. 11)*, International Association of Paper Historians (IPH), Marburg, pp. 164–7.

Rakotonirainy, M., Raisson, M.-A. and Flieder, F. (1998), 'Evaluation of the fungistatic and fungicidal activity of six essential oils and their related compounds', in K. Borchersen (ed.), *25 Years School of Conservation. The Jubilee Symposium. Preprints 18–20 May 1998*, Konservatorskolen, Det Kongelige Danske Kunstakademi, Kopenhagen, pp. 121–30.

Rakotonirainy, M., Leroy, M., Fohrer, F. and Flieder, F. (1999), 'La désinfecttion des papiers par les faisceaux d'électrons et les micro-ondes', in *Les documents graphiques et photographiques. Analyse et conservation. Travaux du Centre de Recherches sur la Conservation des Documents Graphiques 1994–1998*, Direction des Archives de France, Paris, pp. 159–72.

Rebrikova, N. and Manturovskaya, N. (2000), 'Foxing. A new approach to an old problem', *Restaurator* 21 (2), pp. 85–100.

Reissland, B. and Groot, S. de (1999), 'Ink corrosion. Comparison of currently used aqueous treatments for paper objects', in M.S. Koch (ed.), *Preprints vom 9. Internationalen Kongress der IADA, Kopenhagen, 15–21 August 1999*, Royal Academy of Fine Arts, Copenhagen, pp. 121–9.

Rhys-Lewis, J. (2001), *The enemy within! Acid deterioration of our written heritage. A report to the British Library Co-operation and Partnership Programme on behalf of the project Steering Committee*, CCP Project Report, British Library, London.

Salimbeni, R. (ed.) (2001), *Laser Techniques and Systems in Art Conservation. Proceedings of International Symposium on Lasers in Metrology and Art Conservation 2001, held in Munich, Germany, 18–22 June 2001*, SPIE – The International Society for Optical Engineering, Bellingham (WA).

Schmidt, H., Becker-Willinger, C. and Sauer, A. (2000), 'New technologies to combine deacidification and restrengthening of paper within one process', paper read at Mass deacidification in practice. Conference in Bückeburg, Germany, 18–19 October 2000.

Shahani, C., Hengemihle, F.H. and Weberg, N. (1995), 'The effect of fluctuations in relative humidity on library and archival materials and their aging within contained microenvironments', in J.-M. Arnoult et al. (eds), *Proceedings of the Pan-African conference on the preservation and conservation of library and archival materials. Nairobi, Kenya: 21–25 June 1993*, IFLA, The Hague, pp. 61–70.

Shahani, C.J. et al. (2000), *Accelerated Aging of Paper. I. Chemical Analysis of Degradation Products. II. Application of Arrhenius Relationship. III. Proposal for a New Accelerated Aging Test*, Draft Report provided to the Institute for Standards Research of ASTM, Preservation Directorate, Library of Congress, Washington, DC.

Smith, A. (1999), *The future of the past: preservation in American research libraries*, Council on Library and Information Resources, Washington, DC.

Smith, A.W. (1997), 'Effects of aqueous treatments on the mechanical properties of paper', in S. Bradley (ed.), *The Interface Between Science and Conservation*, The British Museum, Occasional Paper No. 116, pp. 59–65.

Steemers, T. (2000), 'Mass deacidification in practice', paper read at Mass deacidification in practice. Conference in Bückeburg, Germany, 18–19 October 2000.

Stevens, N.D. (1988), 'The Alkaline Attack', *Alkaline Paper Advocate* 1 (5).

Strang, T. (in press), 'Principles of heat disinfestation', in *2001: A Pest Odyssey, London, UK, 1–3 October 2001*.

Strlic, M. and Kolar, J. (1999), 'Use of a model Fenton system for studies of paper antioxidants', paper read at the European Workshop on Iron-Gall Ink Corrosion, 16–17 December 1999, General State Archives, The Hague.

Strlic, M. and Kolar, J. (2000a), 'Stability of alkaline paper – Can chemiluminescence foretell the future?', *PapierRestaurierung – Mitteilungen der IADA*, vol. 1, Suppl., pp. 69–74.

Strlic, M., Kolar, J., Pihlar, B., Rychlý, J. and Matisova-Rychlá, L. (2000b), 'Chemiluminescence during thermal and thermo-oxidative degradation of cellulose', *European Polymer Journal* 36, pp. 2351–8.

Strlic, M., Kolar, J. and Pihlar, B. (2001), 'Some preventive cellulose antioxidants studied by an aromatic hydroxylation assay', *Polymer Degradation and Stability* 72, pp. 157–62.

Strlic, M., Radonic, T., Kolar, J. and Pihlar, B. (in press), 'Anti- and pro-oxidant properties of gallic acid', *Journal of Agricultural and Food Chemistry*.

Svensson, I.-L. (1998), 'A papermaker's view of the standard for permanent paper, ISO 9706', paper read at the 64th IFLA General Conference, 16–21 August 1998, Amsterdam, Netherlands.

Tagle, A. (1999), 'Science at the GCI', *Conservation, The Getty Conservation Institute Newsletter* 14 (1), pp. 4–8.

Tétreault, J. (1999a), *Coatings for Display and Storage in Museums*, CCI Technical Bulletin No. 21, Ottawa.

Tétreault, J. (1999b), 'Summary of control procedures to prevent damages caused by contaminants', paper read at the IAP Meeting, Indoor Air Pollution: Detection and Prevention 26–27 August 1999, Instituut Collectie Nederland, Amsterdam, Netherlands.

Teygeler, R. (2001), *Preservation of archives in tropical climates. An annotated bibliography*, International Council on Archives/National Archives of the Netherlands/National Archives of the Republic of Indonesia, Paris/The Hague/Jakarta.

Vergès-Belmin, V. (2001), *Les Lasers dans la conservation des oeuvres d'art. Lasers in the Conservation of Artworks, LACONA IV. Paris 11–14 Septembre 2001*, Elsevier, Paris.

Vilmont, L.-B., Gervason, G. and Brandt, A.C. (1996), 'Etude comparative des procédés de renforcement mécanique des papiers par thermocollage et clivage', in *ICOM Committee for Conservation preprints (2), 11th Triennial Meeting, Edinburgh*, ICOM, Paris, pp. 552–9.

Wächter, W., Liers, J. and Becker, E. (1996), 'Paper splitting at the German Library in Leipzig. Development from craftmanship to full mechanisation', *Restaurator* 17, pp. 32–42.

Wang, J., Heiner, C. and Manley, S.J. (1996), 'The photodegradation of milled-wood lignin. Part II. The effect of inhibitors', *Journal of Pulp Paper Science* 22 (2), pp. J58–J63.

Wills, P. (1987), 'New directions of the ancient kind: conservation traditions in the Far East', *The Paper Conservator* 11, pp. 36–8.

Zou, X., Uesaka, T. and Gurnagul, N. (1996), 'Prediction of paper permanence by accelerated aging. I. Kinetic analysis of the aging process', *Cellulose* 3, pp. 243–67.

Zou, X. et al. (1998), *Canadian Co-operative Permanent Paper Research Project: The Impact of Lignin on Paper Permanence. Final Report*, Pulp and Paper Research Institute of Canada/Canadian Conservation Institute.

6 Sound recordings: problems of preservation

Dietrich Schüller

INTRODUCTION

Sound recordings belong to the group of audiovisual records (photographs, films, multimedia, videograms and sound recordings). While textual documents are representations of human thoughts, generally expressed by a chain of symbols (letters) representing the spoken word, all audiovisual documents are representations of static or dynamic physical phenomena (light, sound and so on). Textual documents have a high degree of redundancy and fault tolerance. In contrast, each detail of audiovisual documents is – potentially – information, and any damage to the carrier causes a loss of information. While a speck of mould, generally, does not render a book unreadable, it may cause significant loss of information, even unreadability, with an audiovisual carrier. As a consequence, by their very nature all audiovisual carriers require a significantly higher degree of physical integrity than textual documents.

STABILITY OF CARRIERS AND THEIR COMPONENTS

The specific physical and chemical nature of audiovisual carriers in general, and of sound carriers in particular, is a factor in their increased vulnerability, as compared to paper-based documents. It must also be taken into account that the replay of such carriers has an influence on their integrity. Therefore, in surveying the most widespread types of audio carriers in archival holdings, their susceptibility to material degradation – be it by inherent instability, by external factors, or by replay – will be briefly examined.

MECHANICAL CARRIERS

Cylinders

With cylinders, the information is recorded in a vertically modulated groove along the surface of a cylinder. Two types of cylinders have to be distinguished: self-recorded cylinders, which are unique, and mass replicated cylinders, which were produced by the early phonographic industry. Self-recorded cylinders always consist of one of several compositions of wax, while replicated cylinders may consist either of wax or of a celluloid (cellulose nitrate) tube over a supporting plaster core (Burt, 1977).

All kinds of cylinders, wax as well as celluloid, are extremely vulnerable to embrittlement. Additionally, wax cylinders are extremely susceptible to mould growth under humid storage conditions (Gibson, 1988). The replay of cylinders requires specialized equipment and skills. For all these reasons, libraries and archives are strongly encouraged to contact the few specialized institutions around the world for a state-of-the-art replay of such holdings. Amateur attempts to transfer these historical holdings will only lead to a poor-quality reproduction of the sound and, almost certainly, irreversible damage to the cylinder.

Coarse groove discs ('shellacs')

Coarse groove or 'shellac' discs were produced from around 1900 to the mid-1950s. The main formats are 25 and 30 cm at 78 rpm. As a replication format, these discs consist of a variety of mineral substances held together by organic binders (Isom, 1977). The signal is recorded in a laterally modulated groove. Although extremely fragile if handled without due care, these records are chemically fairly stable unless exposed to high humidity. Replay requires specialist equipment and experience. The transfer of small collections should be outsourced to specialists, while for bigger collections (more than several thousand items) the installation of a transfer project in house may be feasible.

Instantaneous discs

Before the availability of magnetic tape, 'instantaneous discs' were used for making sound recordings which could be replayed immediately after recording. The most widespread are so-called 'lacquer discs', also called 'acetates', which were originally recorded in the same coarse groove lateral cut format as the 'shellacs', later in the microgroove (LP) format. A typical application was their use in radio stations when a time shift between the recording and its transmission on air was required. They were in use from the mid-1930s until well into the 1960s.

Lacquer discs generally consist of a cellulose nitrate coating on an aluminium plate. Glass or steel plates were also used. With ageing the lacquer coating becomes brittle and shrinks, which leads to a sudden crazing of the surface of the disc and a subsequent flaking-off of the information-carrying material. Much of the worldwide stock of these discs has already been lost. As the life expectancy of those still in playable condition is unpredictable, their transfer is of utmost urgency. A similar policy of urgent transfer must be applied to all other 'instantaneous discs' (gelatine, waxed cardboard and so on). Expert advice is imperative.

Microgroove discs ('vinyls')

Microgroove discs succeeded the shellac discs as mass replicated formats and were produced from the late 1940s to around 1990. The main formats are 25 and 30 cm at 33 rpm (long plays – LPs) and 17 cm at 45 rpm (singles and extended plays – EPs). They consist of a polyvinyl chloride–polyvinyl acetate (PVC–PVA) co-polymer which generally does not exhibit systematic stability problems (Khanna, 1977). The grooves are either laterally cut for mono, or diagonally at an angle of 45 for stereo discs. Because of the softness of the material they are extremely vulnerable to mechanical damage by improper handling or poor-quality replay equipment.

Apart from optical replay equipment, which is available for laterally cut mono and stereo discs, conventional mechanical reproduction of all mechanical carriers is a major potential deteriorating factor which must be kept to the absolute minimum. Such carriers, therefore, cannot be used as access sources in library and archives.

MAGNETIC TAPE

Magnetic tape consists of two main parts: the support or base film and the magnetic layer. The latter can be split again into the magnetic pigment and the binder that holds the pigment together and secures it to the support (Edge, 2000; Gilmour, 2000).

Historically, the support material was cellulose acetate (mid-1930s to mid-1960s) which – mainly due to hydrolysis, nourished by the omnipresent humidity in air – deteriorates by shrinking and becoming brittle. Its successor was polyvinyl chloride (PVC, from 1944 to about 1980), which was mainly used by German manufacturers. As with vinyl discs, to date no systematic failure of this material has been experienced. From the mid-1950s onwards polyethylene-terephthalate (PET, commonly called polyester) was introduced, which is now used for all kinds of audio, video and computer tape. It is considered to be chemically fairly stable.

Of the magnetic materials, iron-oxide (-Fe_2O_3), as used for all reel-to-reel audio tapes and analogue audio cassettes type IEC I, does not exhibit particular stability problems. Chromium dioxide (CrO_2) and chromium substitute (cobalt doped iron oxide), as used for analogue audio cassettes type IEC II as well as for most video

115

consumer formats, are of some concern. Metal particle tape, used for analogue audio cassettes type IEC IV, for the digital audio cassette format R-DAT, and for some analogue and all digital video formats, is of considerable concern in terms of chemical stability. Once metal particles corrode they also lose their magnetic properties and, therefore, their recorded information. It must be noted that, apart from the chemical concern expressed for metal particle tape, the magnetic stability of oxidic pigments is not a major concern of audio preservation. Apart from problems with cobalt doped tapes in the early 1970s, the magnetic properties of state-of-the-art products are fairly stable and there is no reason to be overly concerned about the possibility of magnetically recorded signals deteriorating with time.

The greatest problem affecting magnetic tape stability is that of modern pigment binding materials introduced since the mid-1970s when polyester-polyurethane (PE-PU) binders were introduced (Gilmour and Fumic, 1992; Bradley, 1992, 1999). Hydrolysis – triggered and nourished by the humidity of the atmosphere – weakens the properties of the binder, which leads to a smear-off of pigment particles. These swiftly clog the replay heads and the quality of the replay signal is severely reduced. Processes have been developed to render affected tapes playable, which are all based on the principle of dehumidification. This is either achieved by elevated temperatures, environments of lowest possible humidity or low pressure, or a combination of such measures. Tapes generally recover, at least for a short period, long enough to copy them on to new carriers. It is yet unknown whether this pigment binder hydrolysis will, sooner or later, affect all magnetic tapes. There is also no method yet available to assess the life expectancy of unaffected tapes. Knowledge of the life expectancy, however, is a prerequisite for any meaningful preservation strategy (Schüller and Kranner, 2001).

Magnetic tape is generally much less vulnerable to damage in replay than mechanical carriers. A tape will survive several hundreds of replays before the quality is affected, provided well-serviced equipment of recent production is used.

OPTICAL DISCS

Since the early 1980s, the compact disc (CD) has rapidly replaced the vinyl disc almost completely in the market. Replicated CDs consist of a polycarbonate body covered by a reflective layer, generally aluminium, which is protected by a layer of varnish which also carries the label information. Since the early 1990s, recordable CDs (CD-Rs) have also been available. With CD-Rs, the digital information is embedded in an organic dye. In general, compact discs are susceptible to mechanical damages (scratches) that deviate or obstruct the microscopic laser beam that reads the information. Chemically, the most critical part is the protective varnish. Its failure causes oxidation of the reflective layer, which renders CDs unreadable. This was a major problem of early CDs (Fontaine, 1999; AES28-1997).

Most endangered are CD-Rs because of the inherent instability of the organic dyes which carry the information, mainly due to the influence of light. CD-Rs may fail after only a few years of storage (AES38-2000; Fontaine, 2000; Trock, 2000; Kunej, 2001; Psohlavec, 2001).

DVDs (digital versatile discs) function in the same basic way as CDs, and are prone to the same stability problems. Their increased data density (a factor of 7 per layer) also leads to increased vulnerability. Double-layer as well as double-sided DVDs are available but specific experience concerning their particular vulnerability or susceptibility to deterioration is not yet available.

The mass replicated MiniDisc (MD) works like a CD. Recordable MiniDiscs use the magneto-optical principle, which has been used for computer back-up formats before and proved fairly reliable in the mid-term. Its long-term stability, however, is as yet unclear (AES35-2000).

The replay of optical discs does not influence the quality of the carrier.

In concluding this section on carrier stability, it can be seen that the most endangered sound carriers are instantaneous discs, modern magnetic tape of all kind, and – ironically– CD-Rs, which are widely used as target formats for digitization projects to preserve endangered analogue carriers of various kinds (text, image and sound).

RECOMMENDATIONS FOR STORAGE AND HANDLING

The various endangering factors, as well as recommendations for storage and handling, are discussed for all audio carriers (Pickett and Lemcoe, 1959/1991; Knight, 1977; St-Laurent, 1991; Van Bogart, 1995; AES22-1997; Boston, 1998; Varlamoff and Schüller, 2000). Significant differences between the different types of carrier are mentioned where they apply.

HUMIDITY AND TEMPERATURE

As outlined above, water, the most dangerous natural agent, is omnipresent as vapour in the air. It causes chemical deterioration like hydrolysis (for example pigment binder of magnetic tapes) and oxidation (metal particles, for example reflective layers of CDs). As a secondary danger it furthers biodegradation, specifically at a relative humidity in excess of 65 per cent, causing fungus growth on almost all types of sound carriers, most significantly on cylinders and tapes. This has been most recently reported also to affect CDs.

The temperature range most comfortable for human life (10–30 C) is not directly harmful for sound carriers of any kind. Temperatures in excess of 40 C, however, may begin to affect some magnetic tape pigment binders, and temperatures in excess of 60 C are harmful for PVC (tape and vinyl discs) as well as for several types of reels, cassette housings and so on. Generally, however, temperature has an important indirect influence, as it determines the speed of chemical processes: an increase of 10 C accelerates a chemical process by a factor of two, while a drop in temperature of 10 C retards a reaction to half its speed. As a matter of principle, therefore, lower temperatures are preferable for long-term storage as any kind of chemical deterioration will be slowed down.

Finally, temperature also influences the dimension of materials, which is of specific concern for the integrity of magnetic tape. While old acetate and PVC tapes are prone to an elongation with rising temperature, thereby loosening their tape pack (and vice versa with decreasing temperatures), polyester reacts differently. The thermal extension of the pre-tensilized polyester is much higher for the thickness than for the length of the tape. Therefore, a wound-up tape swells with increased temperature, thereby tightening the tape pack, exhibiting considerable forces. This may lead to mechanical tape deformation, which is of concern for high data density recording, in audio specifically for R-DAT. This is one of the reasons why thermal shocks in either direction must be absolutely avoided. It is also of concern when applying any elevated temperature treatment to tape suffering from binder hydrolysis.

It must be noted that humidity and temperature are interrelated: the higher the temperature, the more vapour it can hold – the lower the temperature, the less moisture. If an environment is cooled without simultaneous dehumidification, the relative humidity rises until the dew point is reached. Superfluous vapour then condenses on the coldest surfaces of the environment. Therefore, temperature and humidity must always be controlled simultaneously.

At the time of writing, two different standards are recommended for humidity and temperature: one for 'access storage' and one for 'preservation storage'. Access storage is for frequently used holdings of a sound archive. For these collections the following parameters are recommended:

> humidity 40% RH   5%
> temperature 20 C   3 C

Technical laboratories where tapes are handled must have the same climatic parameters.

Preservation storage is recommended for archival masters or safety copies (parallel copies to the archival masters kept in a different place):

> humidity: 30% RH and lower, with minimal fluctuations
> temperature: 8–10 C   1 C

It must be noted that holdings kept under preservation storage conditions must be slowly acclimatized before use. Swift changes in temperature and humidity may cause significant problems, in particular, condensation. For these reasons, two different standards have been defined. It is most important to understand the simultaneous control of humidity and temperature. The greatest misunderstanding is to cool storage environments without any dehumidification. In some tropical countries this has led to catastrophic failure within a short time (Schüller, 1996).

DIRT AND FOREIGN MATTER

With mechanical carriers, dirt interferes with the path of the stylus in the groove, causing audible effects (clicks). In magnetic tape replay the closest possible tape-to-head contact is of paramount importance, especially for modern carriers of high data density. Dirt or debris from the magnetic tape surface or other sources accumulating on the head surface impairs the replay signal by lifting the tape away from the head and, effectively, muffling the high frequencies. In severe cases this may cause a substantial loss of information. With optical discs, dirt obstructs the path of the laser, thus creating reading errors which – in severe cases – may also lead to a complete loss of signal.

In arid countries, dust or sand from outside the archive, which is very difficult to control, is the greatest enemy. In rich countries with moderate climates, the prevailing dust originates from textiles, both from clothing and from carpeted floors, and from human skin. Carpeted floors must, therefore, not be used in audiovisual collections. Clean protective overalls for the staff, worn only within the archive, will also help control dust.

A second group of foreign matter is of concern because of its potential chemical interaction with the carriers. The foremost sources are fingerprints, which also form a perfect adhesive for other foreign matter. Food and drink may have a variety of negative influences on audio carriers and, therefore, eating and drinking within storage and handling areas must be forbidden. Obviously chemical substances may have a dramatic influence on the integrity of sound carriers and must, therefore, be kept apart from storage and handling areas. Finally, environmental pollution has an influence on the chemical integrity of the stored materials. Specifically, in industrial areas expert advice should be sought.

A powerful protection against dust and other foreign matter is air filtering, which should always be installed when air conditioning is installed. Mechanical filters will offer protection against dust while chemical pollution can be controlled to a certain degree by appropriate additional measures. To keep them effective, it is important to clean, or exchange, filters on a regular basis.

CLEANING

As with replay, the cleaning of cylinders and instantaneous discs should absolutely be left to specialists.

Shellac and vinyl discs are commonly washed, assisted either by machines to loosen the grit by brushing and sucking the dirty liquids off the surface, or by submerging the grooved part of the discs in an ultrasonic bath. For a cleaning liquid, distilled water with a small percentage of neutral detergent is most successful. For vinyl discs a mix of ethyl alcohol or isopropyl alcohol (isopropanol) with distilled water is also widespread. There are also procedures for CD cleaning which are intensively discussed because any mechanical operation may scratch the surface, thus endangering the readability of the carrier.

For all kinds of tapes, mechanical cleaning using lint-free tissues is recommended if tapes are dusty or exhibit a tendency to shed dry pigment. Expert advice must be sought for all sticky tapes suffering from pigment binder hydrolysis and from 'bleeding' tape splices. The removal of such sticky and gluey deposits is generally possible. The cleaning agent, however, has to be carefully chosen in order to avoid the chemical dissolution of the tape and its components.

MECHANICAL DEFORMATIONS

The mechanical integrity of all data carriers is of utmost importance. Generally the historical mechanical carriers, cylinders and shellacs, are extremely fragile, while all mechanical carriers, specifically instantaneous discs as well as vinyl discs, are very prone to information loss during the replay process. In addition, they are easily scratched. In order to avoid damage, replay equipment must be in excellent and calibrated condition and operating personnel must be fully trained in careful handling of the carriers, which must never be handed over to library users. In contrast to the publicity accompanying the introduction of compact discs, it must be noted that these are as sensitive to mechanical deformation as vinyl discs. They must, therefore, always be stored inside their original containers and never put on any surface in order to avoid scratching when being lifted up. Preservation copies of CDs must not be used as part of the access collection in libraries. All discs apart from soft instantaneous discs must be stored in an upright, not leaning, position.

The mechanical integrity of tapes is one of the most underrated aspects of audio preservation. Any deformation of the tape may lead to signal imperfection during the replay process or even, with high data density carriers like R-DAT, to the complete breakdown of the signal. Mechanical deformations occur as a result of malfunctioning replay equipment, careless handling and uneven winding in open reel and cassette tapes. Because of the tension in wound-up tapes, the tape edges of unevenly wound tapes become wrinkled, which is a particular danger for thin tapes. In order to avoid deformations of this kind, all open reel and cassette tapes must be wound in a single operation over their entire length before being put into storage. Generally this provides flat tape pack surfaces. If not, the machine in use needs repair or exchange. Reel-to-reel tapes and cassettes should be stored upright; tapes wound on flangeless hubs must be suspended by their hubs to avoid a flat being formed in the round tape pack where the tape is in contact with the shelf.

LIGHT, ULTRAVIOLET RADIATION, X-RAYS

Some organic materials are specifically sensitive to light. Amongst audio carriers the greatest light-sensitivity occurs with recordable CDs and DVDs. Recent experiments have shown that after a few weeks' exposure to daylight, CD-Rs begin to fail (Kunej, 2001). Any unnecessary exposure to light has, therefore, to be strictly avoided. Light and ultraviolet radiation also affects polymers like PVC. Finally, it must be noted that electric light as well as sunshine is generally associated with elevated temperatures which will, additionally, endanger carelessly placed carriers. X-rays such as those used for baggage checking in airports and so on does not, in the small doses used, affect audio carriers.

MAGNETIC STRAY FIELDS

Magnetic stray fields may endanger magnetic tape recordings, as well as magneto-optical discs (recordable MiniDiscs). Most endangered are linear analogue recordings, which form the vast majority of all analogue audio tape formats. The permissible threshold of magnetic fields is quoted as 5–10 Oe (Oersteds) for AC fields, and 25–50 Oe for DC fields (Geller, 1972, 1976; Aschinger, 1980).

Archivists should be concerned about the following sources of magnetic fields which are commonly used in audio archives: dynamic microphones and headsets, dynamic loudspeakers, and analogue level meters. Systematic measurement of field strengths exhibited by such equipment reveals that only direct contact or close proximity between tapes and magnetic instruments is of concern. As field strengths decrease in a square root function with distance, even the strongest magnetic instrument is harmless at a distance of 15 cm. Magnetic holders for metallic advertising boards, magnetic shutters for cabinets, and magnetic locks for wallets should not be used in archives and by archivists as one cannot exclude accidental direct contact with these gadgets. Care must be taken that strong motors, such as those used for elevators, and big transformers, and so on are not situated immediately adjacent to storage racks for magnetic tape. It must be noted that walls of conventional building materials form no shield against magnetic stray fields.

Finally, the position of the lightning conductor must be of concern as it is the source of a strong magnetic field in the case of a lightning strike. Generally, buildings have several lightning conductors. Each should be at the maximum possible distance from storage areas. Care must also be taken that the plumbing system is not connected to the lightning conductor system (Knight, 1977).

The permissible thresholds for magnetic field strengths given above apply for linear (not FM modulated) magnetic recordings on iron oxide tapes of medium coercivity. In keeping to these values, all other types of magnetic recordings (FM modulated signals as for video and hi-fi audio tracks on video tapes, and all digital recordings, specifically those on tapes with high coercivity as MP tapes, as well as magneto-optical discs) will be safe, as they would require higher field strengths for their deterioration.

PRINT-THROUGH

Print-through is a storage-related phenomenon. It originates from direct layer-to-layer contact in the wound-up tape. Low coercivity particles in the magnetic pigment, which never can be fully avoided, are magnetized by the fields from the adjacent layers. These become audible as echoes when strong signals are neighbouring low-level signals or silent portions of the recordings. Print-through occurs from the first moment of layer-to-layer contact when the tape is wound up on the spool. It increases, however, only logarithmically with time. It is further dependent on the percentage of low-coercivity particles in magnetic pigment, on temperature, and on the thickness of the tape (Bertram et al., 1980). Being a result of low-coercivity this is also the key for its removal: if tapes are wound several times before replay, the magnetostrictive effect of this process diminishes the built-up print-through to very low and generally unnoticeable levels (Schüller, 1980). Failure to remove the print-through, however, before a tape is copied will render this parasite signal a permanent part of the new recording; it cannot be removed at a later date.

PACKING, STACKS AND STORAGE AREAS

Packing materials, housings and boxes delivered with audio carriers of all kinds are mainly intended to protect the carriers adequately against mechanical damage and pollution – particularly dust. Unfortunately it must be noted that many of the original packing materials and containers are inadequate or at least sub-optimal. Specifically, products of the 1950s and 1960s must be suspected. Paper and cardboard often contain acidity, which may trigger deterioration, while early plastic bags, mainly made of PVC, may suffer from plasticizer exudation, which – instead of protecting them – may negatively affect the carriers, especially vinyl discs.

All packing materials should be checked, and changed if necessary. All paper and cardboard materials must be acid-free, and plastic materials, such as polyethylene or polypropylene, must be chemically inert.

Another source of concern is dust from paper deriving from inlays, booklets and so on, specifically in association with high-density recordings, such as R-DAT.

Finally, it must be taken into account that dust and pollution from outside is not the only cause of deterioration. Many chemical processes, such as hydrolysis of acetate cellulose or of pigment binder, are autocatalytic, which means that such a process produces a catalyst for its further acceleration. It is essential, therefore, that carriers prone to autocatalytic reactions, such as acetate tapes, should never be kept in airtight boxes. Generally, a trade-off between exogenous and endogenous sources of degradation must take place. Archives in an arid and dusty environment may, therefore, justifiably use plastic bags, while archives in northern urban environments may consider endogenous dangers a higher risk than dust and other pollution from outside. In order to support such strategies it is good practice to equip air-conditioning systems with effective dust and – if necessary – chemical filters and keep the collections in comparatively airy surroundings.

Originally, storage stacks were recommended to be of aluminium or wood, as iron was suspected to have a bad influence on magnetic tapes. This is not the case, however, if provisions are made to ensure that stacks will not become part of the lightning conducting system in the event of a strike. When ordering such stacks it should be specified that shelves must be free of remanent (or residual) magnetism. Aluminium stacks are fully acceptable but the choice of wood should be considered because chemical protective agents may evaporate and interact with carriers with unknown results. This applies especially to shelves made from chipboard and other boards made of reconstituted wood.

The floors of storage areas should be made of dust-free and chemically inert materials, such as concrete sealed with two-component varnishes. The colour should be chosen to render dust and dirt visible, and not to camouflage it, in order to trigger its prompt complete removal.

Storage areas are frequently located underground. Such locations, however, need careful planning as they are prone to water influx from various sources (Lotichius, 1981). As floods are generally unpredictable, the lowest shelves should be well above the floor in order to allow time for rescue measures. Also, excellent air conditioning is necessary to de-humidify such areas, especially when the ambient climate is warm and humid, and increases the humidity in cool underground areas. It is advantageous, therefore, to locate storage areas on the ground and upper floors, preferably in the centre of a building, in order to keep climatic fluctuations to a minimum. A slightly elevated position and a water-resistant ceiling will help to provide protection against an unexpected influx of water.

FIRE PROTECTION

Cultural goods need optimal fire protection, which must be planned in consultation with experts in this field. Generally, it is essential to install an adequate fire alarm system throughout a building that houses a valuable collection and to split the building into several sectors by fire division walls. Additionally, storage areas should be given enforced fire protection. The optimal protection can be achieved by the installation of automatic fire extinguishing systems. The preferred agents are halon replacement gases. Pure CO_2 is considered too dangerous to personnel who may be trapped when the gas is released.

It is a well-established traditional practice, and in some countries a legal requirement, to install water sprinkler systems. Because of the devastating effects of water on any kind of audio carriers the installation of such systems should be avoided if possible. This recommendation is reinforced by the fact that all automated systems are prone to false alarms and false releases of extinguishing agents. In the recent past, however, water-based extinguishing systems have been developed that create a misty atmosphere by using a comparatively low quantity of water with additional safety measures against false alarms. Some daring audio archivists have approved the installation of such systems.

Hand-held fire extinguishers to be used in offices, laboratories, studios and so on should preferably contain CO_2 or foam. The use of powder-extinguishers is strongly discouraged, because the removal of the released powder can be an extremely time-consuming and costly task.

SAFETY AND WORKING COPIES

As explained, because of their specific nature as audiovisual documents audio carriers require the highest possible degree of physical and chemical integrity. Any change or deterioration is associated with a loss of information. Because of the inherent instability of all audio carriers in one respect or another and because of their inherent vulnerability, accidental loss can never be excluded. The above-mentioned specific and general risks threatening audio carriers call for a consistent policy of duplication of audio holdings. The governing motto is 'One copy is no copy'.

In the case of industrially produced audio carriers two copies should be acquired by an archive and their integrity tested; one should then be placed in a master store, the other in a safe storage area, preferably located in a safe area a considerable distance away. For unique original recordings, archive master and safety copy should ideally be produced simultaneously as first-generation copies. For distribution and access, working copies must be prepared. In the past these have often been audio cassettes of a lower quality than the original. At the time of writing, cassettes are increasingly being replaced by recordable CDs and, where servers are available, by MP3 files.

OBSOLESCENCE OF HARDWARE

All audio carriers are machine-readable documents and in need of specific equipment for their replay. Even if the carriers did not suffer from any degradation, the retrievability of the stored information would always rely on the availability of the required hardware. With further development of technology, specifically in the domain of digital recording, formats and equipment are of high and ever-increasing levels of sophistication. Additionally, due to the accelerated pace of technical development, the commercial lifetime of recording systems – that is, the carriers and the associated hardware and software – becomes ever shorter. Some formats have been developed, such as the Digital Compact Cassette (DCC), that have never achieved any significant market penetration.

It must be kept in mind that it is possible to construct new cylinder replay machines which retrieve the information contained on cylinders better than the original historic equipment. It is totally impossible, however, to rebuild a CD player once the last player has failed and no dedicated spare parts are available.

Presently, cylinder and 78 rpm record players and accessories can be obtained from expert manufacturers at a price. LP replay equipment is still available on the market. The range of equipment, however, is shrinking. It must be noted that the standard analogue quarter-inch tape format is now seriously endangered by the obsolescence of replay equipment as prominent manufacturers of equipment cease their production of analogue replay machines.

Of the digital formats, R-DAT may become obsolete in the mid-term, while the CD seems to have a fairly solid position.

CHANGE OF PARADIGM: DIGITAL MASS STORAGE SYSTEMS

Audio archivists, like all other archivists and museum custodians, originally pursued a basic archival principle: to preserve the objects placed in their care. By the end of the 1980s it became apparent, however, that such a strategy was becoming increasingly unviable. None of the carriers was of a specified stability, unlike most of the paper documents, nor was there any hope that recording and replay systems with a designed long life expectancy would ever become available in the market. Moreover, the use of recording and replay systems that were stable over long periods of time would swiftly – in view of the rapid technical development – render such systems technically outdated.

In the light of this situation it became obvious that the old paradigm of looking for stable audio carriers and formats would not only be in vain, but counter-productive. The successful future preservation of sound demands that the content be the target and not the carrier. This is achieved by copying the material from one carrier and system to the next. Such a strategy can, however, work only in the digital domain, which makes possible such subsequent copying without loss of information. Consequently, the self-checking and self-regenerating archive was envisaged. Digital mass storage systems (DMSSs) – juke boxes accessible by a robotic system – hold digital carriers. These carriers can be loaded and replayed by remote control, which offers totally new dimensions for access, especially for national and radio sound archives. Additionally the data integrity of such systems can be controlled automatically. Whenever the error rate rises above a given threshold, a copy is made to a new carrier before uncorrectable errors occur (refreshment). If, because of technical development or market forces, the whole system is threatened with obsolesence, the contents can be migrated to a new system with a minimum of manual labour.

Around 1990 this new concept (Schüller, 1992) was met with great scepticism. From 1992 onwards, however, this idea was systematically pursued by the radio archives of the German public broadcasting stations (ARD), and has now become state of the art (Matzke, 2001). A number of archives, including national archives and research archives, are setting up DMSSs. The carriers currently used by such systems are magnetic tape cartridges specifically developed for storing large amounts of computer data. The most common formats used in audio applications so far are DLT, AIT2, and the upcoming LTO format. It may well be that in future a suitable recordable optical carrier will also be widely used for such purposes.

At the time of writing, such DMSSs are costly, mainly due to the fact that each system is more or less tailor-made. Additionally, previous typical customers for such systems were wealthy organizations such as banks, insurance companies and defence organizations. With the ever-growing demand for large-scale data storage by offices, the market will respond and reduce prices for small and scaleable systems ('Personal' DMSSs, Schüller, 2000). However, although DMSSs provide an extremely high degree of data security, appropriate disaster preparedness will imply either the installation of a mirror archive in a different location, or at least the 'manual' deposit of second copies of the carriers in a safe place.

TRANSFER OF CONTENTS INTO DMSSs

A greater challenge than setting up DMSSs is the transfer of data from conventional carriers, be they analogue or digital, into the 'eternal' environment (Schüller, 2001; IASA TC, 2001). For digital originals this is comparatively easy, as it is only necessary to retrieve a fully corrected, un-interpolated signal from the originals. The transfer of analogue sources, on the other hand, implies a series of considerable problems of principle and practice.

The major governing principle is that all data must be transferred unmodified. No subjective interpretations, restorations or aesthetic manipulations must be carried out. It is also important that no data reduction ('data compression') based on perceptual coding is used. For digital originals, the original format and resolution should be the ideal target format too, provided that this format is not a proprietary one but an openly defined standard.

For analogue signals the choice of an adequate digital target resolution is more complex. It is not solely the audio signal that must guide this choice but also the fact that an audio document has to be preserved with all its distortions and artefacts introduced by the historical recording process, and all those added during the life of the carrier by deterioration or damage. In order to represent the signal and its inadequacies in the best possible form, the highest technically and financially feasible resolution at the time of transfer must be chosen. This additional accuracy will be beneficial for any future restoration process.

The practical problems related to analogue-to-digital transfer embrace the increasing obsolescence of equipment, the lack of adequate understanding of historical formats, and the always underestimated time factor for such transfers. Radio sound archives holding uniform source materials produced under specified and controlled conditions can make use of digital audio work stations which assist in controlling the quality of the source signals and their transfer, thus allowing one technician to operate several work stations at once (Lee and Wright, 2001). Apart from the considerable financial input necessary for such installations, the source material of heritage collections is rarely of uniform and standardized character. Therefore, for magnetic tape, the transfer requires, as a minimum, three times the duration of the original. For historical mechanical carriers, this factor of three has to be increased considerably. Depending on the size of the collection, the transfer of entire holdings may, therefore, take many years if not decades.

Consequently, the order in which materials should be transferred has to be carefully considered. Materials which are immediately endangered by deterioration must come first, as well as all those materials in frequent demand. Unfortunately, however, the life expectancy of materials currently in good condition is difficult to predict. It is hoped that valid tests to predict the life expectancy of magnetic tape and CD-Rs will be developed soon. This will prevent stable materials being transferred by a time-consuming procedure while unstable materials deteriorate beyond retrievability (Schüller and Kranner, 2001).

INTERMEDIARY SOLUTIONS BEFORE DMSSs

Many archives and libraries are being forced to transfer materials for preservation and access purposes into the digital domain before DMSSs become affordable.

Although the preferred digital target format of such projects is the CD-R, some projects also use R-DAT. Such a strategy is possible, but its success depends on strict adherence to elaborate and time-consuming procedures (IASA TC, 2001).

In principle, the performance of DMSSs has to be imitated manually. This means that each digital target carrier produced has to be checked for data integrity after its production and, subsequently, at intervals in the course of its life. It must also be noted that the digital target carriers produced should have the least possible number of correctable errors to give the greatest possible safety margins before additional errors are introduced by carrier deterioration. Records of these checks have to be kept and a new carrier has to be produced of the fully corrected digital data stream (refreshment). This must be done well before the error rate reaches the point at which the errors become uncorrectable. Eventually, contents have to be migrated to a new system before the old systems (carrier and related hard- and software) become obsolete.

It is a matter of concern that many digitization projects use the CD-R as a digital target format without checking data integrity in the manner described above. In view of the unknown life expectancy of CD-Rs and of the ever-growing compatibility problems between writers and blank CD-Rs, which often leads to high error rates in the recording process, the results of such projects may be unreliable and not of archival standard. Consequently, some transfer projects already jump the CD-R by recording their digital signals on to computer tapes like DLT, which are 'manually' shelved like conventional carriers and may later be incorporated into DMSSs. High-resolution signals at 96 kHz/24-bit, which it is not practical to store on a CD-R, can be easily accommodated on such a carrier. It view of the time-consuming testing associated with the use of CD-Rs, such a strategy may, in general, be more cost-effective, although the initial investment in drives and the current cost of tapes may be higher.

SUMMARY

This chapter has reviewed the major problems related to the preservation of sound carriers. As far as magnetic tape is concerned, many of the principal and practical aspects also relate to magnetic video tape recordings. The section related to optical discs is also applicable to the preservation of replicated and recorded CD-ROMs and upcoming DVD-ROMs of whatever content. The literature referenced in the text is not exhaustive. It concentrates on publications which themselves are pointers to more specific references. Readers are invited also to specifically study the respective general publications (Ward, 1990; Varlamoff and Schüller, 2000), conference proceedings (Orbanz, 1988; Boston, 1992, 1999; Aubert and Billeaud, 2000; AES, 2001) and standard documents (AES standards, IASA TC, 2001).

Audio preservation has become a specialist discipline which is constantly faced with new problems and insights. Readers are, therefore, encouraged to take this chapter just as a general introduction and to seek expert advice for their specific preservation problems, especially if unique heritage material has to be safeguarded. For the latest advice the International Association of Sound and Audiovisual Archives (IASA) and its Technical Committee should be contacted over the Internet.

REFERENCES

AES22-1997, *AES Recommended Practice for Audio Preservation and Restoration: Storage of Polyester-Based Magnetic Tape*, Audio Engineering Society, New York.

AES28-1997, *AES Standard for Audio Preservation and Restoration: Method for Estimating Life Expectancy of Compact Discs (CD-ROM), Based on Effects of Temperature and Relative Humidity*, Audio Engineering Society, New York.

AES35-2000, *AES Standard for Audio Preservation and Restoration: Method for Estimating Life Expectancy of Magneto-Optical Disks (M-O), Based on Effects of Temperature and Relative Humidity*, Audio Engineering Society, New York.

AES38-2000, *AES Standard for Audio Preservation and Restoration: Life Expectancy of Information Stored in Recordable Compact Disc Systems. Method for Estimating, Based on Effects of Temperature and Relative Humidity*, Audio Engineering Society, New York.

AES (ed.) (2001), *Proceedings of the 20th AES International Conference, Archiving, Restoration, and New Methods of Recording, Budapest*, Audio Engineering Society, New York.

Aschinger, E. (1980), 'Report on Measurements of Magnetic Stray Fields in Sound Archives', *Phonographic Bulletin* 27, pp. 13–20.

Aubert, M. and Billeaud, R. (eds) (2000), *Image and Sound Archiving and Access: The Challenges of the 3rd Millennium. Proceedings of the Joint Technical Symposium Paris 2000*, Centre national de la cinématographie, Paris.

Bertram, N., Stafford, M. and Mills, D. (1980), 'The Print-through Phenomenon', *Journal of the Audio Engineering Society* 28 (10), pp. 690–705.

Boston, G. (ed.) (1992), *Archiving the Audio-visual Heritage. Proceedings of the (Third) Joint Technical Symposium, Ottawa 1990*, Technical Co-ordinating Committee, Milton Keynes.

Boston, G. (ed.) (1998), *Safeguarding the Documentary Heritage. A guide to Standards, Recommended Practices and Reference Literature Related to the Preservation of Documents of all kinds*, UNESCO, Paris. Web version: http://www.unesco.org/webworld/mdm/administ/en/guide/guidetoc.htm Extended CD-ROM version: see Varlamoff and Schüller (2000).

Boston, G. (ed.) (1999), *Technology and Our Audio-Visual Heritage. Proceedings of the Fourth Joint Technical Symposium, London 1995*, Technical Co-ordinating Committee, Milton Keynes.

Bradley, K. (1992), 'Restoration of Tapes with a Polyester Urethane Binder', *Phonographic Bulletin* 61, pp. 87–93.

Bradley, K. (1999), 'Anomalies in the Treatment of Hydrolysed Tapes: Including Non-Chemical Methods of Determining the Decay of Signals', in Boston, G. (ed.), *Technology and Our Audio-Visual Heritage. Proceedings of the Fourth Joint Technical Symposium, London 1995*, Technical Co-ordinating Committee, Milton Keynes, pp. 70–83.

Burt, L.S. (1977), 'Chemical Technology in the Edison Recording Industry', *Journal of the Audio Engineering Society* 25 (10-11), pp. 712–17.

Edge, M. (2000), 'Approaches to the Conservation of Film and Sound Materials', in M. Aubert and R. Billeaud (eds), *Image and Sound Archiving and Access: The Challenges of the 3rd Millennium. Proceedings of the Joint Technical Symposium Paris 2000*, Centre national de la cinématographie, Paris, pp. 35–43.

Fontaine, J.-M. (1999), 'Relevance of the Parameters Defining the Quality of CDs', in G. Boston (ed.), *Technology and Our Audio-Visual Heritage. Proceedings of the Fourth Joint Technical Symposium, London 1995*, Technical Co-ordinating Committee, Milton Keynes, pp. 96–109.

Fontaine, J.-M. (2000), 'Eléments de caractérisation de la qualité initiale et du vieillissement des disques CD-R', in M. Aubert and R. Billeaud (eds), *Image and Sound Archiving and Access: The Challenges of the 3rd Millennium. Proceedings of the Joint Technical Symposium Paris 2000*, Centre national de la cinématographie, Paris pp. 113–36.

Geller, S.B. (1972), *The effects of magnetic fields on magnetic storage media used in computers*, National Bureau of Standards technical note 735, Washington, DC.

Geller, S.B. (1976), 'Erasing Myths about Magnetic Media', *Datamation* 65.

Gibson, G. (1988), 'Decay and degradation of disc and cylinder recordings in storage', in *Audio preservation: A planning study*, Silver Spring, MD: Association for Recorded Sound Collections, pp. 186–99.

Gilmour, I. (2000), 'Media Testing in Audiovisual Archives. Why is my Tape Falling to Bits?', in M. Aubert and R. Billeaud (eds), *Image and Sound Archiving and Access: The Challenges of the 3rd Millennium. Proceedings of the Joint Technical Symposium Paris 2000*, Centre national de la cinématographie, Paris, pp. 79–87.

Gilmour, I. and Fumic, V. (1992), 'Recent Developments in Decomposition and Preservation of Magnetic Tape', *Phonographic Bulletin* 61, pp. 74–86.

IASA Technical Committee (2001), *The Safeguarding of the Audio Heritage: Ethics, Principles and Preservation Strategy* (= IASA Technical Committee – Standards, Recommended Practices and Strategies, IASA TC-03), Version 2. Web version: http://www.llgc.org.uk/iasa/iasa0013.htm

Isom, W.R. (1977), 'Evolution of the Disc Talking Machine', *Journal of the Audio Engineering Society* 25 (10–11), pp. 718–23.

Khanna, S.K. (1977), 'Vinyl Compound for the Phonographic Industry', *Journal of the Audio Engineering Society* 25 (10–11), pp. 724–8.

Knight, G.A. (1977), 'Factors Relating to Long Term Storage of Magnetic Tape', *Phonographic Bulletin* 18, pp. 15–45.

Kunej, D. (2001), 'Instability and Vulnerability of CD-R Carriers to Sunlight', in *Proceedings of the 20th AES International Conference. Archiving, Restoration, and new Methods of Recording, Budapest*, Audio Engineering Society, New York, pp. 18-25.

Lee, A., and Wright, R. (2001), 'New Technology for Broadcast Archive Preservation', in *Proceedings of the 20th AES International Conference, Archiving, Restoration, and new Methods of Recording, Budapest*, Audio Engineering Society, New York, pp. 92–5.

Lotichius, D. (1981), 'Measures for the Preservation and for the Protection of Archived Program Property on Sound Carriers', *Phonographic Bulletin* 31, pp. 37–9.

Matzke, A. (2001), 'Introducing Computer-Based Audio Archives in German Public Broadcast Stations', in *Proceedings of the 20th AES International Conference. Archiving, Restoration, and new Methods of Recording, Budapest*, Audio Engineering Society, New York, pp. 83–6.

Orbanz, E. (ed.) (1988), *Archiving the Audio-visual Heritage. Proceedings of the (Second) Joint Technical Symposium, Berlin, 1987*, Stiftung Deutsche Kinemathek, Berlin.

Pickett, A.G. and Lemcoe, M.M. (1991), *Preservation and Storage of Sound Recordings*, Washington 1959, Reprint by Association of Recorded Sound Collections.

Psohlavec, St. (2001), 'Practical Experience with Long-Term CD-R Archiving', in *Proceedings of the 20th AES International Conference. Archiving, Restoration, and new Methods of Recording, Budapest*, Audio Engineering Society, New York, pp. 15–17.

Schüller, D. (1980), 'Archival Tape Test', *Phonographic Bulletin* 27, pp. 21–5.

Schüller, D. (1992), 'Towards the Automated "Eternal" Sound Archive', in G. Boston (ed.), *Archiving the Audio-visual Heritage. Proceedings of the (Third) Joint Technical Symposium, Ottawa 1990*, Technical Co-ordinating Committee, Milton Keynes, pp. 106–10.

Schüller, D. (1996), 'Preservation of Audio and Video Materials in Tropical Countries', *IASA Journal* 7, pp. 35–45, reprint *International Preservation News*. Newsletter of the IFLA PAC, 21/2000, pp. 4–9. Web version: http://www.unesco.org/webworld/audiovis/reader/7_5.htm

Schüller, D. (2000), '"Personal" Digital Mass Storage Systems – Viable Solutions for Small Institutions and Developing Countries', *IASA Journal* 16, pp. 52–5. Web version: http://www.unesco.org/webworld/points_of_views/schuller.shtml

Schüller, D. (2001), 'Preserving the Facts for the Future: Principles and Practices for the Transfer of Analogue Audio Documents into the Digital Domain'. *Journal of the Audio Engineering Society* 49 (7/8), pp. 618–21.

Schüller, D. and Kranner, L. (2001), 'Life Expectancy Testing of Magnetic Tapes – A Key to a Successful Strategy in Audio and Video Preservation', in *Proceedings of the 20th AES International Conference. Archiving, Restoration, and New Methods of Recording, Budapest*, Audio Engineering Society, New York, pp. 11–14.

St-Laurent, G. (1991), *The care and handling of recorded sound materials*, Commission on Preservation and Access, Washington, DC.

Trock, J. (2000), 'Permanence of CD-R Media', in M. Aubert and R. Billeaud (eds), *Image and Sound Archiving and Access: The Challenges of the 3rd Millennium. Proceedings of the Joint Technical Symposium Paris 2000*, Centre national de la cinématographie, Paris, pp. 104–12.

Van Bogart, J. (1995), *Magnetic tape storage and handling: A guide for libraries and Archives*, Commission on Preservation and Access, Washington, DC.

Varlamoff, M.-Th. and Schüller, D. (eds) (2000), *Safeguarding our Documentary Heritage* (CD-ROM). UNESCO, Paris (extended CD-ROM version of Boston, 1998).

Ward, A. (1990), *A manual of sound archive administration*, Gower, Brookfield, VT and Aldershot, UK.

7 Preservation management: sources of information

Graham Matthews

INTRODUCTION

There have been considerable developments in preservation management in libraries over the last thirty years or so and many of these are reflected in the professional and academic literature. There is now a range of publications to which librarians, archivists, academics, students and others can turn for information about the various aspects of the topic. In recent years, textbooks, policy statements, guidelines, reports, bibliographies, periodicals and journal articles have been published by a variety of commercial publishers, research institutions, national libraries, cooperative consortia, academics and practitioners.

Over the last five years or so, the development of Web sites available over the Internet has greatly facilitated finding and disseminating information about preservation management in libraries and archives. Such sites offer a wealth of information in their own pages and often point to printed materials and organizational or personal contacts elsewhere. The usual caveats when using Web sites should be heeded – check, for example, for authority and reputation of the provider or publisher of the site, and the accuracy and currency of the information presented. That said, much useful information and many links to further helpful sources may be found using a relatively small number of Web sites provided by different organizations around the world. (URLs of Web sites included in this chapter were 'live' in December 2002.)

The focus of this chapter, in terms of subject scope, is preservation management. Conservation, although it is an integral element of effective preservation management, is excluded, other than where it is part of a source on preservation management, or the work is of a more general than technical nature. One area where there has recently been a considerable explosion of activity and publication is digital preservation. The section below dealing with this has been particularly selective given the space available here. The emphasis is on English-language material although some Internet sources offer several European languages. It is hoped that the coverage is sufficiently international in scope to make the chapter of use to those outside the UK.

Many of the sources contain suggestions for further reading and bibliographies of older material, some of which may still be of interest and use. The emphasis here is on current and recent sources (from 1996 onwards) that provide information and details of other potentially useful sources. Reviews of the development of preservation management activity over the last thirty years or so and bibliographies also provide access to previously published material (see Bibliographies below).

The approach taken in this chapter is to move from general to subject specific sources. Sources are therefore presented under the following headings, in this order:

- Textbooks
- Bibliographies
- Periodicals, general
- Web sites, general/international and national
- Collections care – storage and environment, exhibitions and loans
- Audiovisual materials
- Surrogacy/substitution
- Digital materials
- Disaster management
- Security
- Preservation needs assessment
- Preservation policy
- Research
- Education and training

Sources are generally presented within and/or following a brief introduction under each heading, which permits some contextualization.

It should be remembered that general sources should not be overlooked when seeking information on specific aspects of preservation management as they are often divided into specific topic categories and contain information of a specific as well as a general nature.

TEXTBOOKS

Textbooks provide an introduction to the history and development of the subject, outlines of its key component parts, and basic explanations of the technical aspects – they are useful starting-points, with references and suggestions for further reading. Those mentioned here also provide an insight into different national perspectives and influences.

Feather, J. (1996), *Preservation and the management of library collections*, 2nd edn, Library Association, London.

Harvey, D.R. (1993), *Preservation in libraries: principles, practices and strategies for librarians*, Bowker-Saur, London and Melbourne.

Ogden, S. (1999), *Preservation of library and archival materials: a manual*, 3rd edn, Northeast Document Conservation Center, Massachusetts. (Also available at: http://www.nedcc.org/plam3/manhome.htm)

Swartzburg, S.G. (1995), *Preserving library materials: a library manual*, 2nd edn, Scarecrow, Metuchen, NJ.

BIBLIOGRAPHIES

Several Web sites (see below) offer general and subject specific bibliographies. A comprehensive and authoritative bibliography (which follows on from earlier editions) has recently been published:

Schare, R.E. Jr, Swartzburg, S.G. and Cunha, G.M. (2001), *Bibliography of preservation literature 1983–1996*, The Scarecrow Press Inc., Lanham, MD and London (826pp, author and subject index).

Occasional bibliographies and/or literature reviews or reviews of preservation management activity with substantial references also appear in the literature. See, for example,

Jordan, S.K. (2000), 'A Review of the Preservation Literature, 1993–1998', *Library Resources and Technical Services*, 44, pp. 4–21.

Matthews, G. (1997), 'Preservation management', *Library & Information Briefings*, issue 73.

PERIODICALS, GENERAL

On a global basis, for reports of IFLA's activities and events that support efforts to preserve materials in libraries and archives worldwide, see its newsletter, *International Preservation News* (see: www.ifla.org/VI/4/pubs.htm for further details). The *Abbey Newsletter: preservation of library and archival materials (1978–)* (also available online at: http://palimpsest.stanford.edu/byorg/abbey/an/) provides short articles, reviews, announcements and general information with a North American emphasis. 'Preservation News', a regular, monthly one-page feature by Jane Hedberg in *College and Research Libraries News*, is worth checking for announcements of new products, publications and developments, mainly North American. In the UK, the National Preservation Office's *NPO Journal* (1999– ; supersedes *Library Conservation News*, 1983–98), provides short articles on topical preservation-related activities, news of people and initiatives, book reviews and information about conferences, meetings and events. Naturally, the general academic and professional periodicals of library and information management will contain papers and other information on aspects of preservation management. Familiar abstracting and indexing services such as *Library and Information Science Abstracts* and *Library Literature* can be used to identify these. Periodicals covering archives and conservation also contain information about preservation management but are often of a specialist nature. In the UK, for example, the *Journal of the Society of Archivists* and *The Paper Conservator: the Journal of the Institute of Paper Conservation*, contain academic and review articles. Some organizations also publish newsletters, for example, *Paper Conservation News* (Institute of Paper Conservation). *Restaurator* (K.G. Saur) is an international journal for the preservation of library and archive material whose articles are mainly of a technical nature.

Other periodicals of a more specific subject nature are mentioned as relevant in the sections below.

WEB SITES

Web sites are published and maintained by a variety of organizations (for example, international professional associations, national libraries, regional cooperatives, commercial companies, individual libraries and archives) with an interest or active role in preservation management and associated subjects. They range from those that attempt general, broad coverage of different aspects of the topic to those with a particular focus. In either case, they can provide much useful information, either in themselves or through the links and contacts they offer. They often contain references to significant older sources as well as contemporary ones. Increasingly, they offer rich visual material to supplement their textual content and, in some cases, practical examples or case studies of particular issues. Where they are regularly updated, or offer 'news' sections, they can also be scanned for updating purposes. Some contain mailing or discussion lists that are also a useful way of seeking information of a specific nature or opinions on practical applications, and so on. It is not possible to give comprehensive details of each Web site's coverage; rather, the annotations are intended to give a flavour of this, and some include examples. Publications of Web site hosts are also included throughout this chapter.

GENERAL/INTERNATIONAL

Conservation Online (CoOL)
(http://palimpsest.stanford.edu/)
A most comprehensive Web site in terms of coverage of preservation (not just conservation as its title implies) for libraries, archives and museums. It is produced by the Preservation Department of Stanford University Libraries and thus has an emphasis on North American sources but also includes much of broader worldwide interest either in its content or via links. All CoOL documents can be searched, but the site also offers helpful categorization by topic, for example, audio materials, disaster planning and response, electronic media, environment, pest management, survey results. These topics are further divided into appropriate sections to facilitate retrieval and browsing. It also groups together bibliographies, resource guides, dictionaries and glossaries, and provides links to other organizations' Web sites and mailing list archives.

European Commission on Preservation and Access (ECPA)
(http://www.knaw.nl/ecpa/)
The European Commission on Preservation and Access (ECPA), established in 1994, acts as a focus for discussion and cooperation in preservation and access issues for heritage organizations throughout Europe. It is based at the Royal Netherlands Academy of Arts and Sciences. The Web site aims to be a gateway to information on the preservation of the documentary heritage in Europe and contains routine, but useful, information on news and resources, its own publications, notes on training, links to other sites (worldwide) and a discussion list, EPIC-LST. It also offers other significant resources, including the *Preservation map of Europe* that provides information about preservation activities and contacts in over forty European countries, and a *Virtual exhibition of the ravages of dust, water, moulds, fungi, bookworms and other pests*, that illustrate their damaging effects.

UNESCO Memory of the World Programme
(http://portal.unesco.org/ci/ev.php?URL_ID=1538&URL_DO=DO_TOPIC&URL_SECTION=201&reload=1037357654)
The UNESCO Memory of the World Programme, Preserving Documentary Heritage, offers access through its Web site to wide-ranging information on preservation of worldwide interest. The site (available in English or French) offers information on news and events, links and publication). A leaflet, *Safeguarding the documentary heritage of humanity*, provides details of the programme, its aims, projects and activities (available at: www.unesco.org/webworld/mdm/leaflet_en.pdf3). Another document, realized on behalf of UNESCO, by IFLA-PAC (see below), Boston, G. (ed.) (2000), *Safeguarding the documentary heritage: a guide to*

standards, recommended practices and reference literature related to the preservation of documents of all kinds, offers information on the preservation of different media, for example, photographic materials, magnetic materials and optical media, along with subject-specific information, a bibliography of printed sources for disaster planning, a directory of Web sites covering deterioration agents and damaged documents and risk management, and contact details of 'where to turn for advice' organizations (available at: http://webworld.unesco.org/safeguarding/en/).

International Federation of Library Associations and Institutions (IFLA)
IFLA Core Programme for Preservation and Conservation (PAC)
(http://www.ifla.org/VI/4/pac.htm)
The IFLA Core Programme on Preservation and Conservation was established in 1984 'to focus efforts on issues of preservation and initiate worldwide cooperation for the preservation of library materials'. The focal point for PAC is hosted by the Bibliothèque nationale de France and there are six other regional centres: Washington (Library of Congress), Caracas (Biblioteca Nacional de Venezuela), Tokyo (National Diet Library), Canberra (National Library of Australia), and Moscow (Library of Foreign Literature). The Web site provides details of projects, publications (see, for example, Manning, R.W. and Kremp, V. (2000), *A reader in preservation and conservation*, IFLA Publications Series 91, K.G. Saur, Munich), programmes, annual reports, and useful addresses and contacts.

IFLA Section on Preservation and Conservation
(www.ifla.org/VII/s19/sconsv.htm)
The section provides an international forum for the discussion, dissemination and development of issues relating to theories, policies and practices for the preservation of recorded knowledge and works closely with the IFLA Core Programme (above). Announcements, newsletter and annual reports are available, along with contact details of officers.

International Council on Archives (ICA)
(http://www.ica.org)
'ICA is dedicated to the advancement of archives worldwide.' Its Web site has information for members, researchers and the curious. Details of its organization (for example, branches, sections and committees) and publications are provided. Sections cover a range of archives and related issues; these include sections on archival education and training, business and labour archives, archives of churches and religious denominations, university and research institution archives, among others.

138

International Centre for the Study of the Preservation and Restoration of Cultural Property (ICCROM)
(http://www.iccrom.org/eng/news/iccrom.htm)
This intergovernmental organization, established in 1959, has a worldwide mandate 'to promote the conservation of all types of cultural heritage'. The information available on its Web site reflects its main areas of activity: training, information (bibliographic resources), research (for example, international ethics and standards for conservation practice), cooperation and advocacy (for example, teaching materials and workshops).

NATIONAL

Many Web sites of national or regional associations, organizations and libraries contain information of interest and use to those in countries elsewhere. The following, from the UK, the USA and Australia, are significant key sites, which also serve here as examples of the variety of such sites, the organizations that provide them, and the wealth of information they offer. Similar sites hosted by like organizations in other countries can also be found.

United Kingdom

National Preservation Office, based at the British Library
(www.bl.uk/services/preservation/national.html)
The National Preservation Office, established in 1984, aims 'to provide an independent focus for ensuring the preservation and continued accessibility of library and archival material held in the United Kingdom and Ireland'. It is supported 'by the British Library, with additional financial support from the Public Record Office, the National Library of Scotland, Trinity College Library Dublin, the Consortium of University Research Libraries, Cambridge University Library, the National Library of Wales, the Bodleian Library Oxford, the National Library of Ireland, the Public Record Office of Northern Ireland and the Standing Conference of National and University Libraries'. It has developed and coordinated national preservation strategy and offers an information and referral service. Its Web site provides information about its activities (including strategic plan), committees and publications (free and priced; it produces a range of guidance leaflets on preservation management, security, conference reports, seminar papers, videos and promotional materials) and links to other sites, as well as a 'What's new' feature.

The Society of Archivists
(http://www.archives.org.uk)
In addition to standard information such as information about the society, its membership, panels, regions, groups, education and training, the annual

conference, publications, a diary of events and contact lists, the Web site includes cover stories and spotlights latest features.

United Kingdom Institute for Conservation
(www.ukic.org.uk/)
'UKIC is the representative body for professional conservators and restorers in private and institutional practice in the UK.' Its Web site provides details of a range of publications and training on conservation, and has specialist sections addressing topics such as paintings and textiles. It publishes a newsletter, *Conservation News*, *Grapevine*, a calendar of events, and *The Conservator*, an annual journal of refereed papers.

Museums Association
(www.museumsassociation.org)
'The largest association representing Museums and Galleries in Great Britain', the MA's Web site offers information on a wide range of events, for example, conferences, seminars and training, and other topics such as policy in progress, professional development, trusts and funds, and publications. A useful source for keeping up to date with collection care developments in museums.

University of Oxford Library Preservation Services
(http://www.bodley.ox.ac.uk/dept/preservation/)
The Bodleian Library has recently published a series of Web pages offering guidelines for staff and readers on good practices in handling library materials. With colourful illustrative supporting material, this offers an appealing ten-minute introduction aimed at reducing damage to library materials.

United States

Library of Congress, Preservation Directorate
(http://lcWeb.loc.gov/preserv/)
The Preservation Directorate offers a brochure series which includes: *The Deterioration and Preservation of Paper: Some Essential Facts, Saving the Written Word: Mass Deacidification at the Library of Congress* and *Caring for Your Family Treasures.* The Caring for the Library of Congress Collections pages include sections on binding and collections care, preservation reformatting, photographs and films, emergency preparedness and conservation.

Council on Library and Information Resources (CLIR)
(http://www.clir.org/)
CLIR's projects and activities 'are aimed at ensuring that information resources needed by scholars, students, and the general public are available for future

generations'; it is supported by major US institutions and funders. It offers a forum for discussion and change and undertakes a variety of activities and projects, including those in the areas of preservation and digital libraries, and produces a range of publications, including reports such as: Smith, A. (1999), *The future of the past: preservation in American research libraries*, pub 82, Commission on Library and Information Resources, Washington, DC, and Council on Library and Information Resources Task Force on the Artifact in Library Collections (2001), *The evidence in hand: the report of the Task Force on the Artifact in Library Collections*, pub 103, CLIR, Washington, DC, (see: www.clir.org/pubs/reports/pub103/contents.html for details and availability). Anne Kenney, its Director of Programs, is currently conducting, in conjunction with other associations, a project on *Examining the state of preservation programs in American college and research libraries.*

Northeast Document Conservation Center (NEDCC)
(http://www.nedcc.org)
This Web site asserts that NEDCC, founded in 1973, 'is the largest non-profit, regional conservation center in the United States'. It offers a range of publications and services, including conferences, workshops, international exchange programmes, information on funding, suppliers and services, and disaster assistance. It also makes available *Preservation 101: an Internet Course on Paper Preservation*, a well-thought-out and presented programme. Lesson 6, for example, deals with emergency preparedness and offers strategies and tips for writing a disaster plan, with details of printed and online resources.

Regional Alliance for Preservation
(www.rap-arcc.org/)
A cooperative programme with fourteen member organizations throughout the USA, its mission is 'to provide comprehensive preservation information to cultural institutions and the public throughout the United States'. It was initially funded in 1997 as a pilot project of the Commission on Preservation and Access; participants later decided to continue RAP and expanded its membership to include the Association of Regional Conservation Centers. Its Web site provides information about RAP and members, education and outreach, conservation services and publications, and links to related sites. It also provides a bibliography under headings such as environmental control, health and safety, packing and shipping, and security.

Research Libraries Group (RLG)
(http://www.rlg.org/toc.html)
'Research Libraries Group is a not-for-profit membership corporation of over 160 universities, national libraries, archives, historical societies, and other institutions

with remarkable collections for research and learning.' The focus is on collaborative work that addresses shared goals of members. RLG develops information resources for members and non-members around the world. Of particular interest in the preservation context are: the RLG and Preservation pages, in particular, *Long-term retention of traditional research materials* (www.rlg.org/preserv/index.html), and *Long-term retention of digital research materials* (www.rlg.org/longterm/). Details of policies, initiatives, service and publications (including reports and RLG DigiNews) are given.

Solinet Preservation Service
(http://www.solinet.net)
'The Southeastern Library Network is a not-for-profit library cooperative providing resource sharing for the educational, cultural, and economic advancement of the southeastern United States.' Founded in 1973, it now has a membership of over 2100 libraries of all kinds. Its Web site's Preservation Services pages provide information on topics including: field and consulting services, workshops, disaster services, microfilm service, publications and Internet resources. A 'What's new' page keeps readers up to date with new publications and events.

The Getty Conservation Institute
(www.getty.edu/conservation/institute/)
'The Getty Conservation Institute works internationally to advance conservation and to enhance and encourage the preservation and understanding of the visual arts in all of their dimensions – objects, collections, architectures and sites.

The Institute serves the conservation community through scientific research; education and training; field projects, and the dissemination of results of both its work and the work of others in the field.' It publishes a range of resources and offers grants for conservation.

Australia

National Library of Australia
(http://www.nla.gov.au/preserve)
The National Library Web site offers a range of useful information under its Preservation Activities pages. For example, its preservation policy, collection disaster plan, policy on preservation microfilming and a preservation needs assessment survey outline are available as is information about the PANDORA (Preserving and Accessing Networked Documentary Resources of Australia) Archive. The Library also hosts PADI (Preserving Access to Digital Information) – see Digital Materials below. Other pages include staff papers and articles and information on community heritage grants.

Australian Museums and Galleries Online (AMOL)
(http://amol.org.au/about_amol/about_amol.asp)
'A comprehensive Internet site to help Australian museums and galleries make information about their collections available to a world-wide audience' and to act as a gateway for those working in Australian museums and galleries. *reCollections: caring for collections across Australia*, now available online (http://amol.org.au/collections/), has been developed by the Heritage Collections Council as a set of guidebooks for use by non-conservators. It explains how to apply preventive conservation techniques to cultural objects and collections.

For Web sites specifically concerned with digital materials, see Digital Materials, below.

Discussion lists: Discussion lists can be a useful way of monitoring developments and contributing to discussion of topical issues; they can also be helpful in seeking information, advice or opinion from others.

See the Web sites above for details of discussion lists they provide (for example, CoOL's Conservation DistList http://palimpsest.stanford.edu/byform/mailing-lists/cdl/) and how to take part in them; they often provide details of other lists, too. In the UK, details of some lists can be found at JISC's National Academic Mailing List Service (see www.jiscmail.ac.uk). Three useful ones are: conservation-nccr@jiscmail.ac.uk (a multidisciplinary list for discussion of developments in all aspects of the conservation of the moveable heritage); lis-libhist@jiscmail.ac.uk (for information professionals with a common interest in library and book history); and digital-preservation@jiscmail.ac.uk (provides information and announcements on the preservation of digital materials).

COLLECTIONS CARE – STORAGE AND ENVIRONMENT, EXHIBITIONS AND LOANS

The last five years in the UK have seen considerable attention paid to collections care, with libraries and archives increasingly looking towards museums for examples of practice there, and working together, sharing practice and expertise where appropriate. The 1989 British Standard for the storage and exhibition of archival documents was reviewed and superseded by a new version in 2000 (British Standards Institute, 2000, *Recommendations for the storage and exhibition of archival documents (BS 5454)*, British Standards Institute, London). Older material on aspects of collections care can still be helpful. See, for example, Baynes-Cope, A.D. (1989), *Caring for books and documents*, 2nd edn, British Library, London; Hickin, N. (1992), *Bookworms: the insect pests of books*, rev. edn by

143

Edwards, R., Richard Joseph Publishers, Farnham, Surrey; National Preservation Office (1989), *Handling printed books*, National Preservation Office, London (Videocassette); Petherbridge, G. (ed.) (1987), *Conservation of library and archive materials and the graphic arts*, Society of Archivists, Institute of Paper Conservation, Butterworths, London.

Research leading to guidelines for practitioners has been undertaken, including Bell, N. and Lindsay, H. (2000), *Benchmarks in collections care for UK libraries*, Library and Information Commission Research Report 55, Library and Information Commission, London. Such work relating to libraries in the UK has also drawn on the experience of museums. See, for example, Keene, S. (1996), *Managing conservation in museums*, Butterworth-Heinemann, Oxford; Winsor, P. (1998), *Levels of collection care. A self-assessment checklist for UK museums*, Museums and Galleries Commission, London; and Museums and Galleries Commission (1998), *Ours for keeps? A resource pack for raising awareness of conservation and collection care*, Museums and Galleries Commission, London. The National Preservation Office (UK) has produced a series of leaflets which cover this topic, see: *Good handling principles and practice for library and archive materials* (2000), NPO Preservation Guidance Preservation Management Series, National Preservation Office, London; and *Guidance for exhibiting archive and library materials* (2000), NPO Preservation Guidance Preservation Management Series, National Preservation Office, London.

Other useful sources which illustrate the ongoing international interest in the different aspects of the subject are:

Adcock, E. (comp. and ed.) with the assistance of Varlamoff, M.-T. and Kremp, V. (1998), *IFLA principles for the care and handling of library and archival materials*, International Preservation Issues Number One, International Federation of Library Associations, Paris.

Australian Museums and Galleries Online (AMOL) (http://amol.org.au/craft/conservation/re-collections.asp) *reCollections: Caring for Collections across Australia*, developed by the Heritage Collections Council, aims to offer a set of practical guidebooks covering subjects including conservation and assessment planning, disaster prevention planning, and assessing the significance of cultural heritage objects and collections.

Corr, S. (2000), *Care for collections. A manual of preventive conservation*, Heritage Council of Ireland Series, Heritage Council of Ireland, Kilkenny, Ireland.

Giovannini, A. (2000), 'Architecture and preservation: fighting the same battle', *International Preservation News*, 22–23, pp. 15–18.

Kingsley, H., Pinniger, D., Xavier-Rowe, A. and Winsor, P. (eds) (2001), *Integrated pest management for collections: proceedings of 2001: a pest odyssey, pre-prints of the conference '2001: A Pest Odyssey' held 2–3 October 2001 [London]*, English Heritage, London.

Ling, T. (1998), *Solid, safe, secure. Building archives repositories in Australia*, Canberra, National Archives of Australia.

AUDIOVISUAL MATERIALS

Recent years have seen more widely available guidance for those seeking assistance in tackling the preservation problems associated with audiovisual materials, for example: Harrison, H.P. (ed. and comp.) (1997), *Audiovisual archives: a practical reader*, edited and compiled for the General Information Programme and UNISIST, (CII-97/WS/4), UNESCO, Paris (also available at: www.unesco.org/Webworld/audiovis/reader/contents.htm); Farley, J. (1999), *An introduction to new media*, Introduction to Archival Materials Series, The Public Record Office, Kew, Surrey; Dale, R. et al. (1998), *Audio preservation: a selective annotated bibliography and brief summary of current practices*, American Library Association Association for Library Collections and Technical Services, Preservation and Reformatting Section Photographic and Recording Media Committee, Audio Preservation Task Force, Chicago (also available at: www.ala.org/alcts/publications/audiopres.pdf); Gibbs, J.R. (2001), *Audio preservation and restoration including some links to film and video tape preservation*, Music Library, University of Washington (available at: www.lib.washington.edu/Music/preservation.html).

Photographic material, in particular, seems to have received increased attention. See, for example: Wilson, D. (1997), *The care and storage of photographs. Recommendations for good practice*, NAPLIB, London; Ball, S., Clark, S. and Winsor, P. (1998), *The care of photographic materials and related media: guidelines on the care, handling and storage and display of photography, film, magnetic and digital media*, Museums and Galleries Commission, London; Clark, S. (1999), *Preservation of photographic material*, NPO Preservation Guidance Preservation in Practice Series, National Preservation Office, London; Klijn, E. and Lusenet, Y. de (eds) (2000), *In the picture: preservation and digitisation of European photographic collections*, ECPA Report 11, European Commission on Preservation and Access, Amsterdam; and the Library of Congress Web site listed below. A European Union funded project, SEPIA (Safeguarding European Photographic Images for Access) focusing on the preservation of photographic materials was initiated in 1999; this has developed into SEPIA II (see www.knaw.nl/ecpa/sepia/home.html for further details of SEPIA).

There is now also growing activity relating to moving-image heritage. CoOL (Conservation OnLine) (see above) lists various sources under the heading Preservation of Motion Picture Film (see: http://palimpsest.stanford.edu/bytopic/motion-pictures/), including the National Film Preservation Foundation (USA) (see: www.film-foundation.org/organizations/nfpf.cfm) and the National Film

Preservation Board, Library of Congress (see: http://lcweb.loc.gov/film/ and http://www.loc.gov/preserv). In the UK, the National Film and Television Archive/ British Film Institute 'collect, preserve, restore and then share the films and television programmes which have helped to shape and record British life and times since cinema was invented in the late nineteenth century' (see www.bfi.org.uk/ collections/preservation/). Alban, J. (1999), *Film and sound archive sourcebook*, Society of Archivists, London, includes guidelines on identifying cinefilm and preserving nitrate film.

SURROGACY/SUBSTITUTION

Advances in technology and the digitization of special collections offer increasing access to some items and collections via electronic surrogates. In the UK the National Preservation Office, with funding from the Library and Information Commission, sponsored research into the development of a national strategy for surrogacy (Edwards, A., Matthews, G. and Nankivell, C. (2000), *Developing a national strategy for preservation surrogates*, Library and Information Research Report 54, Library and Information Commission, London). One of the findings of this project was that microfilming to archival standards was still regarded as the most appropriate means for long-term preservation and surrogacy of items; at the time of writing, the long-term preservation qualities of digital copies is unproven, with technologies still developing and a lack of standards. Many digitization projects are under way and some consideration of the advantages and disadvantages of microfilming from the digital copy or from the original has been undertaken (see, for example, Kenney, A. and Chapman, S. (1999), *Digital imaging and preservation microfilm: the future of the hybrid approach to the preservation of brittle books*, Commission on Library and Information Resources, Washington, DC). The journal *Microform and imaging review*, Munich: K.G. Saur, 1972– (quarterly), includes articles reporting on developments.

Useful guides to microfilming include: Fox, L. (ed.) (1996), *Preservation microfilming: a guide for librarians and archivists*, 2nd edn, American Library Association, Chicago and London; *Guide to preservation microfilming* (2000), National Preservation Office, London; *Guidelines for preservation microfilming in Australia and New Zealand* (1998), National Library of Australia, Canberra; and *Photocopying of library and archive materials* (2000), NPO Preservation Guidance Preservation Management Series, National Preservation Office, London. The *European Register of Microform Masters* (EROMM), an international database, hosted by Göttingen State and University Library, Germany (http://e250-039.gbv.de/eromm/), provides information about all works that have already been reformatted, or are about to be reformatted. It also includes information on

146

standards for surrogates, with links to other Web sites and details of useful publications.

In the UK, the successful NEWSPLAN initiative, the nationally coordinated microfilming of local newspapers, continues (see www.bl.uk/collections/nplan. html; and The NEWSPLAN 2000 Project at www.newsplan2000.org/, which includes the *Project handbook: guidelines for those participating in the NEWSPLAN 2000 Project*). *Newspaper Library News*, British Library Newspaper Library, 1980– (semi-annually) is another source which may be checked for news in this field.

Edwards, A. and Matthews, G. (2000), 'Preservation surrogacy and collection management', *Collection Building*, 19, pp. 140–50, puts surrogacy and substitution in the current context of collection development in the UK, including the impact of digitization initiatives.

DIGITAL MATERIALS

From the mid-1990s, considerable attention has been paid to the preservation of digitally created, or 'born-digital', materials. The seminal report, Waters, D. and Garrett, J. (1996), *Preserving digital information. Report of the Task Force on Archiving of Digital Information commissioned by the Commission on Preservation and Access and the Research Libraries Group*, Commission on Preservation and Access, Washington, DC (available at: www.rlg.org/ArchTF/) informed similar activity elsewhere in the world. A useful overview of this activity with its focus on the UK but covering significant developments and initiatives from elsewhere is available (Feeney, F. (ed.), (1999), *Digital culture: maximizing the nation's investment. A synthesis of JISC/NPO studies on the preservation of electronic materials*, National Preservation Office, London). IFLA has recently attempted to survey digitization and preservation activity worldwide: Gould, S. and Ebdon, R. (comps and eds), under the direction of M.-T. Varlamoff (1999), *International Federation of Library Associations and Institutions Core Programmes for Preservation and Conservation (PAC) and Universal Availability of Publications (UAP) and UNESCO memory of the World Programme, IFLA/UNESCO survey on digitisation and preservation*, International Preservation Issues Number Two, IFLA Office for UAP and International Lending, Boston Spa, West Yorkshire.

An extremely useful site to track current worldwide developments is the National Library of Australia's *Preserving access to digital information* (PADI) (see below), a subject gateway to digital preservation resources. The Higher Education Funding Councils in the UK through the Joint Information Systems Committee (JISC) (see www.jisc.ac.uk) eLib (the Electronic Libraries) programme (see www.ukoln.ac.uk/services/elib/) have funded the development of digital applications in UK university libraries. Those concerned with preservation have been undertaken with the

National Preservation Office. See, for example; Beagrie, N. and Greenstein, D. (1998), *A strategic framework for creating and preserving digital resources. A JISC/ NPO study within the Electronic Libraries (eLib) Programme on the Preservation of Electronic Materials*, eLib Studies, Library Information Technology Centre, South Bank University, London; and, Lievesley, D. and Jones, S. (1998), *Digital preservation needs of universities and research funders. A JISC/NPO study within the Electronic Libraries (eLib) Programme on the Preservation of Electronic Materials*, eLib Studies, Library Information Technology Centre, South Bank University, London.

Following on from earlier work (such as Hendley, T. (1996), *The preservation of digital material*, British Library Research and Development Department Report 6242, British Library Research and Development Department, London; Hendley, T. (1998), *Comparison of methods and costs of digital preservation. A consultancy study conducted by Tony Hendley, Technical Director, Cimtech Ltd, University of Hertfordshire*, British Library Research and Innovation Centre Report 106, British Library Research and Innovation Centre, London), papers exploring the practical issues and guides and handbooks to digital preservation are now appearing worldwide. See, for example:

Hunter, G.S. (2000), *Preserving digital information. A how-to-do-it manual*, How-to-do-it manuals for librarians, no 93, Neal Schuman Publishers Inc., New York.

International Council on Archives' Committee on Electronic Records Report (1997), *Guide for managing electronic records from an archival perspective*, ICA.

Jones, M. and Beagrie, N. (2001), *Preservation management of digital materials: a handbook*, The British Library, London. (This is maintained and updated by the Digital Preservation Coalition in collaboration with the National Library of Australia and the PADI Gateway; available at www.dpconline.org/graphics/handbook/index.html.)

Kenney, A.R. and Rieger, O.Y. (2000), *Moving theory into practice: digital imaging for libraries and archives*, Research Libraries Group, Mountain View, CA.

Lee, S. (2000), *Digital imaging: a practical handbook*, Neal-Schuman Publishers in association with Library Association Publishing, New York, London.

Ross, S. (2000), *Changing trains at Wigan: digital preservation and the future of scholarship*, NPO Preservation Guidance Occasional Papers, National Preservation Office, London.

Rothenberg, J. (1999), *Avoiding technological quicksand: finding a viable technical foundation for digital preservation*, Commission on Library and Information Resources, Washington, DC.

Youngs, K. (2001), *Managing the digitisation of library, archive and museum materials*, NPO Preservation Guidance Preservation Management Series, National Preservation Office, London.

Such is the pace of technological development in this field and the ongoing large-scale funding of real and developmental applications in archives and libraries that new information, electronic and hard copy, proliferates. It is important to scan appropriate Web sites regularly to keep abreast of this.

WEB SITES

PADI (Preserving Access to Digital Information), National Library of Australia, Canberra, Australia
(www.nla.gov.au/padi/)
'PADI is a subject gateway to digital preservation resources on a worldwide basis.' It offers news and discussion through a moderated discussion list (padiforum-l, see www.nla.gov.au/padi/forum/ for details), and contains pages on events, policies, strategies and guidelines and projects, and gives details of organizations and Web sites, bibliographies, discussion lists, journals and newsletters and glossaries. It also offers information on digital preservation topics, such as rights management, data documentation and standards, national approaches and formats and media.

Arts and Humanities Data Service (AHDS)
(http://ahds.ac.uk)
'The AHDS is a UK national service funded by the Joint Information Systems Committee and the Arts and Humanities Research Board.' It aims 'to help create and preserve digital collections in all areas of the arts and humanities'. Among the site's content is information on funding opportunities, the management of digital collections and links to digital collections and archives, including, for example, the Visual Arts Data Service (VADS), 'providing, preserving and promoting digital resources for research, learning and teaching' (www.vads.ahds.ac.uk), based at the Surrey Institute of Art and Design University College. Its *Guide to good practice: creating digital resources for the visual arts: standards and good practice* (http://vads.ahds.ac.uk/guides/creating_guide/contents.html) by C. Grout, P. Purdy and J. Rymer, includes a section on storage and preservation.

Digital Preservation Coalition
(www.dpconline.org/graphics/index.html)
The Digital Preservation Coalition was 'established in 2001 to foster joint action to address the urgent challenges of securing the preservation of digital resources in the UK and to work with others internationally to secure our global digital memory and knowledge base'. Further information and news on the Coalition is available via the digital preservation email list (details at: www.jiscmail.ac.uk/lists/digital-preservation.html).

ERPANET (Electronic Resource Preservation and Access NETwork)
(www.erpanet.org)
A European Union funded project begun in late 2001 which aims to provide 'a virtual clearinghouse and knowledge-base on state-of-the-art developments in digital preservation'. The initiative is led by the Humanities Advanced Technology and Information Institute (HATII), University of Glasgow, with its partners, the Schweizerisches Bundesarchiv, Rijksarchiefdienst in The Netherlands, and the Institute for Archival and Library Science, University degli studi di Urbino, Italy.

Higher Education Digitisation Services (HEDS)
(http://heds.herts.ac.uk)
HEDS provides 'advice, consultancy and a complete production service for digitisation and digital library development' within and outside the higher education sector.

Humanities Advanced Technology and Information Institute (HATII), University of Glasgow
(www.hatii.arts.gla.ac.uk)
'The mission of the Humanities Advanced Technology and Information Institute is to actively encourage the use of information and communication technology to enhance research and teaching in the arts and the humanities.' Among other content, the Web site offers information on research and projects, events and conferences, and digital summer schools.

D-Lib magazine
(www.dlib.org/)
D-Lib magazine is produced by the Corporation for National Research Initiatives (CNIR), Reston, Virginia, USA, and funded by the National Science Foundation (NSF), USA. It includes broad, international coverage of digital library-related issues, including preservation, and is a helpful source of articles and information on current developments.

DISASTER MANAGEMENT

By the mid-1990s, there was a significant development of printed guidance available on disaster management in libraries and archives. (Bibliographies and Web sites above give details of these and occasional bibliographies provide updates, too; see for example, Kilzack, D. and Chapman, C. (1999), 'A Decade of Disaster: a Selected Bibliography of Disaster Literature', *Library and Archival Security*, 15 (1), pp. 7–66). In the UK, a major review of disaster management practice was undertaken and guidelines accompanied publication of its report (Matthews, G. and Eden, P. (1996), *Disaster management in British libraries. Project report with guidelines for library managers*, Library and Information Research Report 109, British Library Research and Development Department, London). Since then much activity in this area has tended to focus on specific issues such as insurance (see, for example, Graham, R. and Prideaux, A. (2000), *Insurance for museums. Guidelines for good practice*, Museums and Galleries Commission, London) and to facilitate access to information and share experience by utilizing the Internet. A useful example of collaborative action here is M25 Consortium of Higher Education Libraries, Disaster Management Group, available at: www.m25lib.ac.uk/M25dcp/home_c.htm. The site provides a Web-mounted disaster plan template and links to other useful sites for use primarily by over 100 academic libraries and archives in the London area. Details of helpful publications and contacts are also provided. Guides to disaster management continue to appear, for example: Alire, C. (ed.) (2000), *Library disaster planning and recovery handbook*, Neal-Schuman Publishers, New York; Kahn, M. (1998), *Disaster response and planning for libraries*, American Library Association, Chicago; and Flowers, D. and Barrett, A. (2002), *Business Continuity and Disaster Management in the Digital Age. A Guide for Libraries, Archives and Information Centres*, London: Facet Publishing. See also Matthews, G. and Feather, J. (eds) (2003), *Disaster management for libraries and archives*, Ashgate, Aldershot, which provides personal accounts from around the world based on experience of different aspects of disaster management such as risk management, dealing with the psychological impact of disasters and the significance of the disaster control plan.

One aspect of this topic that has received renewed attention following recent events has been the impact of war and civil unrest on the cultural heritage. See International Committee of the Blue Shield (ICBS) (www.ifla.org/VI/4/admin/protect.htm): 'The Blue Shield is the cultural equivalent of the Red Cross. It is the symbol specified in the 1954 Hague Convention for marking cultural sites to give them protection from attack in the event of armed conflict.' The ICBS, set up in 1996, covers museums, archives, historic sites and libraries. Its mission is 'to work for the protection of the world's cultural heritage by co-ordinating preparations to meet and respond to emergency situations'. Blue Shield Committees have been formed in a number of countries including Belgium, Italy and The Netherlands. The United Kingdom and Ireland Blue Shield Organisation (UKIRB) Web site (www.bl.uk/services/preservation/blueshield/content.html) provides links to these and offers basic disaster advice with links to Web and other useful sources. The issues involved are well illustrated in the proceedings of a recent conference on the subject: Sturges, P. and Rosenberg, D. (eds) (1999), *Disaster and after: the practicalities of information service in times of war and other catastrophes. Proceedings of an international conference sponsored by IGLA (The International Group of the Library Association), 4–6 September 1998, University of Bristol*, Taylor Graham,

London. A good overview of events in the last century is provided in Valencia, M. (2002), 'Libraries, nationalism, and armed conflict in the twentieth century', *Libri*, 52 (1), pp. 1–15.

Accounts of incidents themselves and their aftermath continue to offer help to others based on experience. A particularly good example is: Colorado State University, *Lessons of recovery* (www.colostate.edu/floodrecovery/. 'Dead' link 16 December 2002). In July 1997, a massive flood hit Colorado State University. The Morgan Library and University bookstore were badly affected. The Web site compilers laudably aim to share information and to add to this as their recovery process continues. The Website offers personal accounts and expert advice, with sections including: lessons from an extreme event – a scholarly review, images from the review, comment from staff and faculty newsletters, news releases, tips from a disaster recovery expert, public relations response to crisis, university emergency operations plans and a specialist in grief talking about coping.

The impact of the events of 11 September 2001 has begun to be assessed and personal accounts published. See, for example, Heritage Preservation (2002), *Cataclysm and challenge. Impact of September 11, 2001, on Our Nation's Cultural Heritage. A report from Heritage Preservation on behalf of the Heritage Emergency National Task Force*, Project Director Ruth Hargreaves, Heritage Preservation: Washington, DC. Available at: www.heritagepreservation.org/NEWS/Cataclysm.htm, a report of a survey of the impact of the events of 11 September on cultural and historic resources at the Pentagon and in Lower Manhattan, with recommendations; and American Library Association (2002), *Loss and Recovery: Librarians Bearing Witness to September 11, 2001*, produced by *American Libraries*, the magazine of the American Library Association, in cooperation with Library Video Network, Chicago: American Library Association. (Distributed by Library Video Network, Towson, Maryland.) (Interviews with some of the librarians who were working in or near the World Trade Center when terrorist attacks occurred. They recall the effects on information and library services and how they have recovered personally and professionally.)

Disaster management is another aspect of preservation management where libraries are looking to archives and museums and other cultural heritage organizations for good practice and possible collaboration. In this respect, see, for example:

Ashley-Smith, J. (1999), *Risk assessment for object conservation*, Butterworth-Heinemann, Oxford.

Batchelor, K. (1999), *Records management: a guide to disaster prevention and recovery*, DISCPD0013:1999, British Standards Institution, London.

Doig, J. (1997), *Disaster recovery for archives, libraries and records management systems in Australia and New Zealand*, Topics in Australasian Library and

Information Studies Number 12, Centre for Information Studies, Charles Sturt University, Riverina, Wagga Wagga, New South Wales.

Dorge, V. and Jones, S. (comps) (1999), *Building and emergency plan. A guide for museums and other cultural institutions*, Getty Conservation Institute, Los Angeles, CA.

East Midlands Museums Service (2001), *The EMMS Emergency Manual for historic buildings and collections*, East Midlands Museums Service, Nottingham. (Available as interactive CD-ROM; for further details see: www.emms.org.uk.)

Society of Archivists, Scottish Region, Disaster Preparedness Working Group (1996), *Disaster preparedness: guidelines for archives and libraries*, Society of Archivists, London.

SECURITY

There appears to be little published in recent years on security and libraries, particularly in the UK. This is perhaps surprising in light of the findings of a survey of theft from libraries there (Burrows, J. and Cooper, D. (1992), *Theft and loss from UK libraries: a national survey*, Police Research Group Crime Prevention Unit Series paper no. 37, Home Office Police Department, London). The National Preservation Office (UK) offers a series of free leaflets on security matters (see: www.bl.uk/services/preservation/freeandpaid.html). The Museums and Galleries Commission also addressed this issue in Museums and Galleries Commission (1997), *Improving museum security*, Museums and Galleries Commission, London. More recently this lack of coverage of this topic in the UK has been addressed on the Resource Web site, Resource: the Council for Museums, Archives and Libraries (2002), *Information. Advice and Guidance: Security*. Available at: www.resource. gov.uk/information/advice/00security.asp.

These Web pages provide a range of advice for libraries, archives and museums in the UK, including, for example, security specifications, government indemnity scheme and invigilation guidance.

More activity seems to have taken place in the USA, with the publication of a handbook, Shuman, B.A. (1997), *Library security and safety handbook*, American Library Association, Chicago, IL; and a manual, Cravey, P. (2001), *Protecting Library Staff, Users, Collections and Facilities: a how-to-do-it Manual*, How-To-Do-It Manuals for Librarians, New York, London: Neal-Schuman Publishers; and in the rare books field, including Association of College and Research Libraries, American Library Association, *Guidelines for the security of rare books, manuscripts, and other special collections*, prepared by the ACRL Rare Books and Manuscripts Section's Security Committee. Final version approved July 1999. Originally published in *College and Research Libraries News*, October 1999. Available at:

www.ala.org/acrl/guides/raresecu.html). The journal, *Library and archival security*, Haworth Press, 1975– (twice yearly) is a useful source of information for librarians and researchers on security planning, policies, procedures and strategies for libraries and archives.

PRESERVATION NEEDS ASSESSMENT

As national libraries or regional or state-wide cooperative initiatives have considered the development of preservation policies to address preservation issues in a formalized manner, the significance of the ability to survey collections to identify and quantify preservation needs has been more keenly felt. The information gleaned from such assessments or surveys can be used to determine priorities, to plan preservation programmes and to bid for funding and other resources for preservation and conservation. Preservation and condition assessments were developed in the USA in the 1980s and 1990s, culminating in off-the-shelf packages such as CALIPR, for which see California State Library, *Calipr: preservation planning software* (available at http://sunsite.berkeley.edu/CALIPR).

In the UK, recent years have seen the development of a preservation assessment survey (Eden, P., Dungworth, N., Bell, N. and Matthews, G. (1998), *A model for assessing preservation needs in libraries*, British Library Research and Innovation Report 125, British Library, London). This owed much to earlier work in the USA (the project report contains a helpful bibliography which provides details of this) and elsewhere (see, for example, National Library of Australia, Community Heritage Grants Programme (1997), *Preservation needs assessment survey*, National Library of Australia, Sydney, available at: http://www.nla.gov.au/chg/assess.html), and other domains (for example, Museums and Galleries Commission (1998), *Levels of collection care. A self-assessment checklist for UK museums*, Museums and Galleries Commission, London). The project aimed to develop a survey with a standard methodology, which would provide locally useful information which, when accumulated nationally with data from other archives, and libraries using it, would paint a picture of the national situation. The UK survey, developed and promoted by the National Preservation Office, is in two parts, a collection assessment survey, and a condition survey, and has been designed and developed to be used by libraries and archives (Walker, A. and Foster, J. (comps) (2001), *Preservation assessment survey for libraries and archives: user's guide*, National Preservation Office, London, available from: npo@bl.uk). The National Preservation Office is involved in pilot studies with museums to determine if a standard methodology for non-print artefacts can be incorporated in the survey tool for use by archives, libraries and museums.

PRESERVATION POLICY

Since the mid-1990s, there has been considerable development in the UK towards a national preservation policy, led by the National Preservation Office. Research addressing libraries (see, Feather, J., Matthews, G. and Eden, P. (1996), *Preservation management. Policies and practices in British libraries*, Gower, Aldershot) and archives (Feather, J. and Eden, P. (1997), *National preservation policy: policies and practices in archives and record offices*, British Library Research and Innovation Centre Report 43, The British Library, London) have fed into this. In the UK, such policy acknowledges the significance of cooperative and collaborative activity (Eden, P. and Gadd, E. (1999), *Co-operative preservation activities in libraries and archives: project report with guidelines*, British Library Research and Innovation Report 161, The British Library, London). Following the election of the Labour government in 1997, the Department of Culture, Media and Sport (http://www.culture.gov.uk/) through Resource: the Council for Museums, Archives and Libraries (http://www.resource.gov.uk/), is fostering greater interaction and collaboration between the three domains, both regionally and nationally. It has recently been developing a *Stewardship Strategy* (see www.resource.gov.uk/action/stewardship/00stew.asp), which includes coverage of collection development and preservation management. The outcome was published in early 2002 as *Preserving the past for the future. Towards a national framework for collections management* (available at: www.resource.gov.uk/action/stewardship/preserv01.asp).

The significance of cooperation and collaboration is not restricted to the UK (see, for example, Banks, P.N. and Pilette, R. (eds) (2000), *Preservation issues and planning*, American Library Association, Chicago; Berthon, H. (2001), 'Preserving together: collaborative library activities in Australia', *International Preservation News*, issue 24, pp. 22–5; and Lusenet, Y. de (ed.) (1997), *Choosing to preserve. Towards a cooperative strategy for long-term access to the intellectual heritage. Papers of the international conference organized by the European Commission on Preservation and Access and Die Deutsche Bibliothek, Leipzig/Frankfurt am Main, March 29–30, 1996*, European Commission on Preservation and Access, Amsterdam).

The importance of policy at local and institutional level is recognized, too, with publication of guidelines to assist its development: Foot, M.M. (2001), *Building blocks for a preservation policy*, NPO Preservation Guidance Preservation Management Series, National Preservation Office, London; and Pickford, C., Rhys-Lewis, J. and Weber, J. (1997), *Preservation and conservation: a guide to policy and practice in the preservation of archives*, Best Practice Guidelines 4, Society of Archivists, London. Funding to develop preservation management activities is not easy to come by; a useful guide to preparing applications in the UK is available, *Preparing funding applications for preservation and conservation projects* (1999),

NPO Preservation Guidance Preservation Management Series, National Preservation Office, London.

Conferences addressing policy in the light of ongoing and future developments are useful sources of information on the key issues and ways to tackle them. See, for example, *Preservation and digitisation: principles, practice and policies. Papers given at the National Preservation Office 1996 Annual Conference, University of York, 3–5 September 1996* (1997), National Preservation Office, London; and *Towards the 21st century. Papers given at the National Preservation Office Conference, held 28 April 1997 in London* (1997), National Preservation Office, London.

RESEARCH

Details of completed and ongoing research projects and publication of results can be found on many of the Web sites above, some of which also offer information about sources of funding for research and development work. In the UK, a particularly useful source in this respect is: Lomax, J., Palmer, S., Jefcoate, G. and Kenna, S. (2000), *A guide to additional sources of funding and revenue for libraries and archives*, 2nd edn, rev. by Sully, R., British Library Co-operation and Partnership Programme, London.

The present author was commissioned by the British Library Research and Innovation Centre (BLRIC) in 1996 to undertake a review of research in preservation management in libraries and archives to inform the development of a research programme in this field. The focus of the research was to provide an overview of research undertaken from 1984 in preservation management appropriate to British libraries and archives. As well as UK research, that undertaken elsewhere (for example, in Australia, Europe and the USA) was also considered. The project identified gaps in research and recommended how these might be addressed. (Matthews, G. (1996), *Research in preservation management*, British Library Research and Innovation Report 30, British Library Research and Innovation Centre, London.) Shortly after this, the newly established Library and Information Commission (LIC) took over BLRIC's research role and developed a research programme for this area (Library and Information Commission (UK). Preservation of and access to the recorded heritage [research programme]. Available at: http://www.lic.gov.uk/research/preservation/index.html).

In 2000 a new government agency, Resource: the Council for Museums, Archives and Libraries (www.resource.gov.uk/home.asp) replaced LIC. Since then, it has been developing policies and strategies and considering where these need underpinning by research. Details of projects it is supporting (such as, Hughes, S. (2001), *Preserving library and archive collections in historic buildings*, Library and Information Commission Report 118, Resource, London) are available on its Web site. Concord: the British Library Co-operation and Partnership Programme Web site is also a useful source to consult for details of cooperative preservation-related projects. See, for example, Rhys-Lewis, J. (2001), *The enemy within! Acid deterioration of our written heritage. A report to the British Library Co-operation and Partnership Programme on behalf of the Project Steering Committee. Results of a feasibility study to investigate and make recommendations for a collaborative approach to mass deacidification as part of the national preservation strategy for the cultural written heritage,* The British Library Board, 2001 (available at: www.bl.uk/concord/ pdf_files/massdreport.pdf).

For those interested in keeping abreast of developments in conservation research, the Commission on Library and Information Resources offers a recent review: Porck, H.J. and Teygeler, R. (2000), *An overview of recent developments in research on the conservation of selected analog library and audiovisual materials,* Commission on Library and Information Resources, Washington, DC.

EDUCATION AND TRAINING

Many of the Web sites above provide details of training programmes, seminars, workshops and other events relevant to continual professional development. Details of educational courses which may offer preservation or related topics may be found at: *World list of departments and schools of information studies, information management, information systems, etc.,* maintained by T.D. Wilson (http:// informationr.net/wl/index.html).

The situation concerning the teaching of preservation in schools or Departments of Information and Library Studies in the UK has recently been reviewed informally. See Feather, J., 'The role of the library and archive schools', in Thebridge, S. (ed.), *Training for preservation management: the next step. Proceedings of the National Preservation Office Annual Seminar held on 26th October 1999 at the British Library.* Also Thebridge, S. and Matthews, G., *Review of preservation management training in the UK and abroad. The main findings of the Library and Information Commission Research Report 48 2000,* London: National Preservation Office, 2000, pp. 19–23.

The situation concerning training is perhaps more fluid, as illustrated by other papers from the same seminar. For a broader perspective than just the UK, see Cloonan, M.V. (1994), *Global perspectives on preservation education,* IFLA publications 69, K.G. Saur, Munich, and Lusenet, Y. de (1998), 'The case of the Dutch hamster: promoting awareness and preservation management training in Europe', *Liber Quarterly,* 8, pp. 458–71. Wiseman, C. and Darby, S. (2001), 'Preservation workshop evaluation', *Library Resources and Technical Services,* 45, pp. 95–103, is an interesting article which considers how to assess the effectiveness of preservation training.

The future of training in preservation will inevitably involve coordination with national training initiatives and closer cooperation between the archive, library and museum domains. This was a key finding of a recent review of preservation management training in libraries, archives and museums (Thebridge, S. and Matthews, G. (2000), *Review of Current Preservation Management Training in the UK and Abroad*, Library and Information Commission Research Report 48, 2000), which, whilst its focus was on libraries, looked to related domains for good practice (see, for example, Museums and Galleries Commission (1997), *Developing and Training Staff in Museums and Galleries*, MGC Guidelines for Good Practice, MGC, London).

A good example of a Web-based tutorial and the role such resources can play in preservation management education and training is: Council on Library and Information Resources and Cornell University (2002), *Library preservation and conservation. Southeast Asia tutorial*. Available at: www.librarypreservation.org/. Funded by the Henry Luce Foundation, the tutorial is aimed at libraries and archives in Southeast Asia. It offers broad preservation coverage, with sections on different aspects such as security and disaster management, offering step-by-step advice, further sources (print and Web-based) and cases for discussion.

ENDNOTE

Digital technologies have opened up both opportunities and challenges for preservation management. Research and development projects are investigating and implementing effective means of preserving digitally born material. Digitization offers the possibility of future alternatives for surrogacy of printed material. The increased awareness of preservation management issues over the last decade has evolved into practical developments, particularly for digital materials. There is worldwide interest and activity. Thanks to technological developments in the same area, particularly those in information and communications technology, individuals and groups globally are able to find and share information and experience much more easily than they could less than a decade ago. With that in mind, this chapter represents a selective snap-shot of sources at the time of writing (late 2002) – keep checking those Web sites and discussion lists for new information and sources, electronic and printed!

8 The Future

Marie-Thérèse Varlamoff

WHICH FUTURE FOR WHICH PRESERVATION?

It is now commonly observed by most senior library and archives professionals that the profession has evolved considerably since they first started their careers. The same situation is reflected in the area of preservation, and the general feeling is that it is going to evolve even more in the future. As Director of IFLA (the International Federation of Library Associations and Institutions) Core Programme on Preservation and Conservation I have been asked to draw a portrait of the future of preservation from an international point of view. The first question that comes to my mind is: what future and what areas of preservation are we talking about? Is it preservation management, collections preservation, staff training and preservation curricula, is it the identification of priorities and the selection of items to preserve, or is it new technologies? I imagine all of these domains need to be taken into consideration. If we think in terms of long-term preservation, it also means that we have to get ready now in order to prepare for the future.

It seems to me that the major change, since I was a student in library school years ago, is that the subject of preservation, which was then limited to a two- or three-hour class during the one-year curriculum, has become a much more important part of today's curriculum and is also a major mission of libraries and archives.

There are several reasons for such a change. First, more and more people, not only scholars and students, now regularly use library and archives services. Second, the volume of publications has been increasing considerably. Third, the quality of the constituting materials of items has continually deteriorated since 1850, and there is a growing threat of losing huge quantities of documents and information. Fourth, publications are now published on new carriers that require different preservation techniques or conservation treatments.

It seems difficult to envisage the future of preservation without first analysing its evolution in recent years. Twenty years ago, not a long time in the life-span of a

159

library, the main concern was not conservation. Although a few national libraries could afford to have conservation laboratories and conservators who could spend several months on the restoration of one unique and costly manuscript, this was not the case with most libraries. Furthermore, although the decay of collections – principally newspapers and paperbacks – had long started, due to the poor quality of the paper in use since 1850, until the late 1970s little had been done to mitigate the damage and few measures had been taken to try to stabilize the situation.

A PROGRAMME FOR PRESERVATION AND CONSERVATION

In 1986, a milestone in the history of preservation, the Conference of the Directors of National Libraries, IFLA and UNESCO jointly convened and supported a Conference on the Preservation of Library Materials. Very much alarmed by the desperate state of preservation of most European collections, participants in the conference decided to react, and IFLA, which had already envisaged the creation of a Core Programme on Preservation and Conservation during its Annual Conference in Nairobi, Kenya, two years before, proposed to officially launch the PAC Programme.

IFLA PAC has one major goal: to ensure that library and archives materials, published and unpublished, in all formats, will be preserved in accessible form for as long as possible. To achieve the goal, its objectives include raising awareness through information, documentation and publication, education and training, promotion of standards, encouragement of scientific research and, last but not least, promoting and facilitating greater cooperation in the field of preservation.

The IFLA PAC Programme was conceived in a decentralized way for greater efficiency: a focal point to manage activities and regional centres, responsible for their choices and policies. PAC was first established at the Library of Congress in Washington with two regional centres: one at the Bibliothèque nationale in France, responsible for Western Europe, the Mediterranean countries and Africa, and another at the Deutsche Bücherei, in Leipzig, responsible for Eastern Europe. Gradually other regional centres were identified to cover the main regions of the world: in 1988, the Biblioteca Nacional de Venezuela in Caracas accepted responsibility for Latin America and the Caribbean, as did the National Diet Library in Tokyo for Central and East Asia in 1989, followed by the National Library of Australia in Canberra for the Pacific and Southeast Asia.

Since its creation PAC has undergone a few changes: the focal point is now hosted by the Bibliothèque nationale de France in Paris and acts as regional centre for Western Europe, Africa and the Middle East, whereas the centre in Washington acts as regional centre for the USA and Canada. The centre in Leipzig closed down in 1997 and its activities were taken up by the Library for Foreign Literature in

Moscow, now responsible for Eastern Europe and the Commonwealth of Independent States (CIS).

While IFLA PAC was developing, preservation was progressively evolving: treatments by the unit have been gradually superseded by mass or semi-industrial treatments and the scope of activities has moved from traditional treatments like restoration towards new reformatting technologies, especially digitization.

When not seen as a masterpiece or a cultural artefact of world interest, the book that contains the information is considered less important than the information itself. Nevertheless, the present situation is not stable and it is most likely that evolution will continue, not only following the changes in and creations of new technologies, but also according to the needs of libraries and in particular of national libraries, committed to their first objective of collecting, preserving and making accessible for future generations their national heritage.

For all those who have kept an eye on preservation during the past fifteen years it is obvious that preservation has been subject to various successive or simultaneous trends. Deacidification, recommended use of permanent paper, paper splitting, lamination, microfilming, digitization, to name just a few, have each represented at one time or another the main, although not necessarily the only, concern of specialists in charge of preservation in their institutions. There is nowadays a deliberate tendency to consider those techniques as the many treatments to be discussed, analysed, budgeted and taken into account when implementing a preservation plan. The general feeling is that preservation is not an exact science and that it can involve several techniques at a time or successively. There is no single approach, but different ones dependent on the type of library, the country, its climate, the economic situation and the number of users. The principle of reversibility that prevails in restoration should also be applied, as far as possible, in preservation.

THE PRESENT SITUATION

Before envisioning the future we must recall the present situation. Does preservation have the same role in all libraries? Certainly not. If European and North American libraries have had quite a long experience in the field, the situation is far from identical all over the world. Even in industrialized countries, for instance in Asia or in Australia, problems differ according to the specific political, economic and climatic situations of each country in general and of each library in particular.

EUROPE

In Europe, the situation is also uneven, and while most countries tend to show a real concern for their documentary heritage there are still too many libraries that have no one on their staff responsible for preservation and, moreover, too many lack the necessary financial resources to manage preservation and cover the related expenses. The recent construction of new national libraries in London, Paris, Frankfurt and Copenhagen has focused the attention of professionals but also of the public at large on preservation issues. The acerbic criticisms from journalists or preservation professionals have proved useful in pointing out the requirements in terms of preservation. In Paris, for instance, even though the architecture of the building was criticized and a number of mistaken statements made in many newspapers, the department of preservation and the conservation laboratories, together with their extension outside Paris, are among, if not actually, the largest and most modern in the world.

NORTH AMERICA

In the USA and Canada the situation seems much more even. Besides the Library of Congress, the National Library of Canada and the New York Public Library, most major university libraries like Cornell or Harvard have their own conservation laboratories. There are also a number of private, non-profit regional conservation centres such as NEDCC (Northeast Documentation and Conservation Centre in Andover, Massachusetts), CCAHA (Conservation Center for Art and Historic Artifacts in Philadelphia, Pennsylvania), SOLINET (Southern Library Network Preservation Services in Atlanta, Georgia) or Amigos Library Services, Inc. (Dallas, Texas). These centres pursue multiple activities: conservation treatments, surveys, preservation planning, organization of workshops and seminars, publications, emergency planning, response and assistance, training, internship, expertise and so on. In the USA, the National Endowment for the Humanities helps to fund many of the regional or national preservation structures. We must also underline the prominent and determining role of organizations such as the Commission on Preservation and Access, which merged in 1996 with the Council on Library Resources to form the Council on Library and Information Resources (CLIR). CLIR's surveys, expertise and publications are appreciated by the entire preservation community and tend to reflect the most recent research and the most up-to-date recommendations and applications. It first denounced the brittleness of books and advocated the use of permanent paper through the well-known video *Slow Fire*, then with the appearance of new technologies shifted to the preservation of digital documents with another video, *Into the Future*. For the North American community, raising awareness of preservation issues does not stop at the door of the library, and some, including the Library of Congress, organize workshops for private individuals to teach them how to preserve their family treasures.

ASIA AND THE PACIFIC

In Asia and in the Pacific area the situation is more diverse. Some countries have long proved their concern for preservation, through installing conservation laboratories in the national library and advocating preservation through the activities of the IFLA PAC regional centres. The National Library of Australia, for instance, which has long worked on traditional preservation issues, is now very much ahead in the preservation of digital documents. The National Diet Library in Tokyo or the National Library of Korea are good examples of what can be done in the field of paper conservation and adequate storage for long-term preservation. Several countries are willing to implement preventive measures and to apply preservation and conservation treatments to their collections. They know how to proceed, they have developed a policy or a project, and sometimes staff have been trained. They do not, however, have the budget to implement the project or, when a project has been implemented, they cannot manage it on a longer-term basis because the economic situation has deteriorated. Even worse is the situation of some libraries in Asia which have suffered from wars, neglect and disrespect and are in such a desperate state that very little remains of what used to be the national library. In such cases huge efforts are necessary to repair the premises, train new staff and rebuild collections. Even if people are aware of the importance of preserving the national heritage, a major problem remains: most of the time there is nothing to preserve, a situation sometimes exacerbated by the lack of interest from the governing authority.

AFRICA

In Africa the situation is far from acceptable. Library schools are rare and preservation is seldom an important item of the curriculum, although a recent expert meeting in Nairobi, Kenya (1998) settled the basis for a preservation curriculum for library schools in Africa. On this continent, where the oral tradition has long been the sole or main information source, implementing traditional preservation activities is not easy. The reasons for this are many: a lack of resources, and difficult climate and environmental conditions are partial explanations. On the other hand governments and politicians in general do not consider libraries or archives as a priority, and therefore allocate no money for the preservation of the collections. Consequently, there is no preservation strategy. Although many library and archive directors are conscious of the problem and of the importance of preservation, they cannot do more than complain about the lack of resources. Even if they seem willing to react against such a situation, the results are often disappointing. That was the experience shared by IFLA and the International Council on Archives, which in 1996 created the Joint IFLA/ICA Committee on

Preservation in Africa (JICPA) in order to help the Africans implement some preservation activities. The preservation workshops in different languages that have been organized throughout Africa by ICA and IFLA do not seem to have been followed up by local preservation activities, except in South Africa where there is a long-standing tradition of conservation treatment and substantial commitment from the conservators.

LATIN AMERICA

A recent survey conducted by IFLA PAC for ABINIA in Latin America and the Caribbean has analysed the state of preservation of national libraries collections. It shows that, apart from three or four national libraries, the others have great difficulties in trying to follow basic preservation practices. More sophisticated measures, such as deacidification, paper splitting or lamination, for instance, are practically unused or even unheard of. Among the priorities that were put forward are the need for better stacks and for air conditioning, although 70 per cent of the libraries equipped with air conditioning confessed that their systems do not work all day and are shut down at night and during weekends and vacations. The next priority is training and the possibility of accessing professional literature in either Spanish or Portuguese. Another need is to have national preservation offices and strategies so as to be guided in their preservation effort and to avoid duplication of effort.

RUSSIA AND THE CIS

The situation in the former Soviet Union has greatly improved in recent years but is still far from satisfactory, despite the effort of the newly created and dynamic PAC Centre in Moscow. The size of the collections and the financial constraints have slowed down the enthusiasm of conservationists and postponed the implementation of consistent preservation policies. In remote countries in Central Asia much remains to be done and the lack of resources of all kinds, human as much as financial, added to difficult climate and environmental conditions, leaves little hope that the situation will improve, at least in the short term.

From this short survey we can see that there is a huge gap between industrialized and developing countries and that the divide between North and South is growing. Some people believe that the gap will be filled in shortly, thanks to the general adoption of digital technology. Although encouraged by numerous top organizations, whether international or non-governmental, this is a lure, and a dangerous one, because although digitization allows many more people to access all sorts of documents, digital preservation is still in its infancy and is not considered by specialists to be a means of preservation. Preserving digital documents requires additional trained staff, constant technological vigilance, and is quite costly. This is a situation that developing countries cannot afford to deal with.

THE FUTURE OF PRESERVATION

In less than thirty years preservation has emerged as one of the core missions of libraries. Almost ignored or left aside forty or fifty years ago, it has gradually become indispensable to all those who are in charge of cultural heritage. It is always a difficult and hazardous task to anticipate or plan the future, and I would not like to be the pythoness or a real Jeremiah. Nevertheless there are a few things that we can predict with a reasonable amount of certainty.

FLEXIBILITY

Flexibility will become the rule. As new technologies emerge, preservation techniques will have to adapt. Paper conservators, for instance, despite their knowledge and training in the treatment of paper documents, cannot claim to understand the preservation of digital documents unless they receive the appropriate training. This means that, either individually or at an institutional level, staff will have to be trained in order to shift from the preservation of traditional carriers to the preservation of new technologies. Simultaneously Library and Information Science schools will have to adapt their curricula. The skill required from a conservator is different from the qualities required from a digital preservationist. Just as librarians have seen their tasks evolve, conservators as well as preservationists will have to count upon and cooperate with computer scientists and technicians where digital preservation is concerned.

Flexibility will also be required for adapting standards to the particular economic, climatic and environmental conditions of each library. It would be misguided to believe that standards, guidelines and best practices can be applied indifferently to all types of libraries or archives. In the near future, HVAC systems will certainly be extended to most occidental countries, but I am not sure of their utility in tropical or subtropical countries, where power failures are frequent. In those regions traditional architectural techniques and materials appear still to have a future. To equip a building with a double roof allowing the air to circulate or to establish natural ventilation by means of well-distributed windows is certainly a more efficient, safer and less costly measure than to install an expensive HVAC which will never be working 24 hours a day all year around.

Likewise, the recommended levels of temperature and relative humidity are difficult to maintain in certain climates. Standards should therefore not be applied across the board but should be adapted to each situation, making sure that severe fluctuations are avoided.

COOPERATION

Another important factor in the success of preservation in the future will be cooperation at all levels. This means not only cooperation among libraries of the same type or in the same area or city, but also with other cultural institutions, that is, between libraries, archives and museums at a national, regional or international level. This leads us to envisage another form of cooperation, that between industrialized and developing countries, in order to eradicate, as much as possible, the gap between the 'preservation rich' and the 'preservation poor'. As we can observe that it is in the developing countries that the cultural and documentary heritage is most at risk because of lack of resources of all sorts, it is the duty of more prosperous nations to help them in their preservation efforts. This attitude is in line with what already exists in the humanitarian sector with organizations like the Red Cross or *Médecins sans Frontières*. Recent years have witnessed the development of a strong tendency towards implementing and developing structures for the preservation of cultural heritage, especially in the event of disasters.

SHARING RESPONSIBILITIES

Sharing responsibilities will certainly be among the priorities in the future. Preservation has a cost and is time-consuming and resource-intensive. If people learn to cooperate they will avoid duplicating effort and reinventing the wheel. The sharing of responsibilities is not new. Union projects like EROMM (European Register of Microform Masters) or catalogues such as the National Union Catalog of the Library of Congress or the online *Catalogue Collectif de France* have proved their utility and efficiency in terms of resource saving. Sharing responsibilities also implies knowing who is doing what and, if possible, deciding this beforehand, according to respective fields of excellence and resources. It is commonly accepted that each nation is responsible for the preservation of its own publications and should be responsible for collecting and preserving the publications related to that country. This rule will be maintained in the future, but should not prevent solidarity when one country proves no longer able to assume the preservation of its national heritage, for whatever reason, be it war, civil disorder or an exceptionally disastrous economic situation. In a case such as this, other countries could volunteer and bring help. Sharing responsibilities also relates to libraries with similar objectives and missions regarding acquiring and preserving publications. This has been the policy of the Bibliothèque nationale de France with the *Pôles Associés*.

These are libraries whose field of excellence entitles them to develop their collections in one specific domain. The Bibliothèque nationale de France relies on them to cover all acquisitions in the domain and for ensuring the long-term preservation of the collection. For example, the University Library of Marseilles specializes in acquisitions concerning the Mediterranean area. The National and University Library in Strasbourg collects all documents concerning religious studies and Germanic studies. It is a reasonable assumption that, in the future, with the development of digital technologies that will make long-distance access easier, this type of policy will become more generalized.

Selecting which documents need to be preserved in the long term or what can be preserved effectively is likewise a shared responsibility. A librarian should not have to decide alone the kind and number of items to be put aside for preservation. This is the kind of decision that should be taken in consultation with users and scholars because the final choice will have an influence on research in the future.

SHARED INSTALLATIONS

Shared equipment, especially in respect of a costly installation, will become more and more the rule, particularly as the volume of documents to be treated gradually increases. Except in the case of small repairs or the restoration of unique costly pieces, mass treatments tend to supersede treatments by the unit. Deacidification plants or splitting units are already in use in Europe and in the USA. It is not clear at present whether such plants will in the future be privatized or run by libraries, although the tendency seems to be towards privatization.

As many libraries are built in city centres or on university campuses, they have limited possibilities of expansion and it becomes more and more necessary, as time passes and collections grow, to find space to store collections that are not much used. The construction of vaults or back-up stacks to be shared by several institutions is a trend. We find the same tendency regarding emergency equipment. In the USA, for instance, three university libraries (Binghamton, Rochester and Syracuse) have joined Cornell to form a regional mutual-aid emergency response team and to install a freezer facility in case they need to secure water-damaged collections. This type of joint action is exactly the way decision-makers should now manage preservation issues: sharing responsibilities and costs in order to cut down expenses and to maximize resources.

BUDGETING AND OPTIMIZING COSTS

As has been pointed out, preservation costs money. In the future, the cost of preservation will become an even more important part of the overall budget of an institution. Such costs will have to be calculated on a long-term basis, and analysed according to various criteria. For instance, when calculating the cost of microfilming newspapers, one must take into account not only the cost of the microfilm itself (including staff salary), but also the cost of the reading machines and their maintenance, and compare this with the money saved by reducing the space needed for storage of the paper copies, or with the money saved by cutting down on conservation or preservation treatments such as splitting, lamination or binding.

Another good example of the trend is preventive measures taken to reduce future maintenance costs. For instance, the extensive use of library binding applied to open-access and loan collections is an initial treatment that effectively protects the book and avoids many further small repairs and postpones its replacement.

Nevertheless preservation will remain expensive, and, as the library market is a small one, it remains unlikely that suppliers will lower their prices.

FUNDING AND SUPPORT

At present, library funding comes from different agencies, depending on the country and the type of library. For instance, in the USA many libraries are supported by private funding, and preservation costs are covered by sponsors. In France national, public and university libraries are financed by the state (ministries, city councils, regional councils, and so on). Very few libraries are supported by private sponsors, which explains why preservation is to a certain extent rejected in favour of acquisitions or new technologies, which are much more gratifying for a sponsor in terms of publicity. When money is scarce or limited, priorities must be established. Preservation is not often considered one of them.

Preservation in the future will require increasing amounts of money. Moreover, the growing use of digitization and new technologies in general will increase expenses even more, since preserving digital materials implies regularly migrating or emulating data. Funding will have to be shared, and private support will have an increasingly important role, especially in developing countries that cannot afford to spend much on preserving documents when they do not have enough money to feed their people and provide basic health care.

Fund raising will become a necessity, and will have a higher profile, even in the library or preservation community. Library schools will have to teach students how to present a project to potential donors and how to defend the project in order to persuade eventual sponsors.

WHAT TO PRESERVE IN THE FUTURE?

What are we going to preserve for future generations? This is for some of us a very difficult question. We are all facing lack of space in our stacks. We are all facing some degree of financial shortage, at least when it comes to implementing appropriate measures for long-term preservation. Consequently we have to make a choice, which will influence research in the future. Contrary to what seems obvious, masterpieces do not always constitute the most important holdings in a library. Although we should take good care of them and ensure that they are well preserved, there are other collections, less prestigious in appearance, which may prove to be just as important for research in the future, for example newspapers. We should keep in mind that they are important mainly because of the information they contain. That is why we should preserve this information in the first place, by reformatting the contents on microfilm or digitally. For very special events we may want to preserve not only the information, but also the newspaper itself, as a testimony. Newspapers announcing the outbreak of the First World War or the first landing on the moon will certainly be valuable to those who intend to organize an exhibition on the subject. Some libraries have disposed of their collections of newspapers after microfilming, but some are now reconsidering that policy.

When it comes to making a list of all the different items to be preserved, we must not forget that an important part of the world heritage is intangible. The oral tradition that has been and still is prominent in many parts of the developing world should be given greater consideration. Often it is too late, because when an old man dies, a part of his cultural background dies with him. It is urgent that campaigns for recording oral traditions be implemented wherever possible. Another point to be underlined is that what seems a good candidate for preservation in one place may not necessarily be a good candidate elsewhere. For instance, it may be a high priority in Africa to preserve recordings of old stories told in an almost defunct dialect, whereas the New York Public Library may take a major interest in safeguarding all documents relating to Broadway shows. Shakespeare's complete works will certainly stand among the Stratford-upon-Avon Public Library's priorities, but they probably would not have the same priority for a lending library in Madagascar. Therefore, it is important to analyse what users will need and ask for now, as well as also in the future.

Audiovisual documents and some paper documents, such as photographs, maps or posters, complement and illustrate the information to be found in books or newspapers. Sometimes they are the only testimony that we have about an event, in which case it is of the utmost importance to preserve those documents as well.

Digital documents represent an enormous problem, especially born-digital documents. It is well known that NASA lost a great deal of the data about the first voyage to the moon. At the time of writing, an enormous amount of vital data is accessible mainly or only in digital form. What will happen in fifty years, maybe sooner, when someone decides to close down a nuclear plant and cannot access the original plans because the digital data cannot be read due to digital obsolescence?

169

Preserving digital documents also means preserving the Web, which represents another very difficult task because of the quantity of information that is continually being updated. It is commonly admitted that not every bit of information on the Web deserves to be preserved, but who will make the selection? Some Nordic countries are collecting all the data concerning their country, but such a policy cannot be applied in the USA, for instance, because of the enormous amount of information. Moreover, once the decision to preserve a Web site is taken, which data are to be preserved, and when? Should we preserve new data each time the site is updated? How shall we know it has been updated? In this domain as well, it is necessary to establish a consensus between librarians, scholars and users to decide on a common documentation policy for the future.

HOW TO PRESERVE IN THE FUTURE?

How all these documents will be preserved in the future depends on the type of carrier publishing them, as each different type requires a different method of preservation. Two alternatives then arise: should we preserve the originals only whenever possible or, if they are too damaged, only the copies we have made on microfilms or in digital form, or both the originals and the copies? The last solution means that we shall be facing an enormous increase in the quantity of documents that we wish to preserve. It may be necessary to use out-of-town building vaults for this purpose, perhaps sharing such facilities with several institutions, which will cut down on building maintenance and staff expenses.

For a long time to come, reformatting will remain the best preventive measure to make sure that the information contained in traditional and non-digital documents will be preserved and accessible in the long term. Conservation treatments, while preserving the original, do not allow access to several users at the same time or in different places. On the other hand, microfilming and digitization both offer the possibility of storing the information in a different place from the original which is a good way of enforcing security and constitutes a very safe and reliable preservation measure.

Reformatting treatments and expenses can also be shared. We have already covered initiatives like EROMM. The past few years have seen new global digitization initiatives flourish everywhere. The project *Bibliotheca Universalis*, for instance, launched in 1995, gathers digitized documents from thirteen libraries around the world (mainly Europe, North America and Japan) with the theme 'exchange among people'. A number of documents related to travelling have already been digitized. Some of them are also part of a national digitization project. This is the case for 'American Memory: Meeting of frontiers' between the USA and Russia and digitized by the Library of Congress, of *Gallica: Voyages en France et Voyages en Afrique*, digitized by the Bibliothèque nationale de France or of *Memoria Hispanica: Clásicos Tavera* on the relationships between Spain and America and digitized by the National Library of Spain.

Although we must underline that up to now digitization cannot be considered a means of preservation because of the problems raised earlier about obsolescence, it will be more and more used as a reformatting option, not least by developing countries who are sometimes tempted to skip the microfilm option. Nevertheless, a new concept has emerged, as discussed earlier: the possibility of operating both microfilming and digitizing techniques simultaneously so as to answer the problem with a hybrid solution. A master microfilm is kept safe in a back-up repository and is only accessible in case the copy for reproduction or duplication is damaged or missing, whereas the digitized copy can be used for larger or long-distance access.

Born-digital documents or digitized copies for access will of course have to be checked regularly or automatically where possible, and migrated or emulated according to the selected, recommended or standardized technique. As mentioned earlier, preserving expanding collections in the long term is such a demanding task that sharing responsibilities will be the rule, together with the establishment and general adoption of national preservation policies.

Last but certainly not least, the future of preservation lies in the development of preventive measures rather than in curative treatments. Mass treatments will be favoured and treatments by the unit will be kept for outstanding and unique documents; they should of course remain exceptional.

During the next decades we shall probably see more and more staff trained in preservation management, so that preservation will no longer be a matter of mere technique and *savoir-faire* but a much more business-like activity with a full range of side activities like user surveys, collection surveys, cost accounting, statistics, long-term forecasting, planning, human resources management, staff training and of course fund raising.

The new digital era will force preservation staff to acquire knowledge in the preservation of digital documents and in new reformatting techniques such as migration or emulation. To reach this goal they will have to cooperate with information technicians. They will also have to work with scholars before selecting what is to be preserved for future generations. The role of consultants and experts will probably become more important as technology evolves new means of preservation and curative treatments.

WHERE AND BY WHOM WILL DOCUMENTS BE PRESERVED?

Although national libraries and archives will remain responsible for the preservation of their respective national documentary heritage, in some cases the work will be undertaken more efficiently by preservation centres, either private or non-profit. Such centres will either be devoted to one sole type of treatment – this is the case of Bookkeeper (a system developed by Preservation Technologies), which has established deacidification units in the USA, the Netherlands and Australia – or will cover multiple activities and treatments in a particular field like the Zentrum für Buch-Erhaltung in Leipzig, which proposes to offer among its services deacidification, digitization, disaster management, treatment of water damage and splitting.

In coming years, supranational entities, either non-governmental or intergovernmental organizations, will undoubtedly play an important part in safeguarding the world memory. UNESCO, which created, developed and maintains the *World Heritage* Programme and the *Memory of the World* Programme, must be mentioned for its leading role in raising awareness of the fragility of our heritage and of the respect owed to it.

Respect for the world's cultural heritage is one of the aims of the *International Committee of the Blue Shield* (ICBS). Created in 1996, ICBS is a global network of preservation, conservation and restoration specialists committed to safeguarding cultural heritage from the effects of both natural and human-made disasters. Founded under the auspices of UNESCO, ICBS comprises four non-governmental and cultural organizations: the International Council on Archives (ICA), the International Council of Museums (ICOM), the International Council on Monuments and Sites (ICOMOS), and the International Federation of Library Associations and Institutions (IFLA). The Blue Shield has its origins in The Hague *Convention on the Protection of Cultural Property in the Event of Armed Conflict*, 1954. This is the first worldwide international agreement that specifically addresses the protection of cultural heritage during hostilities. It was drafted and signed in the wake of the Second World War and the whole-scale destruction and theft of art that had occurred. Nation states then realized their obligation to protect the world's cultural objects and centres from deliberate or unnecessary destruction. An emblem representing a blue shield was designated as the internationally recognized symbol to be used to mark buildings and sites to be expressly exempted from deliberate attack, by either bombing or theft.

The world cultural heritage, also referred to as cultural property, covers monuments, museums, houses of worship, arboretums and cemeteries as well as archives and libraries. Cultural heritage reflects the product of human activity in its many forms and among the entire world's many peoples. ICBS operates on the principle that the loss of any people's cultural expression is a great loss to the global community as a whole. It claims that it is vital that nations, regions and communities preserve such treasures for future generations. We have seen that the problems faced by our cultural and documentary heritage are numerous, ongoing and ever-widening. The three basic categories of disasters are:

- natural disasters, such as fire, floods, earthquakes, tsunami, landslides and hurricanes;
- man-made disasters, which have become more and more deliberate. In recent years a rise in arson and terrorist attacks has been noted;
- the ravages of time itself. Preservationists and conservationists are always in a race against time in respect of deterioration of materials and the effects of pollution.

ICBS works closely with scientific, legal and art experts around the globe to ensure that each region and country is both aware of and able to implement the steps necessary to ensure that its people's heritage will be preserved in the event of a disaster. ICBS coordinates and advocates the creation and establishment of national Blue Shield Committees to teach respect for the cultural heritage, implementing preventive strategic measures and organizing teams to respond to disasters. In Europe, national Blue Shield Committees have been established in Belgium, the United Kingdom, France, the Netherlands and Italy, and others are in preparation in Poland and Russia. It is expected that many more will be created in the next few years. Essentially, the Blue Shield intends to become the cultural equivalent of the Red Cross. Its unrivalled body of expertise will be capable of giving advice and assistance as well as training professionals or volunteers for response or recovery operations. Its role is also to identify resources for disaster prevention and for rapid intervention in emergencies.

Trying to consider what preservation will be like in the future is not an easy task and this chapter is not the place for technical advice on best practice in the third millennium. The technological changes of the last decades have been so important that we may expect further large-scale changes in the years to come. I sincerely hope that library and archives professionals are persuasive enough to convince information and computer suppliers of the necessity of working together on the long-term preservation of digital documents, given that our future depends so greatly on our past. We can hardly expect to educate our children if we do not teach them how to respect their heritage and keep track of their cultural memory.

Our documentary heritage has a manifold role – human, scientific, economic, cultural and educational. Since the end of the Second World War we have seen fashions and trends following each other according to an ever-accelerating rhythm. This trend seems exponential. Nevertheless, the one thing that we must always remember is that the documentary heritage conserved in our libraries and archives is a treasure and is the memory of mankind. We must do our best to preserve it, in all its integrity, and use technology to make it accessible to as many people as possible, now and in the future. Preservation without access is meaningless.

Index